*Saso Seminars*
514 PRADA DR.
MILPITAS, CA 95035

# SAGA

D0188169

# SAGA

## EDITORIAL BOARD

### EDITOR
JONATHAN YOUNG, JOSEPH CAMPBELL ARCHIVES & LIBRARY

### CONSULTING EDITORS
PATRICIA BERRY, JUNGIAN ANALYST, CAMBRIDGE, MA
WILLIAM G. DOTY, UNIVERSITY OF ALABAMA
CHRISTINE DOWNING, SAN DIEGO STATE UNIVERSITY
LINDA SCHIERSE LEONARD, JUNGIAN ANALYST, BOULDER, CO
DAVID L. MILLER, SYRACUSE UNIVERSITY
THOMAS MOORE, INSTITUTE FOR THE STUDY OF IMAGINATION
GINETTE PARIS, UNIVERSITY OF QUEBEC, MONTREAL
HUSTON SMITH, SYRACUSE UNIVERSITY

# SAGA

## BEST NEW WRITINGS
## ON MYTHOLOGY

### VOLUME 1

EDITED BY
## JONATHAN YOUNG

WHITE CLOUD PRESS
ASHLAND, OREGON

Copyright © 1996 by White Cloud Press. All rights reserved.
No part of this book may be used or reproduced in any manner whatsoever
without written permission except in the case of brief quotations
embodied in critical articles and reviews.
Inquiries should be addressed to:
White Cloud Press, P. O. Box 3400, Ashland, Oregon 97520

00 99 98    2 3 4 5

Cover Design by Daniel Cook

Cover illustration, "Creation Myth," © Betty LaDuke

Printed in Canada

ISBN 1-883991-13-7

ISSN 1086-1769

ACKNOWLEDGMENTS
Grateful acknowledgment is made to the following for permission to reprint material
from the sources listed below. White Cloud Press is not authorized to grant permission
for further use of copyrighted selections reprinted in this book without permisssion
of their owners.

"In Search of Hidden Wonder," by John Matthews.
Copyright © 1995 by John Matthews.
"On Pilgrimage: An Interview with Jean Shinoda Bolen" by Mary S. Nolan.
Copyright © 1995 by C. G. Jung Institute of Chicago.
"This Question of Images," by James Hillman.
Copyright © 1995 by James Hillman.
"Developing a Mythic Sensibility," by Thomas Moore
Copyright © 1995 by Thomas Moore.
"Persephone Abducted," by Rita Dove.
Copyright © 1995 by Rita Dove.
"Revisiting the Myth of Demeter and Persephone," by Christine Downing.
Copyright © 1995 by Christine Downing.
"Adult Liberation and the Mature Trickster," by Allan B. Chinen.
Copyright © 1995 by Allan B. Chinen.
"The Fire is in the Mind," by David L. Miller.
Copyright © 1994 by David L. Miller.
"Face in the Wind . . . Protect the Flame: An Interview with
Clarissa Pinkola Estés" by Charlene Sieg.
Copyright © 1994 by Clarissa Pinkola Estés.
"St. George, the Dragon, and the Virgin," by Robert Bly
Copyright © 1994 by Robert Bly.
"Story Food," by Robert Bly.
Copyright © 1993 by Robert Bly.
"Stepping Over the Threshold" by Marion Woodman.
Copyright © 1993 by Marion Woodman.
"In the Beginning," and "The East Wind: Bead Woman's Dress," from *Global Myths*
by Alexander Eliot. Copyright © 1993 by Alexander Eliot.
Used by permission of Dutton Signet, a division of Penguin Books USA Inc.
"Psycho-Erotica: Pursuing the Perverse with Madonna," by Patricia Reis
Copyright © 1993 by Patricia Reis.
"Hermes and the Creation of Space," by Murray Stein.
Copyright © 1995 by Murray Stein.
"Pitfalls in Faërie," by Verlyn Flieger. Copyright © 1994 by Verlyn Flieger.
"Allen Ginsberg in India: An Interview" by Siranjan Ganguly.
Copyright © 1993 by *ARIEL: A Review of International English Literature.*
"Coming Back from the Silence: An Interview of Ursula LeGuin" by Jonathan White.
Copyright © 1994 by Jonathan White.
"Language Alone Protects Us," by Toni Morrison.
Copyright © 1993 by The Nobel Foundation.

# ACKNOWLEDGMENTS

It is good to have a chance to thank Joseph Campbell for showing me a way back to the sacred, and Jean Erdman Campbell for her grace throughout the forming of the Joseph Campbell Archives & Library—also James Hillman and Marija Gimbutas for allowing me to initiate their archives.

Certain professors deepened my love of stories, particularly Rollo May and Viktor Frankl—later, colleagues and students were supportive of my efforts to pass along ideas at the Pacifica Graduate Institute, Antioch University, University of California, Santa Barbara, the Carl Jung Societies, and St. Edmund's Hall College of Oxford University.

Favorite booksellers helped at The Earthling and Chaucer's in Santa Barbara, The Bodhi Tree in Los Angeles, Midnight Special in Santa Monica, Black Oak in Berkeley, A Clean, Well-Lighted Place for Books in Larkspur, Village Books in Bellingham, Thunderbird Books in Carmel, and Powell's in Portland.

Journalists and broadcasters gave precious attention, including: Dave Bemis, Deanna Brady, Kedron Bryson, Joan Crowder, John Detro, John Dotson, Allan Hartley, Gali Krononberg, Gordon Legge, David McIntyre, Susanne Ohrvik, Pythia Peay, Guy Rathbun, Sue Reilly, Lesley Tipton, and Nancy Walbeck.

Religious leaders offered forums, such as: Nancy Anderson, Sarah Moores Campbell, Carol Carnes, Duane Cox, Robert Gale, Howard Hamilton, Luzette Hoff, Doris Gallagher, Michael Gerdes, Stuart Grayson, Sandy Jacob, Lloyd Klein, Virginia Kluth, Colleen MacGilchrist, Carolyn McKoewn, Michelle Medrano, Marcia Pearce, John Pearsall, Patrick Pollard, Shirley Price, Michael Rann, Alice Ross, Mary Murray Shelton, Sandy Shipley, Kennedy Shultz, Jayne Taggart, Joan Tomlinson, Frank White, Bets Wienecke, and Kathryn Yates.

Writer friends have been generous with their encouragement, including: Abigail Albrecht, Anne Bach, Shannon Creaven, Susan Gulbranson, Sojourner K. Rolle, Aaron Kipnis, Linda Schierse Leonard, Perie Longo, Anne McClaughery, Andrew Samuels, Terry Lynn Taylor, Connie Zweig and many at the Santa Barbara Writer's Conference.

May these and the other good souls who helped along the way have marvelous journeys and many enchanted stories to tell.

# CONTENTS

# INTO THE STORIES:
## AN INTRODUCTION

### BY JONATHAN YOUNG

*S*LOWLY, WE TAKE OUR PLACES AROUND THE campfire. At first, there is only silence and anticipation. Then, the village elders begin the ritual telling of the tales. We have heard some of the stories before. Others are new to us but are as old as the tallest trees. These are the accounts of people, like us, making their long journeys through this life. We listen closely. There is much to learn.

Whether we hear mythic stories in ceremonial situations or read them in paperbacks during vacations, the lure is eternal. The tales nourish something in us. We reconnect with universal patterns that move the human heart and soul. In some new way, we see the rich beauty and significance of ordinary life. When we enter the mythic imagination, we are participants. As we read the adventure, we go as seekers in quest of the grail and face each test we come across. Along the way we might find ourselves gaining greater understanding of the challenges we face in the search for meaning.

The gifts of stories are many. They can wrap themselves around our imaginations and enchant us with magical events. Sometimes, they show us the way through situations we have not been in before. It is also possible to find a tale with parallels to one's own journey and then locate the present moment in the unfolding account. The remainder of the story offers possible glimpses into the future. The actions of the characters may suggest the outcomes our choices will create. In an example from Greek myth, Demeter's responses to the way her beloved daughter Persephone leaves home may provide insight into one's own difficult moments in parenting.

Stories let us see through the eyes of others and learn that the rich variety of events goes far beyond what any one person can experience. When Rapunzel lets her hair down and the prince climbs to be with her in the tower, we enter a situation that is at once familiar and more unusual than what we have seen ourselves. Perhaps our task has been to escape the enchantments of our favorite perspectives that would keep us emotionally locked away as if in a tower, removed from others. Possibly, like the prince, we have had to scale obstacles to reach an experience of beauty.

Stories can also keep us company through long nights and sometimes even give courage to carry on in the face of difficulties, both obvious and unseen. In mythology, folklore, and legend, an amazing array of precious wisdom is available to us from ancestral voices. Just as the great sorcerer Merlin counseled the knights and ladies of the court, we can receive the assistance of the sages as handed down in great teaching stories.

In times of individual and societal troubles, when there is less certainty about familiar guideposts, we may do well to reach back for the timeless lessons of the ancient stories. Every large event that comes along these days, personal or shared, takes us into unfamiliar territory. Mythology helps us face the best moments and the worst.

One gift of the mythic vision is that it provides us with maps. We do not have to start from scratch. Those who traveled this way before have carefully left bits of guidance for us. The sagas and epic poems of the Nordic and other traditions are not just richly crafted tales. They carry the insights needed to live a worthy life. For example, when an initiatory story describes the deep bond that forms with an animal guide, it is telling how important it is to be one with nature.

By listening closely to the sacred stories of all times, we can become more aware of the symbolism that is present in familiar rituals. The rice and almonds at weddings symbolize fertility. The lights at winter holidays represent the divine spark of the life force. The pageantry of a graduation marks an initiate's return from a quest for knowledge. Once we begin to see events through the mythic imagination, rituals, sacred images, and epic tales seem to fill our lives. The sense of fulfillment is immediate. The sacred dimension is not far away at all. We discover that rich meanings have always already been operating right here in daily events.

*SAGA: Best New Writing on Mythology* strives to gather the most stimulating recent thinking in the fields of mythology, folklore and legend. A primary focus is the psychological symbolism seen in images, stories, and rituals. In the last decade, there has been a tremendous increase of interest of mythology and symbolism. The rediscovery of timeless wisdom in stories has led to a great wave of new insights. *SAGA* honors some of the leading writers in the current mythic revival.

These articles remind us of how mythology can put us in touch with unseen beauty. We see legendary characters face issues much like those in our own lives. Examples from around the world illustrate the universal qualities of the great narratives. The ideas are powerful, but the form is accessible. Stories can speak to us in several ways at once. The practical aspects of our personalities appreciate the assistance they provide in prudent decision-making. The playful child-like energies find the stories to be great fun. The quiet, spiritual side is grateful to have some time invested in reflection.

Mythology allows us to reconnect with a dimension beyond ordinary time. In this moment in history, consumer values dominate the media. Ancient stories give us a chance to visit with eternal characters involved in primal adventures. This can provide perspectives that go beyond trendy concerns with possessions or appearance. Also, issues that are too large to grasp in a single lifetime become accessible. Great shifts of history or dramatic changes in the natural environment often occur so gradually that they are hard to recognize or understand. The mythic imagination presents large issues in human form, with recognizable personalities acting out vital dramas. The great dynamics may be played out by goddesses of ancient Greece, or by lost orphans in a fairy tale. In either case, the characters and situations lay bare the quandaries of existence, and, by seeing the choices they make, we can gain some guidance on how to deal with large questions.

The stories reveal the shape of cosmic relationships. The mythic characters need each other, despite all their impressive powers. This human quality reveals the ultimate interdependence of all creation. Mythology reminds us that we must honor this great mutuality if we are to maintain balance on the planet. We also learn that the needs of the gods and goddesses extend to mortals. These are our epic tales. We are not bystanders. We are the seekers and elders. Our particular lives manifest the great patterns of history. Once we see that mythology has to do with how to live, we see that we each participate in the unfolding of creation. We each have many crucial roles to play in the living of the mutual sagas. Seeing this can enlarge one's sense of place and purpose. The recurring themes in the world's key teaching stories reveal that living on a shared globe in human form is a kindred experience for all peoples.

Sacred stories continually show us how to align our energies and attention with the forces of the natural world. Such a connection often requires quieting ourselves in some formal way in order to be more receptive. In myth, we can see that it is from a silent attunement that we can get the crucial energy for the tasks that life sets before us. In the lore, shamanic healers use lengthy meditations and extensive rituals to be open to the magic that comes directly from the vitality of the living environment. As we ponder these wonders, we become aware that the world is animated by invisible threads that are beyond our conscious knowing.

The tales provide an unforgettable sense of place for each adventure. They take us beyond our particular locales and we realize our concerns really involve the larger world community. The creation myths told by indigenous people of the Amazon take us into the animated moist density of that tropical jungle. The Nordic sagas take us into glacial wastelands. The visits to exotic settings can also enrich our sense of the specific mythologies of our home communities.

It is notable that the animals and trees are active members of the ensemble of players. These are constant reminders that we, too, are animal beings and essential components of nature, not mere observers. The birds that befriend Cinderella let us know that the resources to resolve her situation come from the natural world. This sense of union with nature connects us with a deep ecological awareness that permeates the mythic world view.

Many of the articles in *SAGA* point out how symbolic patterns can reveal hidden wisdom about the journey of the soul. Through metaphoric reading, we become open to the significance all around us. We speak in metaphors when we say "that dancer can fly," or "that politician is a wind-bag," or "the ocean is moody." In strict terms, these statements are not true. On a deeper level, such figures of speech reveal a greater truth than mere factual statements can deliver. Exploring how each image or action in a story can represent truths beyond the obvious yields the treasures. It becomes clear that the apparent world has always had abundant meanings that we had overlooked in lives busy with practical concerns.

In the teaching stories, every feature is necessary to the whole. Also, all of the often bountiful characters are important. A minor figure can hold the secret to the whole tale. The brief appearance of what may seem to be an inconsequential maidservant may end up being the turning event of the story. This helps us to enlarge our perceptions to be aware of the many possibilities in difficult situations. We begin to see the abundance of options in our surroundings. The psychological counterpart is valuing the many aspects of ourselves and others. Symbolic images in stories represent and can evoke previously unclaimed facets of our inner selves. One's least honored attribute may come to the rescue on some fateful day when circumstances require that very quality.

The mythic stories are powerful psychologically partly because they have mysterious qualities. Unexpected developments in the tales remind us that experience is not orderly. The plots propel us past our expectations into something larger, such as when Raven does trickster magic in Native American stories. As we read, we allow supernatural powers to seize our imaginations. Gradually, we can learn to allow the divinities to speak to us, and invite personal revelations, such as may come from dreams and fantasy, to become involved in our decision-making processes.

The tales have their own lives, each with unique eccentric qualities. Part of the richness is that the same story will have different lessons for each person who listens. Stories can be like the Holy Grail, which, when it passed from person to person, let them drink what they alone desired. Also, when we come back to the same story after a time, it will tell us new things. This unpredictable element keeps the encounter lively. It may also show us something about the way our lives are caught up in currents that are larger than ourselves. Even such obvious powers as the flow of history, family dynamics, and natural disasters take us to places we do not choose. The more we can know about the dynamics of these and other forces, the better chance we have of taking the best actions.

Finding the story that reflects most closely on one's individual life is a great accomplishment. Carl Jung made it his task of tasks to find the myth that was living his life. Once the general pattern of the tale becomes evident, the challenge is to participate in the rewriting of one's own story. We may not be able to create the rivers that carry us along, but we can certainly navigate the little boats of our lives. There are many variations on each theme to choose from. We each have the opportunity to shape a novel of great complexity that stays fascinating to the last scene.

In mythic stories, we see that the characters do not resolve contradictions so much as they learn to tolerate them with grace and humor. It becomes clear that there are multiple answers within each story. One would have a hard time distilling a list of right answers from these tales. In the Grimm fairy tale, the princess must keep the promise she made to the frog. Later, it is the act of refusing to keep her word that is crucial to the lesson. Differing situations at various points call for different responses. Rather than giving us clear solutions, pondering stories helps us find our own answers. Learning from stories is an interactive process.

Between the covers of this book, you will find many key ideas in the appreciation of myth and ritual. The articles repeatedly underscore the central importance of initiation. The pilgrim in the story may have to survive desert ordeals and perform feats of physical courage. In our lives, the tests may be mustering enough self-discipline to reach a worthy goal, or completing a backpacking vacation without moaning and groaning excessively. The principles are the same. One enters the realm of initiation to make allies, develop strengths, learn lessons, and return a wiser person.

The writers who have contributed to *SAGA* are masters of the tales who artfully evoke the vitality of the immortal characters. The reader feels the presence of the deities. In these presentations we can see the enchantment of the age-old stories. Such wisdom can open perceptions so that we begin to sense a vast web of interconnected being. In this collection, we have insights on how to live with each other and how to live wisely on this earth. The soul of the planet speaks to us through the mythic imagination.

To conclude on a personal note, it has been a rich delight to arrange this collection. The discussions with many of the authors have provided opportunities to reconnect with friends and colleagues. Many of the contributors I met while organizing the Joseph Campbell Archives. Some of these marvelous people, such as Christine Downing, James Hillman, and Marion Woodman have also given lectures in my courses at the Pacifica Graduate Institute. Others, such as Robert Bly, Jean Shinoda Bolen, Allen Ginsberg, Ursula Le Guin, Thomas Moore, and Murray Stein have presented seminars for Pacifica. David Miller gave many hours of his exceptional expertise when I was developing a graduate program in mythological studies. Patricia Reis is a former graduate student in Pacifica's program in depth psychology who has gone on to write books of great insight into mythology. This is an exceptional community of thinkers. These friends and colleagues have given me many gifts of grace and kindness in recent years. Once again, they have been most generous, this time in allowing me to present their work in *SAGA*.

This task has reminded me of the importance of community. There is a lively network of lovers of mythology. Lately, when I travel to speak on rediscovering stories, the experience is one of visiting friends and kindred spirits all over. We all rely on so many others. My work draws on the years of research done by the scholars included in this volume. Getting to spend time pondering the insights of their explorations in the mythic imagination is endlessly fascinating and enriching. I heartily recommend following up the discoveries you make in these pages by seeking out books by these writers. You might also take a look at the unique publications from which I chose these articles for further reading along these lines.

The people featured in this book are vital source of inspiration in these times. They are the leading teachers of mythology and symbolism. They devote their energies helping others on the quest. These scholars are the keepers of the lore. It is an honor to have gathered some of their wise writing.

Santa Barbara, California
September, 1995

# IN SEARCH OF
# HIDDEN WONDER

### *by* JOHN MATTHEWS
### *from* **Parabola**

WHEN THE TWELFTH-CENTURY POET CHRÉ-
tien de Troyes left his poem *The Story of the Grail* unfinished, he
created a mystery which has stirred the imagination of countless seekers
ever since. Yet the mystery refuses to be codified, identified, or pinned
down to a specific time or place. The setting is most often the Middle
Ages and the elements of the story follow their own pattern: the Grail
itself, variously described as a cup, a dish, a stone, or a jewel; the
presence of its guardian, the wounded King who rules over a devastated
Wasteland; the Company surrounding the King; and the questing knights
who must pose the right question to heal both King and land. Yet
despite the millions of words written every year about the Grail, it
remains an object of mystery; it is hidden, secret, as the medieval knight
and poet Wolfram von Eschenbach wrote in his telling of the myth,
where the Grail is:

The wondrous thing hidden in the flowergarden
   of the king
where the elect of all nations are called.[1]

The great mythographer Joseph Campbell has a passage in one of his books, which, though in fact referring to Biblical studies, sums up the attitude of many seekers for the Grail.

> It is one of the prime mistakes of many interpreters of mythological symbols to read them as references, not to mysteries of the human spirit, but as earthly or unearthly scenes, and to actual or imaginal historical events . . . Whereas it is one of the glories of the tradition that in its handling of religious themes, it retranslates them from the language of imagined facts into a mythological idiom; so that they may be experienced, not as time-conditioned, but as timeless; telling not of miracles long past, but of miracles potential within ourselves, here, now, and forever.[2]

It is for this reason that the Grail is *hidden*—though the hiding is in plain sight. As Campbell said elsewhere, why should the medieval knights have needed to look for the Grail—which they saw as a chalice—when there was a chalice to be found on every altar in Christendom? In the same way, why do we still seek the Grail when it is in fact everywhere around us—and within us?

The Grail can be many things: it may be without form, it may appear in more than one form, or it may not even exist at all in this dimension. The important thing is that it provides an object for personal search, for growth, and human development. In fact, those who seek it are often less concerned with the *object* than with the *actions* of the Grail—the way it causes changes to happen—in the heart, in the mind, in the soul.

In Western alchemical traditions, this is reflected in the mystery surrounding the transformational quality of the Great Work which lies at the center of the alchemist's striving for earthly perfection. The transmutation of base metal into gold is a metaphor for the transformation of the human spirit, a transformation which takes place within the alembic of the Grail. Those who encounter the mystery are never the same again. They are caught up into an entirely new frame of existence, no longer bounded by time and space: they are transformed by the process of what they encounter.

We are dealing here with a mystery that is almost too much for us. But we can learn, and grow, from studying it. Whatever else it may be, the Grail story is first and foremost pure myth, and like all myths, it is filled with archetypes.

As we follow the Quest Knights of the Arthurian legends we see many turnings which lead to different places in the map of the soul's journey. Nearly all of the characters are in some way archetypal, as are their adventures, their sufferings and their realizations. It would be wrong to regard the stories too literally, but at the same time, they were never intended as parables. This is why we need to go back to the texts as often as possible—to their infinite variety, complexity and subtlety, where we may find ever new meanings.

The thirteenth-century romance of Perlesvaus, for example, seems to say a great deal about the reasons for the quest, now as much as then. The scene is set not long after the Arthurian era. The Grail Castle, where so many strange and wondrous things have taken place, is described as ruinous and empty, a place of ghosts, with its once sacred and mysterious nature already beginning to be forgotten. To this place come two young knights in search of adventure, after the manner of the old heroes of the Table Round:

> They were fair knights indeed, very young and high spirited and they swore they would go, and full of excitement they entered the castle. They stayed there a long while, and when they left they lived as hermits, wearing hair-shirts and wandering through the forests, eating only roots; it was a hard life, but it pleased them greatly, and when people asked them why they were living thus, they would only reply: "Go where we went, and you will know why."[3]

Many people have been "going there" ever since, seeking the mysterious object of which they have heard such marvelous reports—more often than not failing, but sometimes, like the two young knights, discovering things about themselves and their own inner state. The Grail itself remains hidden, elusive, yet most have found that its "secret" is indissolubly linked with the idea of service.

This brings us to the mysterious Grail "Question" which, sooner or later, everyone who seeks the Grail has to ask, and answer: whom does the Grail serve? It may seem an odd thing to ask when you have traveled many hundreds of miles, undergone countless adventures and trials and arrived at last in the presence of the Wounded King and his entourage of Grail maidens and youths.

According to the legend, the Grail is borne through the hall in procession with the spear that drips blood, a large shallow dish, and either a candelabra or a sword.

The Wounded King is then fed with a wafer from the chalice. In some versions this is all, in others the entire company is fed with the food they most desire, which can be interpreted as actual *or* spiritual food. The point is that, in the literal sense, the Grail serves either the Grail King or the Company. Why then, the question?

In part, of course, it is a ritual question, requiring a ritual response which in turn triggers a sequence of events: the healing of King and Kingdom, the restoration of the Wasteland. The texts indicate that the Grail serves the King, the Company, and all who seek it, and it is this last possibility that concerns us.

Here, the Grail is shown to be a gateway, a nexus-point between two states of being—the human and the divine, the worldly and the otherworldly. We can see this in the very shape most often assumed by the Grail, that of a chalice. The upper portion is open to receive the downpouring of blessings of the spiritual realm; the lower half, stem and base, form an upward pointing triangle which represents human aspiration; and the two meet and are fused in the center. The Grail operates its wonderful life-giving properties so that we are each served in the way that the Fisher King is served.

But this only happens in response to the need, urgency, and the drive of the quester—the Grail serves us according to the way we serve it. Like the king who serves the land as the land serves him, we stand in similar relation to the Grail. Our service, love, hope, or desire is offered up to be accepted and transformed into pure energy. If we have be-haved in a right manner on our quest, we will reap the rewards, the divine sustenance of the Grail. And, if we open this out still further, our service will help transform the land on which we live and walk and have our being. The Grail does not need to be in view—it is present all around us, in every act of service we do, whether it be, symbolically, for the king or the land.

While the king and the land are suffering, the Grail cannot pass openly among us. It is as though a gap had opened between two worlds, leaving us shut out, lost in the twilight looking for the shining power of the Grail . . . or, as some texts suggest, inhabiting a land where there are no chalices, no means of expressing our own love or hope for the world we inhabit.

Charles Williams sums it up in a passage from a modern Grail story, *War in Heaven*. After many adventures, the moment has come when a celebration of the Eucharist is to be made, using the Grail itself as the chalice. Standing before it, one of the modern questers reflects on its mysterious power:

> Of all material things still discoverable in the world the Graal had been nearest the Divine and Universal Heart. Sky and sea and land were moving, not towards the vessel but to all it symbolized and had held . . . and through that gate . . . all creation moved.[4]

Here, the most important thing is not the Grail itself, but what it symbolizes—"through that gate all creation moved." The object is as mysterious and as "hidden" as ever.

What we have to understand is that the Grail serves us in proportion to our service to the land and to the world about us. It is not some wonderworking artifact but an active principle touched off by the accumulated longing of humankind for what was once ours—for the perfect state of being which can still be ours. It is this which gives the aura of a lost golden age to Arthur's realm and acts.

The Grail is a symbol for our time as much as it is for any time, a contemporary symbol of an utterly current aspiration. The King—call him Arthur or Christ or the World Soul—is wounded *by* as well as *for* us. His wounds impinge upon everyone, and when he is healed, so shall we all be. It is the same story, an utterly simple one: the Grail serves us; we serve the Grail; it will heal us when we use it to heal the wounds of creation.

Each one of us is *already* engaged upon this quest. Each has a chance to redeem the time in which we live, to awaken the Sleeping

King, to bring the Wasteland back into flower. We are indeed all "grails" to some degree, and the true object of the quest lies in making ourselves vessels for the light that will bring about these things.

Only then can we ourselves be healed, the Fisher King within us regain his strength, and the land flower. When that moment comes there will no longer be any need for a Grail, it will be everywhere about us, no longer hidden but openly recognized, its presence felt in every particle of our being. As another contemporary writer, Vera Chapman, writes:

> Like a plant that dies down in winter, and guards its seeds to grow again, so you . . . must raise the lineage from which all Arthur's true followers are to grow—not by a royal dynasty, but by spreading unknown and unnoticed . . . . Names and titles will be lost, but the story and the spirit of Arthur [and the Grail] shall not be lost. For Arthur is a spirit and Arthur is the land of Britain. So shall Arthur conquer, not by war, nor by one kingship that soon passes away, but by the carriers of the spirit that does not die.[5]

We are all carriers of that spirit, and by seeking the inner reality of the Grail *behind* the symbols and stories, we are taking part in an ongoing work without which all we hold most dear would long ago have perished. And if people look at us askance as we wander through the world with a strange look in our eyes, we have only to give the same answer as those knights who visited the ruined Grail Castle: "Go where we went, and you will know why."

Notes

1. Wolfram von Eschenbach, *Parzival* (Harmondsworth, Middlesex: Penguin, 1980).

2. Joseph Campbell, *The Masks of God* (London: Souvenir Press, 1968).

3. John Matthews, *At the Table of the Grail* (London: Arkana, 1993).

4. Charles Williams, *War in Heaven* (Grand Rapids, Mich.: Eerdmans, 1988).

5. Vera Chapman, *The Three Damosels* (London: Methuen, 1978).

*JOHN MATTHEWS* is the author of over forty books in the mythological field, with particular emphasis on the Arthurian and Grail legends, on which he is a noted authority. His latest titles include **King Arthur and the Grail Quest**, **The Arthurian Tradition** and **The Encyclopedia of Celtic Wisdom**, co-written with his wife, Caitlin Matthews. He gives courses throughout Britain and North America, and lives in Oxford, England.

Reprinted from *Parabola*, Winter 1994. 656 Broadway, New York, NY 10012-9824. (800) 783-4903. Subscription: $20/year.

# ON PILGRIMAGE

*An Interview with* JEAN SHINODA BOLEN

*from* **Transformation**

***In a wide-ranging conversation with Mary Nolan,
Jean Shinoda Bolen discusses the stages and tasks of adulthood.***

**Mary Nolan:** Adulthood seems to be made up of transitional periods and then times between when one is extremely busy but nothing much seems to be happening in terms of personal change. And some of the transitional times come without one seeking them, in a sense, as when the children leave home, and the parents, especially the mothers, must work with that.

**Jean Shinoda Bolen:** And some of them we can see coming at a distance. We certainly have a sense of when the children are going to be starting off to college and the nest might be empty. Others happen when a relationship or a job or our health is suddenly different than it was, and we have to adapt to circumstance that we had no preparation for—then it's an abrupt transition to adjust to. Life is full of both kinds.

Maturity, wisdom, learning from experience essentially have a lot to do with being adaptable, having some attitude that truly wonders, even in the midst of things being very stable, about what might be coming next—the assumption that seasons and weather and life are in continual change. We can either go with the changes and welcome them as a part of life, or we can resist or be upset about them, and then we have great difficulties. These have to do in part with not accepting that this is what life is and posing that it should be different, that these things shouldn't happen. If this were a perfect, just world, a lot of things wouldn't happen that do happen, so how are you going to meet what happens?

There are periods of stability when we are committed and involved, and we are genuinely using all the energies that we have in being where we are. Then it is "No, thank you!" to any other adventure that comes along. Life is like a creative process, in general: for a period of life we are absorbed, and it's alive, it's deep, it's meaningful.

Then we reach a point, as in a therapy process, for instance, when most of the journey's over. It's nice to be together, but essentially there isn't much "juice" for the experience. If we stay with something that's no longer alive, it is like an artist who does art in a certain way which sells, and gets stuck doing it over and over. After a while, the artist might as well be painting ties; in doing what will sell, the soul goes out of it. A lot of people get caught like that.

At a certain point we then may be going through the form, but the substance is missing. One of the great dangers of adulthood, I think, is being in a form that no longer has any real life to it, any vitality. If we face the truth and risk actively bringing about a transition of one kind or another, we risk change; it may end or it may grow. Instead, we may choose an addiction to numb whatever it is that we're feeling about the emptiness or meaninglessness of our work or relationships or inner lives. That defense, whatever it is, makes us grow further and further away from our own authenticity, so that we begin not to know what it is we feel, because we are working all the time or are using something to distance ourselves from our feelings. People use all kinds of things, television, for example; it's not just the substance abuses, it's process abuses.

*MN:* How do you look at where you're at and judge it in a fair way? Some of us seem to look restlessly for change even when we might perhaps be content.

*JSB:* It isn't about looking for change; it's being attuned to what really is happening and knowing how we feel about it. We actually do know our feelings, and so we know that there is a missing intensity, joy, absorption, that we're bored. Boredom is a major sign that something is amiss and there isn't much energy, more "juice" in whatever it is we're doing. We are just "being present," but not present, really: only our body is there. The more our particular world requires us to be in places that we don't want to be, and the more that we adapt to being just partially there, the more we really lose touch with what is vital.

Apart from how it is we feel, the other thing has to do with what it is we dream. Our dream life is very good at telling us things are being ignored, things are not being addressed, if we listen. People often come into a therapy process with some history of having increasingly bad dreams with similar themes; it's like they don't want to hear it, they don't want to hear it, they don't want to hear it; the dreams get worse, the dreams get worse. Then the circumstance blows up, and there's no choice but they're in it. So much has to do with really being genuine or authentic or real to your own life experience.

*MN:* Is this the primary task for those of us in adulthood?

*JSB:* It's the primary task of being a person at any stage, I like the notion that our task is to keep the best quality of every stage you have been through, so that we do not lose the awe and wonder of the child but in fact keep that child aspect with us, and we don't lose the idealism of adolescence, and that certain kind of sensitivity that is a positive part of adolescence. Adults learn how to be competent in lots of ways, and responsible, and hopefully they integrate their archetypal nature, their instinctual nature, their societal nature into an authentic life. It is a major challenge, because it matters that we adapt so as to be adequate in the eyes of the culture in which we live, so that we have reflected back on us some sense of having met the initiations of adulthood, having competently encountered and experienced what life expects of adults.

It is certainly part of adulthood that we learn to make commitments to relationship and to work, and we learn how to be responsible in lots of ways. How to do that and stay in touch with that child and that adolescent and that instinctual man or woman, and hold the opposites—I think the challenge of holding the opposites as we interact with what draws us is really an adult challenge all the time.

*MN:* Easier for a woman?

*JSB:* I think that things are easier and harder for a woman. Going through menstruation every month and bearing children makes us quite aware that we are acted upon and don't have dominion over a whole lot of things. It makes us feel closer to other people as well as to all life. We don't see ourselves as that different, at some level, from other species. Because they don't have this experience, I think men are able to distance themselves from their connectedness with all life in ways that women who are in touch with their bodies do not. I think that it is more possible for women to have depth friendships and be supported in their interior and emotional lives than men. I think men as a group are more lonely and cut off from the fact that they even feel that. Women have more of a juggling of their different relationships and responsibilities than men do, as a group.

*MN:* What happens when people find that change or growth is needed but feel trapped? I have to tell you that when we were discussing this issue a member of the Editorial Committee came up with a wonderful title: "How to follow Your Bliss and Pay the Rent." There is a lot of that for some of us.

*JSB:* It's true; nobody said it would be easy. It was Frieda Fromm Reichman who said to Joanne Greenberg, in *I Never Promised You a Rose Garden*—"I never promised you a rose garden." If we venture out into the world as an adult, it's not always going to be easy. Period. And whether we choose to make waves or passively acquiesce and stay where we are, we have made choices that will affect who we are and who we will become. The cost of it is what we give up, always; that's basic economics: the price, the true cost of anything is what we give up in order to have it. So if we give up bliss in order to pay the rent, that's the cost. If we go for bliss and don't have the money to pay the rent, that's the cost. If we can hold those opposites and somehow manage to lead an authentic and individuated life, that's the challenge. By holding the opposites, the transcendent function may provide an unexpected resolution. Something shifts; through synchronicity, dreams, or a change in circumstances or in the heart, the polarized conflict dissolves. In my work and life, I know that sometimes we need to hold the opposites, keep faith, and actively wait. I also know that sometimes the need is to act decisively, to step beyond our known world, into the fire or into the void; that there is something that is a now-or-never opportunity and choice. And there are no promises as to outcome.

When I talk to people who are a couple of decades older than I, whom I think of as having some wisdom for having lived as long as they have, I find the things they most regret are usually not what they did but what they didn't do, something that they know really was important, really did matter. I think that Joseph Campbell's idea of following one's bliss means following something that is truly meaningful to us, and the price extracted by the journey and the hardships of it are worth it to us.

When we often choose what others expect us to do, or what is the conservative, cautious thing to do, we sometimes find that the cost is far greater than we expected, in terms of being chronically depressed, being in a life that has form but not much substance, not much joy. There is something about having joy as an accessible part of your self. More women, I think, have a broader range of feeling, including joy, than most adult men. Why? Because we are more attuned to our feelings, but also because we are more spontaneous, we can be more playful, we can laugh more with—not at—other people. We haven't been acculturated always to assess ourselves about "Where am I relative to the other man in terms of power?"

The difference between men and women is something Deborah Tannen wrote about (in *You Just Don't Understand Me*, 1990). She pointed out that women talk in order to express feelings and exchange information about themselves or their relationships. Men talk about objects and facts; communication between them is a means of establishing status, of knowing whether they are one-up or one-down vis-à-vis the other man. This makes conversations between the sexes fraught with misunderstanding, which is the point Tannen makes. Another conclusion that I see, is that women's conversations with friends are opportunities to be real about what we feel and observe about ourselves as well as others. We are free to share our vulnerabilities and foibles, to cry and laugh.

As a gender, however, women have more difficulty than men in acting decisively. Both knowing how we feel and acting upon what we know are necessary in making choices that add up to an authentic life.

*MN:* For some of us it may feel risky, sometimes, to open ourselves, really communicate, change—better to stay where you are than run the risk of following your bliss, or really looking at what your options are.

*JSB:* Vitality, in which we laugh and cry, assumes an open heart that isn't toughened and armored and hidden. I think that overall it is better to love and lose than not to love at all. Loss is always the risk in caring about anyone or anything. But what else is there to do, when the choice is not to care, not to be connected, to be armored, and to grow old. One of the things about watching the years from forty to sixty is the enormous discrepancy between vitality versus chronological age. In forty-, fifty-, sixty-, and seventy-year-olds there can be a world of difference between someone who has lived well and deeply and been involved, who has a youthfulness and a wisdom, versus someone who has lived defensively, closed down, closed off, is, under it all, angry, depressed, hostile.

In adulthood, we have the difficulty and the challenge of holding the opposites—that of individuation vs. responsibility to our more collective or traditional roles. The Jungian point of view leans toward individuation and is an influence that may tip the balance in the direction of change, while the institutions of society—religion, family, marriage, and even professional and corporate institutions—resist individualism and change. Both polarities are within us. Within and without, there may be room to dialogue and bring about change without having to come down on one side of these opposites, but it is often fraught with emotional and spiritual pain, and in the end we may have to face an either-or choice.

In the day-to-day living of life, I see the necessity of being conscious of our feelings and perceptions in order to be real to ourselves and others—which also makes life itself more real and interesting. For so many of us, there is an awareness that the form we're in is stifling and rigid, and yet if we break the form there are children and others who will be affected by the choices we make. By what light do we act? We need to hold the opposites within us until there is some clarity, so that what we do is our choice, not someone else's. People are always willing to tell us how we are supposed to lead our lives. But we have each been given the opportunity to live the particular life we have. We come up to those places where we have to decide to choose, based on who we are and how we call it, knowing that there is no absolute, easy, all-around solution to these quandaries we get into—and I don't see how people avoid them, either. There has to be some risk-taking as to how and what it is we do next.

*MN:* What are the paths to that kind of wisdom?

*JSB:* You're asking a "how-to" question, and there are not exactly "how-do" answers. There is a need to be aware of what is painful in our lives, so that we don't ignore the pain or numb it out, and to accept that we don't have a solution yet. Therapy may be turned to as a means of resolving or responding to any major painful life situation, but it is only one path. Prayer and meditation and solitude, which provide access to the archetype of the Self, are other paths. Whatever the means, we need to stay open to synchronicities and dreams and trust that, if we stay engaged in our own deep process, clarity will come.

The other task often has to do with our willingness to speak the truth about what we are experiencing, whether it's at the job or in a relationship, or whatever. Angeles Arrien, the cultural anthropologist (author of *The Fourfold Way*, 1993), has a wonderful four-point plan. Her precepts are: show up, pay attention, speak your truth, and don't be attached to outcome. It applies beautifully in most situations.

To show up means being truly present, engaged in what is going on. Truly to pay attention means we aren't so caught up in our own "poor-me" story that we don't really look and pay attention to who else is in the story and what is going on with them, what they are saying to us. Then we speak our truth as we perceive it, as we feel it, and that's not easy, especially for women—to speak about what it is we need, what it is we perceive. To say it without being attached to outcome means that we don't have an assumption, just because we say it, about what the response from the other person or the situation will be. We actually assume that the other person has the freedom to respond genuinely to what we have just genuinely said. The outcome gives us more information. It may not be what we wanted to hear, but what we do hear informs us more about how things really are, and that's yet one more part of our process.

*MN:* What about the prayer part?

*JSB:* I think prayer has several different functions. When we take prayer seriously, it means that we have to be very careful about what it is we're praying for; we need some clarity about the "what." Prayer connects us to the Self, the archetype or meaning, whether it's to the Alcoholics Anonymous sense of a higher power, or the Christian sense of God, or the Goddess, or the Tao. When we pray, "thy will be done," I think we are asking to do and learn what we came for: Let me be who my highest self could be. Let me be on a soul path.

In praying for that, or praying to be out of a complex, or to be more forgiving, or less afraid, or for courage, or to be more articulate, there is something about putting the intention in a prayer that helps strengthen that intention. When it comes to praying for other people, I think that there really is an efficacy about it. I am delighted that Larry Dosey, in his book on prayer (*Healing Words*, 1993) is bringing forth research that says that people who are prayed for do better than people who are not, that prayer has a reality, that prayer changes things.

When we start tapping into prayer and seeking to pray for people to be healed, we are invoking the healing archetype, helping it to come through us into the situation. As we pray, we are aligning ourselves to the Self. And if we spend some time aligned to the Self every day, we are better off for it. Meditation, prayer, contemplation are soul enhancing. I like the notion of asking ourselves, is this soul satisfying? You don't even have to be able to define what soul is in order to have some sense that one thing is not soul satisfying while another is.

*MN:* Any final thoughts?

*JSB:* No; I'm still in process!

*JEAN SHINODA BOLEN* is a psychiatrist, a Jungian Analyst, and a clinical professor of psychiatry at the University of California San Fransisco. She writes extensively on the application of mythology in contemporary living as the author of *The Tao of Psychology*, *Goddesses in Everywoman*, *Gods in Everyman*, *Ring of Power*, and *Crossing to Avalon*.

Reprinted from *Transformation*, Summer 1994, C. G. Jung Institute of Chicago, 1567 Maple Avenue, Evanston, IL 60201. (708) 475 4848.

# THIS QUESTION OF IMAGES

### by JAMES HILLMAN

*from* *The Joseph Campbell Archives & Library Newsletter*

THE REASON THAT WE'RE IN THIS CAMP-
bell room is that we're involved in mythic thinking. That's what Joseph
Campbell did. It's important to realize the importance of thinking in
images, especially in a culture that uses images, but doesn't really *think*
in images yet. We watch them—we go to the movies and watch images
and read poetry, but our thinking is still scientistic, explanatory, and
laid out flat. *Explanation* means to lay out flat, putting something out
flat.

What Campbell did was to think in images. That's something
different than thinking critically or thinking analytically or thinking
scientistically or thinking logically. And Campbell opened this up—
this question of images. I think that's the most important thing that he
did. That's why there are so many images in his books. Not only visual
images of cave paintings or of statues or of goddesses and gods and so
on, but poetic images, and if there had been a chance, probably musical

images. (But maybe he left that to his wife—the musical images, the ballet images.)

This movement to thinking in images is part of the movement of our times, because we are going to stop reading linear sentences—one that follows another, and will be watching video screens with three or four windows in them, juxtaposing images. Kids are already doing that. Therefore, the value of Campbell's work is his laying out the richness of images that people will need to use for truly deep images rather than Nintendo games. We'll have an information highway where you sit at your own monitor and you will be able to create a whole world of imagery—paintings, architecture, symbols, ruins. All the museums will be available. A kind of pioneer nucleus of that is the great intellectual and educational value of Campbell's work and his collection.

The way I understand his value is that there are four things that are important that he contributed to our culture. First, the research and collection. He spent his whole lifetime researching cultural images from all sorts of cultures, collecting them, filing them, organizing and publicizing them. His span of the imagination goes from the earliest cave paintings to James Joyce to C. G. Jung to George Lucas, so you get images from one man embracing all that. It's a hero's journey.

The second thing he did—for which scholars disapprove of him— was that he related it to popular culture. He was not afraid of people—which so many academics are. He could understand that learning is also entertainment and enjoyment. Now that's become *info-tainment.* We understand that much better, but he was put down for being understandable, not arcane, not mysterious, not elite, not private, not keeping it as a preserve of scholarship, but making it something that was available to all levels of culture and therefore not dogmatic. He did not have a particular dogma in his research, in his works and collection, that he was trying to prove. He was collecting and comparing and enjoying.

One of the great differences between thinking in images and other kinds of thinking is that it's enjoyable. You enjoy, there's pleasure in it when you look at the picture, read the poems. When your mind works in imagistic ways there's a pleasure in that. Those of you who ever heard Campbell talk know he was humorous and fun. He himself was a man who spread a kind of enjoyment of it all.

A third thing is his extension of the idea of religion. He took it very seriously. *Religio*: linking back, linking again, tying back to something. Religion as re-finding all that has been forgotten, rather than religion as dogma or creed. There's a big difference. This is religion that is rediscovering what has been left behind, what has been called in the Christian culture the pagan past, or tribal cultures, or the cave people. He extended the notion of religion from what you do on Sunday to what is the foundation of a culture, of our whole civilization. In his four volume *Masks of God* he moves from dogma and creed, linking back to the roots of the images of the gods.

He did something else that is the fourth thing that seems so important: he carried on the tradition of great mythologists, because he was a teller of tales. He didn't just talk about it, he would tell the stories and he was a tremendous storyteller. He had that great gift of gab—he would tell the story and it would go on and you were enchanted and delighted. This is in the line of thinking in images that goes back to Plato who told stories in his *Dialogues*, to Michelangelo, to Shakespeare. It's a literary storytelling tradition of thinking which is unlike the drier side that you find in Aristotle and St. Thomas and Descartes and science where your work is not in images.

Those particular points are those that seem of great value to the culture as a whole. Why those films he did with Bill Moyers caught on so, it was as if there was something missing in our culture. Religion meant the creed you either went to or went away from, but you were trapped in one position and narrowed. Your thought always had to be such that you could pass a test or, if you were learned, you had to be academic, not popular. He broke those places. If you studied myth, you had a theory about it, like if you studied art you'd have a theory about it, you wouldn't be a teller of tales or a painter. So by his gift of telling, he was the artist of mythology, not only the organizer of myths. All of that came through in the Moyers interviews. There'd be moments when that would flash. Of course, he was under the pressure of an interview—one of the most horrible inventions—which no one suffered in antiquity. There were no talk shows, there were no interviews, they had no panels. Anybody who's got anything to say today is forced to suffer those three forms of tortuous inquisition invented in our culture. He was under pressure a lot in the Moyers interviews and wasn't able to take off as he might if he were sitting with us and talking.

One of the things about thinking in images or mythical thinking is that there is another level to what is said. You're not only seeing things realistically or naturally. It's like dreams: there's another meaning in there. There's metaphor. Things can happen in images that don't happen in life, for example, if you dream that there's a butterfly swimming around in your aquarium, that's not natural. If you're only thinking naturally, you think there's something wrong. But if you're thinking in images you've got the combination of the butterfly and aquarium and you have a butterfly that can swim. The aquarium is a watery area that will hold butterflies. There's a lot of metaphor happening, but if you're only looking scientistically, then something's wrong. We do this to our dreams all the time. We keep seeing strange things in our dreams and we reflect this against our naturalistic world and think something's wrong. But in the dream there's nothing wrong. The butterfly is happy in the aquarium! We have to extend our mind to a second level and begin to play with it more.

*JAMES HILLMAN* is the founder of Archetypal Psychology. He is the author of *ReVisioning Psychology, The Myth of Analysis, Dream and the Underworld,* and *Kinds of Power.* Dr. Hillman was director of studies at the C. G. Jung Institute in Zurich for ten years and is now professor of psychology at the Pacifica Graduate Institute. This is a slightly edited version of a talk given by Dr. Hillman at the Joseph Campbell Archives & Library on the Pacifica campus.

Reprinted from *Joseph Campbell Archives & Library Newsletter,* 249 Lambert Road, Carpinteria, CA 93013, (805) 969-3626. Membership: $75/year.

# Developing a Mythic Sensibility

*by* Thomas Moore

*from* **Sphinx**

**M**YTH IS ONE OF THE GENRES OF EXPERI-
ence, a way that imagination wraps us in fantasy even as we dream or
live out a day. It accounts for the deepest level of emotion, understanding, interpretation, and valuing in experience. Because it is so deep, it is
collective in tone, full of memory that goes back so far as to feel
antecedent to personal life and even to human life. In it, unfamiliar
plants, animals, geographies, and notable events may take their place
regardless of any connection to actual experience.

Perhaps because myth is so much larger than personality, we tend
to mystify it, and although we want to see daily experience in relation
to myth, we may juxtapose a mythic theme with an event in life and
miss the deep story that is suggested *within* the event. I once sat on a
rock at the top of a New England mountain watching several young
men bind themselves into brightly colored winged gliders and leap off

into the valley below. Some of them soared high above me, catching thermals, they said, that caught them and drew them up into the atmosphere. It seemed as though Icarus had come to life with little disguise in these adventurers who spent more than an hour circling high above like the hawks they admired and emulated.

In this case myth rose to the surface, pure, since what these flyers were doing had no rational or pragmatic purpose. They felt their element, air, against their faces and heard it rush through their wings, and they looked to the hawks as their teachers. To me, the mythic quality of these flights was more in the archaic and elemental nature of the play than in their echoing of the Greek Icarus. I'd rather think that both Icarus and my young neighbors were seized by the same myth.

I think it is helpful to distinguish between myth and mythology. Mythology is a certain kind of story that describes the stratum of myth in imaginal experience. It helps us see myth in ordinary life, just as lyric poetry might teach us to appreciate a lyrical moment or a novel might show us that every episode in life, for all of its immediacy, is a fiction. There are no real people, no real places—only characters and settings. We should not confuse the mythological exemplar with the immediate mythic experience.

At its best mythology can generate a sensibility that appreciates the deep fiction that is myth. It can open up a particular kind of vision, so that we see what otherwise would be hidden beneath a layer of literalism or personalistic fiction. Myth is less personal and more archaic (a word extremely close to archetypal) than the intentional stories we tell or the personal memories we use in order to imagine the present. It is more radical than the novel which uses the imagery of personal life for its fictive construction of experience. It is much closer to emotion and meaning than the reasoning interpretations we drop on experience from moment to moment.

On the other hand, mythology can be used to obfuscate imagination, especially when it is given prominence over the experienced myth. One obvious way, for example, that mythology obscures imagination is what we call fundamentalism. We enshrine the mythology, taking it literally, conceptually, and moralistically and lose imagination altogether. Fundamentalism is not only a problem in religious organizations, whereby the power of religion poetically to generate a sense of the sacred is lost, it is also a block to imagination in our own psychologies and in personal life. If in Jungian psychology, for example, we take the mythic figure of the anima, whose mythic nature generally is preserved in Jung's personal recollections of her, and make her into a concept into which we can pour all the female images of our dreams and daily life, then we are behaving as psychological fundamentalists. If in our own lives we remain attached to a particular story that explains who we are, then we are moving dangerously close to personal fundamentalism.

I know a man, for instance, who explains to everyone that his mother told him never to say much about himself because people would only gain power over him with the information. Therefore, he says, he is a tight-lipped adult who can't be expected to express his thoughts and feelings about things. My sense is that his tale from childhood serves as a protection against the soul's desire to put itself into the world in its stories. He is a fundamentalist, with all the accompanying defensive ploys, in relation to his own unfolding life. We all fall into this kind of fundamentalism, which seems generally to be a defense against the iconoclastic nature of imagination.

Another way mythology is used against the mythic imagination is by enshrining a particular mythological tradition. Although there are good reasons why a particular mythology might be more appealing than another in a certain context, focusing on a single tradition might threaten the fluidity that imagination usually requires. For example, Western language, art and thought is profoundly indebted to Greek mythology, and that is good reason to rely on Greek imagery. Our arts are largely an elaboration of that tradition, and so we have a ready-made substantive body of reading that tradition that is extremely valuable. But Judeo-Christian literature and iconography have equal weight in Western life and thought. The problem is that we tend not to see the mythological nature of these traditions, assuming that to label something mythological is to diminish it, and therefore we get caught in literal arguments. Eastern and African mythology have the advantage of being rather fresh and unfamiliar to the Western mind. They are not loaded down with centuries of canonical readings and therefore can offer new vision.

Many people seem to think that archetypal psychology is a mythological psychology, and Greek in particular. In a discussion on the archetypal nature of an issue, someone will likely say: "Oh, which Greek God or Goddess is involved here?" Archetypal psychology is interested in the myth, but the traditional mythology only amplifies, in the technical Jungian sense, the myth we are trying to perceive.

"Archetypal" refers to an imaginal matrix for the matter under scrutiny, but that imagining may take a number of different genres. Myth is one of the ways life is lived archetypally, but we might also imagine in the mode of fairy tale, Sufi story, Zen koan, parable, novel, and even train schedule. Given that the situation appears to be mythic, then mythology helps us glimpse the particular mythic themes at play here. But myth is never neat and fixed. Just when you think you have discovered the myth in play, then is the time to allow imagination to move on. My flying boys evoked Icarus, but their own myth was unique and could be told in a new story.

All the same, mythology tells us a great deal about myth. For example, mythology is extremely unstable and fluid. A mythological story readily decomposes, so that we find many contrasting versions, great variety in the names of characters, changes in locations, variations in plot and even contradictory outcomes. But this is the nature of experience: facts may seem to remain the same, while our stories are always changing. The campfire game in which one person in a circle tells a story to the one next to him, who tells it to the person next to him, and so on until the last person tells the story with wide variations on the original is not just about memory, it's about the fluidity of imagination. This is a game our mythology has been playing for centuries. We may prefer a different kind of game, one that is not so variable and open to chance, but it is not our part to choose the game.

Mythology also decomposes into fragmentary art forms that keep it alive. We read the myth of Phaedra in Euripides and then find it familiar but radically altered in later poets and playwrights, from Seneca to Eugene O'Neill. Freud claims to find his truth in mythology, and yet his version of Oedipus is a marked variation on Sophocles. A woman dreams of being led by a burglar down into a cellar and calls it a Persephone dream, but this isn't the precise imagery we find in the "Homeric Hymn to Demeter."

Mythology also fragments in stories that appear only in brief, suggestive form. In a sense, mythology is always in ruins, a piece missing here and there, just like the sculptures and paintings that have been reshaped by time and fortune, perhaps in more telling form than in the original. Visit a medieval cathedral, and you will see a character in relief or in sculpture in the middle of speaking a word or making an action. Either the rest of the story is implied, or a piece of myth is all that is necessary to suggest the theme. A moment seized in marble may be a more true evocation of the myth than a story. Isn't this, too, the nature of experience? How often do you feel you are in a complete story, with beginning, middle, and end? We can try to make up stories that seem to apply, but these stories are suspicious. They force an issue or a point of view. Lived experience is more fragmentary, suggestive of themes and plots, but never definite. It may take many different stories to evoke a myth.

Mythic experience as such is not narrative in quality. It is more like a dream—incomplete, volatile, elusive. Its power lies in its images more than in its narrative elements. In literature it is usually not so effective to retell a complete ancient mythological story in modern dress. It's better to insinuate pieces of the mythology so as to suggest the mythic stratum. Myth is made of characters who don't need an author to give them a story. They do quite well walking through life with their own personalities, their stories no more obvious than the stories of any of us who bring our quirks and oddities into every life situation.

A story can be a defense against myth, because if we allow myth to live through us, we can't predict what the characters, given their histories, might do. A story is protective because it gives the illusion of wholeness and singularity. Myth is the soul's deep narrative stuff rolling along on the winds of fate. It is largely iconoclastic, forging meanings that counter the interpretations we lovingly construct and cherish.

"My" in "myth" is the Greek *mu*, which implies shutting the eyes and mouth. I understand this to mean that myth is the story we tell when our mouths are shut. It is a different kind of telling, perhaps the story we live as opposed to the story we say we are living. It is the pieces of story told when our mouths are shut in sleep. It is the story another person tells about us when our mouth is shut—different from the story we tell ourselves. The story told with a closed mouth is indirect. It sneaks out when we are saying other things. It is essentially different from what we intend to say when we open our mouths to speak. I do not tell the myth, but rather one of its characters speaks and the myth comes to life.

Myth is also the tale we behold when we close our eyes in sleep or reverie. It is a world that doesn't operate on the laws of nature. It follows rules of imagination. If we want to perceive the myth, we have to close our eyes to all the usual interpretations of events. We think we know how things work and what they mean, but myth says otherwise. Because it is a deeper story, it is not the same as the one we tell from the surface of understanding. "Deeper" means closer to sacred. Mircea Eliade described myth as the "sudden breakthrough of the sacred that really establishes the World." Mythology speaks in the language of gods and goddesses, and so, too, does myth as it is lived. The closer we move toward a mythic sensibility, the more we appreciate the divine in the everyday. We penetrate through our rational explanations, past our technological methods, and beyond our personal motivations to behold meanings, ways, and reasons that human will and understanding cannot hold. "Myth" and "mystery" are twins, not only etymologically, but also in the nature of things. To appreciate myth is to preserve mystery.

Approaching myth in an ordinary situation, therefore, we ask not "What am I doing?" but rather "What is being done?" To ask, "What does the soul want?"—one of the important questions in the archetypal method—is to inquire about myth, because myth is the story being fashioned by the soul and its fate rather than the one being told and willed, in counterpoint, by personal consciousness. We hang onto and apply our understandings and intentions, but the proper attitude toward myth is response. The word "respond" means to pour a libation. We respond to myth by acknowledging the particular divine mystery hidden and expressed in the fragments of its revelation. The whole idea of talking and doing art mythically is to find those images that give a divine base to a particular human event or tendency. Myth provides the religion we need in order to be saved from the secularism of any particular moment in life. Every episode has its own religion, requiring its own piety, asking for special sacrifices, calling for appropriate rituals. In this sense myth serves the religious attitude—its traditional purpose and the gist of Eliade's remark.

A mythic vision opens our eyes to a world otherwise shrouded by secularism. With the grace of a mythic viewpoint, we see the way medieval painters saw: that saints are alive among us, that our fellow human beings have halos, that miracles are performed daily, that devils peek around every corner. A poem by D. H. Lawrence makes the point gracefully:

> *And a woman who had been washing clothes in the*
>     *pool of rock . . .*
> *now turned and came slowly back, with her*
> *back to the evening sky.*
> *Lo! God is one God! But here in the twilight*
> *godly and lovely comes Aphrodite*
> *out of the sea towards me!*

Myth is not merely a kind of intellectual interpretation of events, it guides us out of the modernistic template that lives by natural law, by perception of the senses and by physical technologies toward a sacred world in which meaning is not limited to human categories and where the laws of imagination have dominance. It generates technologies that are magical rather than mechanical. Therefore, the restoration of a mythic sensibility calls for nothing less than a radically post-modern way of living. It allows a vision, not of Greek mythology once more incarnated, but of the goddess of the sensual body and the sea breaking through in an ordinary passage of time.

We are always in myth, whether or not we appreciate that fact. If we are in it piously, prepared by art and religion to deal with the sacred, then life is given immense depth and we can engage the angels and devils who are always turning up unexpectedly. But if we are convinced of the secular philosophy of the day and ignore the necessary rituals of myth and the technologies of depth, then we suffer the incursions of the divine. Their breakthrough becomes our breakdown. The word "pathos" means either to feel the pathology of the divine breaking painfully into human life or to live the passion of the divine as it arrives. Passion is merely the aura of a god who has been given a place of entry.

Myth cannot survive within the confines of modern psychology, however imagistic and spiritual. Myth urges us toward the restoration of art and religion, toward the end of psychology that has been a temporary stand-in for these while we experimented with secularism. Myth cannot be translated into psychological categories, certainly not to passing themes of gender and personality. Myth has nothing to do with character traits of human beings of any sex. Whenever we translate myth into personal, human qualities we are making one of the most grievous reductions possible. The mystery of incarnation does not mean reducing the nature of divinity to human definitions. It has to do with the mystery by which the archaic world of myth and the supraordinate realm of divinity play their parts in the unfolding of human fate.

Our task, therefore, is to return myth to modern life and thought without reducing it to eighteenth-century notions of reasonable divinity and yet without literal archaism and mythological fundamentalism. We need art that speaks to and from the depths where myth spawns, as well as art that knows its purpose to be in the service of religious sensibility. We need less an appreciation for mythology and more a daring spirit willing to live in a mythic, animated (imagination-filled) world where everything is sacred, where angels appear unexpectedly and in many guises and where devils make it all interesting and complicated.

*THOMAS MOORE* is the author of ***Care of the Soul,*** and ***Soul Mates.*** His earlier books include ***The Planets Within*** and ***Dark Eros.*** He is also the editor of ***A Blue Fire, Selected Writings of James Hillman.*** Dr. Moore is the founder of the Institute for the Study of Imagination in Massachusetts.

Reprinted from *SPHINX, A Journal for Archetypal Psychology and the Arts,* London Convivium for Archetypal Studies, P.O. Box 417, London NW3 6YE, England, UK.

# PERSEPHONE ABDUCTED

## *by* RITA DOVE

She cried out for Mama, who did not
hear. She left with a wild eye thrown back,
she left with curses, rage
that withered her features to a hag's.
No one can tell a mother how to act:
there are no laws when laws are broken, no names
to call upon. Some say there's nourishment in pain,
and call it Philosophy.
That's for the birds, vulture and hawk,
the large one's who praise
the miracle of flight because
they use it so diligently.
She left us singing in the field, oblivious
to all but the ache of our own bent backs.

*RITA DOVE* served as the Poet Laureate of the United States and Consultant in Poetry at the Library of Congress from 1993 to 1995. She is a recipient of the Pulitzer Prize in poetry. Her collections of poetry include **The Yellow House on the Corner, Museum, Thomas and Beulah, Grace Notes,** and **Mother Love**. She also writes short stories, a novel, ans a verse drama.

Reprinted from *Ms. Magazine*; Subscription: $45/six issues, P.O.Box 57132, Boulder, CO 80322-7132. Used by permission of the author.

# Revisiting the Myth of Demeter & Persephone

### by Christine Downing

**I** HAVE LONG BEEN FASCINATED BY THE sacred myths and rituals of initiation through which women and men of the ancient world were helped to discover and become themselves. I have long believed that remembering and reimagining these traditions might help us do likewise. Like James Hillman I believe that although myths don't tell us how, they help us to question, imagine, go deeper.[1] Myths help us to enter the complexity of our situations more deeply, with more love of the perplexities themselves and of those caught up in them.

The myth of Demeter and Persephone stirs the imagination of almost all who hear it. Greek rituals associated with it recognized its relevance to the cycle of vegetal life, to the human fear of death and hope for immortality, to the deep bonds that exist among women, particularly mothers and daughters. Some of these rituals were open only to women, others also included men. The myth appears to have particular resonance for women and many seem to feel that in some sense it is *the* myth for them, as the Oedipus myth may be *the* myth for men. Yet we find amazingly different meanings in it.

My own involvement with Greek mythology and particularly with Greek goddesses was initiated almost fifteen years ago by a dream which led me to remember how my myth-loving mother had welcomed me, her first child, a daughter born on the first day of spring, as *her* Persephone. Continued reflection on this memory and its significance for me as an adult woman led to my book *The Goddess* in which, looking at the myth from the perspective of Persephone, I contrasted my view with that of the Homeric "Hymn to Demeter" which (as the title suggests) adopts Demeter's view, identifying with her grief over the loss of her daughter and her assumption that time spent in the underworld can only be understood negatively. I, by contrast, spoke of the importance of Persephone's being taken out of the role of daughter and taking her own place as goddess of the underworld. I focused on how Persephone initiates us into a recognition of the underworld as a sacred realm and thus into a different relation to periods during our lifetime when we are abducted from our preoccupation with worldly tasks and with others and into a different relation to death.

In the intervening years, I have become fascinated with how this myth has compelled the attention of many other women, and with how differently each of us reads it. This has given me a renewed appreciation of the power of a myth to engender new mythmaking (which is what demonstrates that a myth is still functioning as a myth) and has taught me to value other dimensions of this myth, other ways in which it is pertinent to the lives of contemporary women and men.

Some speak of finding in it resources for the imaginal recreation of a prepatriarchal matristic world. Many, concentrating on the myth's account of Demeter's love of Persephone, see it primarily in terms of how it valorizes the beauty and power of the mother-daughter bond. Others focus on Hades' abduction of Persephone and read the myth as primarily a story about paternal violation, about rape, incest, abuse, about male intrusion into women's mysteries, about the rise of patriarchy and the suppression of goddess religion.

Yet this same myth has also been interpreted as one which might help move us beyond the fantasy of a conflict-free world ruled by an all-giving and all-powerful mother, beyond the illusion of female innocence and perfect love. It has been seen as representing a necessary initiation for women which frees them from being defined by the roles of mother or daughter and as teaching the necessity of coming to terms with loss and limitation and with experiences that provoke rage and grief.

Most feminists have focused on ways of understanding the myth that reveal its particular relevance to women's lives, but many have recognized that the myth is not just about women's psychology but also about gender issues, not just about mothers and daughters but also about the relations between women and men. Some have gone further and suggested that the myth may be profoundly important to the self-understanding of men as well as of women. They note that the Eleusinian mysteries, the most important rites associated with these two goddesses, were open to all, men and women, and that all initiates regardless of gender temporarily adopted names with feminine endings, as though the transformed understanding of human relationships and of death which the mysteries provided required entrance into a female perspective.

An even more inclusive interpretation is suggested by some ecofeminists who, moving beyond seeing the myth primarily through a psychological lens, emphasize its relevance to their concerns about the earth's renewal.

Exposure to these many different perspectives underlies my own re-engagement with this myth which I truly felt I had fully honored long ago. I have come to see the story of Demeter and Persephone as providing us with resources for the articulation of a vision sorely needed by all of us, a vision which may move us beyond an identification with peculiarly female or male perspectives but which is nonetheless unquestionably informed by some of the things we have learned from the matristic past, from our dreams, from one another, and from our bodies. I see myself and most of the others drawn to this myth as not interested only in learning what it meant *then*, in the world of classical Greece or in an imagined prepatriarchal world, but in reimagining it; that is, in using the myth to help us imagine forward to a possible postpatriarchal world.

This imagining forward involves a careful listening to and honoring of the many different explications spawned by the ancient myth. The various interpretations contradict, complement, complicate, and ultimately enrich one another. Just as no one version of a myth is the "real" one, just as a myth *is* its many variants, so no one interpretation is the "right" one, the myth *means* these many different understandings of it.

Even in the ancient world each telling of the myth served a different meaning. There is no original version, no recoverable first telling, no retelling that wasn't already an interpretation. Probably the oldest meaning was about Demeter as a grain goddess, about the seasonal cycle and the introduction of agriculture. By the time of Homer the Greek gods and goddesses were not viewed as aspects of natural world but as humans writ large. In the earliest literary version of the myth available to us, the Homeric "Hymn To Demeter"—which played a central role in expressing and forming the ancient world's understanding of the goddesses and on which most contemporary reinterpretations of the myth are based—the myth is already understood as primarily about interpersonal relationships and about the establishment of a cult which freed initiates of their fear of death.

This Hymn (and the extant traditions about the all-women's ritual, the Thesmophoria) gives us more access than most classical material does to women's perspectives, since the hymn looks at the story of Persephone's abduction from a female perspective, from Demeter's view point, and the Thesmophoria is generally regarded as one of the oldest and least changed of Attic rites.

Yet despite its prominence, the hymn's version of the Demeter/Persephone myth never received canonical status. The Orphic tradition included a very different version, one with which fourth and fifth century Athenians such as Sophocles, Euripides, Aristophanes, and Plato were clearly familiar, one in which Zeus (in the form of a snake) not Hades is Persephone's seducer and the issue of their liaison is the infant Dionysos.

The most influential late classical version is the one included in Ovid's *Metamorphoses*. Ovid, an artist for whom myths are clearly first and foremost good stories, seeks to make manifest myth's power to illumine human psychology, to demonstrate it's enduring power even for those who no longer believe in their gods. In his writing the gods (and the goddesses, too) are reduced to human psychological terms and seen as often arbitrary and cruel. Thus in his telling Demeter's rage is seen as extravagant, Persephone's innocence as also exaggerated—or feigned!

It is generally agreed that the rituals celebrated in honor of the two goddesses, including both the Attic Thesmophoria and the Eleusinian Mysteries, are far older than any literary account of the myth. Archaeologists have found indications that a mystery cult was already established at Eleusis by the middle of the second millennium B.C.E. The place name, Eleusis, probably refers to the underworld in a favorable sense; it may mean something like "place of happy arrival;" the name suggests an allusion to Elysian, the realm of the blessed.[2] Unlike most Greek temple sites, at Eleusis the temple complex is built around a subterranean chamber, making evident the connections to archaic chthonic tradition.

It may be that at one time the Eleusinian rites were open only to women (as the Thesmophoria always continued to be); it is certain that priestesses always played a central role in the administration of the cult. But in historical times the Eleusinian cult was the most inclusive of all Greek cults, open to all who spoke Greek and were free of blood guilt, and who took a vow to keep the ritual secret.

Unlike many other rituals in which one participates on a regular basis, it was felt that to have seen the mystery once was sufficient, although a different status in the celebration was reserved for repeaters. Participation in the ritual created no ongoing bonds among the initiates and implied no further ritual or ethical obligations. The initiates returned to their ordinary life outwardly unchanged. But inwardly, as testimony after testimony confirms, they were transformed, freed from fear of death. As Pindar exclaimed, "Happy is he who, having seen these rites goes below the hollow earth; for he knows the end of life and he knows its god-sent beginning."[3]

What the initiates saw at the climax of the rites is still a mystery, still a secret. The hymn was, of course, public; the myth was known to everyone. The myth was part of the open preparation, elements of it are clearly paralleled by various parts of the preparatory phases of the celebration about which no one felt they must be silent.

But what was enacted, what sacred things were shown, at the climax of the rite which took place within the temple and at night we do not know. As Mylonas says, the maintenance of the secret is amazing when one considers that these rites were celebrated for almost 2000 years and that multitudes from everywhere were initiated. We have the testimony attributed to Aristotle that the focus in the secret part of the rite was on something seen and done that had a transformative psychological effect, not on something taught: the initiates, he says, don't learn anything but suffer, feel certain emotions, are put in a certain frame of mind.

If we want to understand how Demeter and Persephone were experienced in the ancient world, we must also take into account the Thesmophoria, an all women's ritual, celebrated in the fall in honor of Demeter, which provided married women (children and virgins were excluded) an occasion to share with one another the sorrows of motherhood and the anger women feel at men, and, some believe, an opportunity to reclaim their own sexuality.

The myth and the rituals associated with it have given rise to many interpretations, many appropriations. Many of us have experienced that our own understanding of its meaning keeps changing, keeps growing. At a particular time, at a particular life-stage or in relation to a particular life crisis, a new meaning may suddenly emerge. We learn to appreciate a wide range of such meanings by continuing to return to the myth itself, by continuing to seek to understand our own lives in terms of their mythic dimensions—and by listening to what others have found in the myth that speaks to them. There is a sense in which each of the interpretations imagines the myth forward, perhaps by imagining a Demeter who has come to terms with loss or a Persephone who has wholeheartedly taken on her role as goddess of the underworld. The themes of reunion and renewal so prominent in the end of the Homeric hymn seem to encourage such hopeful, though often cautiously hopeful, retellings.

Some retellings have taken as central to the myth its hints of a prepatriarchal matristic world. For instance, Charlene Spretnak's *The Lost Goddesses of Ancient Greece*,[4] offers us a "reimagining" of a lost oral version inspired by meditation on the available ancient sources. If we ask, are her versions of the myths true? We have to answer, yes. Yes, as myths that have had powerful resonance for us. Indeed, many feminists who have written about the Demeter/Persephone myth cite Spretnak's retelling in a way that grants it the full authority of myth.

In her book Spretnak saves the Demeter and Persephone myth for last, perhaps because of her conviction that of all the pre-Homeric goddesses Demeter is the least changed by the male-dominated tradition. She remains a goddess of the earth rather than making her home on Olympus; she claims her daughter as fully her own child. Spretnak's version of the myth proceeds from her assumption that the story of Persephone's rape was added to the Persephone traditions after the rise of patriarchy, indeed, that it is a disguised representation of the patriarchal invasion. In her introduction she reminds us of the many artistic representations of Persephone's descent that omit the rape and sees them as reminders of this earlier account.

"There was once a land with no winter"—thus Spretnak begins her tale. Demeter is goddess of both grain and underworld, but she admits to her beautiful and beloved daughter Persephone that she is so concerned with providing food for the living that she has had to neglect her underworld domain. Persephone chooses to go to the underworld and welcome the confused newly dead. Finding them in despair, she initiates them into their new world and restores them to tranquillity and wisdom. Demeter accepts her daughter's choice and nevertheless grieves at her absence. The fields become barren; winter comes for the first time. But in the spring Persephone returns and the grain and flowers reappear, as they will every year.

The myth paints a picture of an idealized world, a world free of violence, deceit, jealousy; a world filled with peace and harmony. Many scholars would say there was never such a time. There was blood sacrifice, orgiastic worship, even when the goddesses ruled. The ancient religion was inspired by terror as well as by joy. The ancient goddesses were less insipid, less unambivalently benevolent than the ones pictured here. But myths need not describe a world that *was*; they may also picture a world that might have been or that might be.

Probably the most prevalent contemporary understanding of the myth focuses on its picturing of the mother/daughter bond and sees in Demeter an idealized representation of maternal love. I first heard the story of Demeter and Persephone from my mother. Or so I've always said. But actually what she told me was how profoundly Demeter had longed for a daughter to whom she could give the love that filled her heart and how wholly she had delighted in the daughter whom she bore. My mother's telling focused on the love that flowed back and forth between this mother and daughter of ancient times. There was no abduction, no separation forced or chosen, only a mother and a daughter, each full of love for the other.

Or so I remember. And yet when I now read the poems by my mother I included in my book, *The Long Journey Home*,[5] I wonder, "Is that what she told, or only what I remember? Only what I was ready to hear, willing to hear?" When I reread her poems I discover a Demeter who knew, who foreknew, "how much of motherhood is loss" (to use Kerenyi's beautiful phrase); I find a Demeter, aware that Persephone stands poised at the precarious and beautiful transition between childhood and womanhood, who watches her daughter prepare to join her lover and blesses her eagerness. I see Demeter's recognition that though her daughter may miss the upper world, she loves the Hades with whom she shares rule of the nether realm. I read these poems and I sense that my mother has always known of the separation that tears Demeter and Persephone apart. I see that her Demeter had accepted the inevitability of the separation long before it occurred, that her Demeter blessed her daughter's eager embrace of her lover, that her Demeter took pride in her daughter's graceful exercise of her adult powers. And I realize that perhaps it was always I who was attached to the fantasy of a never-broken bond.

Of course, I realize that my mother's vision is still one that idealizes the mother-daughter bond; still a vision of how it might have been, of how she wishes it had been. I could name all the ways it was never quite thus, but then so could she. But the image of Demeter as a representation of the all powerful, all loving mother for whom we all yearn still has enormous power for her, for me, for many of us. Of course, I also know that there are other versions of Demeter, visions of Demeter as a devouring mother, as a narcissistic mother, as a cruel and vengeful goddess, and they, too, have their truth.

Nonetheless, for many the predominant meaning of this myth lies in its powerful evocation of the strength and beauty of the bond that connects mothers and daughters. Adrienne Rich, for example, sees the myth of Demeter and Persephone and the Eleusinian mysteries cele-brated in their honor as an "enduring recognition of mother-daughter passion and rapture." What is most important to her about the story of Hades' rape of Persephone is that it means that the separation of Demeter and Persephone is unwilling and unwilled. "It is neither a question of the daughter's rebellion against the mother, nor the moth-er's rejection of the daughter." Rich honors the sustained, passionate power of Demeter's commitment to her daughter. "It is a mother whose wrath crystallizes the miracle," Persephone's return.[6]

Carol Christ is also moved by this myth as a tale of a mother who puts her relation to her daughter above all else: "What is important for women in this story is that a mother fights for her daughter and for her relation to her daughter. This is completely different from the mother's relation to her daughter in patriarchy." The story encourages "mothers and daughters to affirm the heritage passed on from mother to daughter and to reject the patriarchal pattern where the primary loyalties of mother and daughter must be to men."[7]

The love between Demeter and Persephone has been felt by many to symbolize not only the mother-daughter bond but more generally the intense, intimate connections among women whose loyalty to one another takes precedence over their relationships with men. Thus the myth has been taken to provide us with what Karin Carrington calls "an archetype of lesbian love."

Demeter is represented as a determinedly woman-identified god-dess. Having been separated from her own mother at birth when her father, Kronos, fearful that one of his children might grow up to overthrow him as he had overthrown his father, swallows her, she longs to have a daughter to whom she might give the maternal devotion she had herself never received. Demeter hopes to maintain the intimate connection preceding the recognition of separate existence which we all imagine to have been there "in the beginning," forever, to keep her daughter for herself, and seeks especially to protect their bond from any male intruder.

After her daughter's abduction, she is overtaken by her grief and rage. During this time she spends an evening in the company of an aged dry nurse, Baubo, who succeeds (even if only momentarily) in getting the goddess to smile and even to laugh aloud. She does so by entertaining her with a lewd dance; she takes off her clothes, she spreads her legs, she displays her vulva. Long past her childbearing years, withered, wrinkled and probably flabby, Baubo communicates her joy in her own body, her pride in her female organs, her conviction that her sexuality is *hers*, defined neither by the men who might once have desired her nor the children she may have borne. Conventional beauty, youth, reproductive capacity are all beside the point; she celebrates the pleasure her body can receive and give. The Greeks acknowledged that Baubo was a goddess, that the self-sufficient female sexuality she represents is a sacred reality.

Demeter's laugh suggests that she catches on, if only for a moment, that there is life, female life, even when one is no longer mother. But to Greek women Demeter remains associated primarily with the love that flows between mothers and daughters and with the griefs and losses that seem to be an inevitable corollary of motherhood.

Demeter connects her worshippers to a time when there were no boundaries, when lover and beloved were one. Much of the intensity, the emotional intimacy, women discover in one another comes from the Demeter-Persephone dimension of their bond. I believe that all close bonds between women inevitably conjure up memories and feelings associated with our first connection to a woman, the all-powerful mother of infancy. The pull to re-experience that bond of fusion, of being totally loved, totally known, totally one with another and the fear of re-experiencing that bond of fusion, of being swallowed up by a relationship, of losing one's own hard-won identity enter powerfully into all woman-woman relationships. This does not mean that in a relationship between two women, one will necessarily play the mother role, the other the daughter role, but that both will experience the profound longing to be fully embraced once again and the imperious need to break away.

The connection to the mother is always also a connection to our own mysterious origins and in this sense Demeter is also relevant to the particular power that the sexual dimension of women's love for one another may have. Because all intimate touching between women may invoke a sense of returning to woman, to source, to origin, it may seem for many women a more sacred experience than heterosexual intercourse (no matter how physically pleasurable) can provide. I believe this is especially true of the almost overwhelming sense of touching upon the whole mystery of our own beginnings that is sometimes experienced in entering another woman's vagina, with finger or with tongue. Even though women's lovemaking with women is not literally connected to reproduction, it inescapably calls forth that mystery, the return to the place of origin.

Yet whereas many interpretations focus on the bond between Demeter and Persephone as the central clue to the meaning of the myth, others highlight Hades' disruption of that bond. Rather than seeing the myth primarily in terms of how it evokes images of a woman-centered matristic world, these writers view it in connection with the dominance of patriarchy. Rather than seeing it as celebrating the power of mother love, they see the myth as making painfully evident the vulnerability of the daughter and the disempowerment of the mother. Mary Daly, for instance, believes the myth relates a "primordial mutilation," the ontological separation of mothers from daughters and sisters from sisters. She suggests that we tend to view the reunion of Demeter and Persephone much too sentimentally and bids us notice that when Zeus decides Persephone is to spend only part of each year with her mother, Demeter "sets aside her anger" and Hades now "possesses" the maiden. "The fact that the daughter was *allowed* to return for a 'period' of time," she notes, "says everything about patriarchy."[8]

River Malcolm's poem, "The Two Goddesses"[9] reads the myth of Demeter and Persephone as a story of rape, as a story that happens in our time, as a story about how daughters are raped and the daughters feel betrayed by their mother's failure to protect them and not only by the rapist. In the poem Persephone and Demeter, each in turn, speak of how the rape has changed her life. Persephone communicates the terror of the god's violently wrenching her away from the world she has known, the physical horror of the rape, and her painful awareness that things can never be the same again. Again and again she asks, And where was my mother when the earth swallowed my girlhood? Demeter speaks not only of her loss and her grief but of her culpability. She knows she has failed her daughter, knows the daughter must hate her, knows things will never be the same, knows the daughter will never know how profoundly the mother who was not there when needed most loves her still. Here, in this poem, the mother (perhaps because she is a goddess) can do what our own mothers so rarely can, acknowledge her own guilt without expecting forgiveness, without expecting that can erase what has happened. She is able to see what has happened to her daughter, not simply the external event, but what happened within that has changed her forever.

Other commentators on the Eleusinian myth agree that the abduction is central—not as violation but as initiation. Bruce Lincoln reads the Homeric hymn as a disguised account of a young woman's initiation into a male-dominated culture. He emphasizes Persephone's innocence and terror; he acknowledges the violence of the abduction and father Zeus's role in not only approving but instigating it. Noting that initiations typically mark the transition from one life stage to another in dramatically violent ways and often involve a figurative death experience, Lincoln suggests that Zeus and Hades are playing culturally approved roles designed to transform Persephone from child to woman. Lincoln refers to other Greek myths in which rape, the forcible loss of virginity, is understood as initiatory as it often is in " male-centered, misogynistically inclined cultures. . . The real point being the forcible subjugation of women to male control."[10]

Lincoln interprets the myth as the story of a young woman's initiation into a patriarchal world. Many women, however, read the myth as an initiatory scenario in which Hades serves to help Persephone make the transition to a more authentically female maturity. Jennifer and Roger Woolger see Persephone as the archetypal maiden, innocent and passive, accustomed to depend on others, her mother or her Olympian father, to protect and defend her. "The wisdom of this extraordinary myth," as the Woolgers understand it, "is that the source of Persephone's transformation comes from beneath, from the lower depths of soul." Persephone's "true savior" is Hades not Zeus.[11] Persephone, the "eternal sacrificial victim" needs to get beyond her identification with her passivity and powerlessness and the sympathy and pity these elicit. Only a genuine encounter with Hades that brings the death of all attachment to innocence can free her.

When the emphasis in our viewing of the myth falls on Persephone, we are likely to see the myth as representing a particular life passage, the one that leads from maidenhood to womanhood. If, however, our focal point is Demeter, then her passage beyond her identification with motherhood becomes prominent. For the rape happens to Demeter, too. Indeed, the Homeric hymn concerns itself primarily with Demeter's, not her daughter's, response to Hades' abduction of Persephone.

Helen Luke begins her reading of the myth[12] by noting the difference between Demeter and Gaia who, so the Hymn relates, actually came to Hades' aid. From the earth mother's perspective neither rape nor death seem all that tragic, although from Demeter's they seem well nigh unendurable. Demeter's task is to learn to come to terms with her loss, a loss which signifies not simply the loss of her daughter but more profoundly the loss of her own daughterly aspect. The youthfulness to which she still unconsciously clings represents her resistance to taking on the challenges of the second half of life. The grief is real and appropriate; this is a painful and difficult transition, but a necessary one. Demeter's nine day search symbolizes that after Persephone's disappearance she is pregnant with herself, with the self she must now become. Persephone may return to Demeter but she will not return to her daughterly role, not regress to an identification with her mother; for Luke believes that Persephone swallowed the pomegranate seeds voluntarily, signaling that she is ready to assimilate her underworld experience. Because for Luke Persephone represents an aspect of Demeter this means that Demeter, too, has now come to terms with what this passage requires of her.

Patricia Berry is less sanguine. She, too, sees the rape as at the heart of the myth. She suggests that Gaia not only condones and aids the rape but understands it as a necessary experience for Demeter to undergo. "At Eleusis," Berry says, "rape was elevated to the state of a mystery."[13] Which does not mean, as James Hillman makes explicit, that rape is always necessary. There is a particular style of consciousness, Persephone's exaggerated innocence, Demeter's denial of all but upperworld reality, that resists other modes of descent to underworld experience and so constellates rape, the forced descent.[14]

Although like Luke, Berry understands Persephone as an aspect of Demeter, Berry sees Persephone as representing not Demeter's daughterly or maidenly aspect, not the youthfulness and innocence to which Demeter still clings, but precisely as Demeter's "in the underworld" aspect. What Persephone's rape means, in terms of Demeter's perspective, is precisely Demeter's suffering. Demeter needs the underworld experience into which Persephone initiates her—that is what she is seeking as she engages in her search for Persephone. Her suffering over the loss, her extravagant grief and rage, are as Berry understands them, an expression of her "compromise" with the rape, her both experiencing it and refusing it. Her immersion in her suffering is psycho-pathology, soul-suffering, expressed as profound depression and in destructive behavior. Her involvement with the household and nursery in the Eleusinian palace represents a way of evading "the needs of her own deepening."

Berry seems unsure that the reunion of Demeter and Persephone at the end of the myth represents that full entering into loss for which Demeter's soul seems to long. Deep suffering in itself does not guarantee transformation. Demeter could stay stuck in her neurosis forever. It is not clear that she has really let go of the perspective which grants reality and value only to the upperworld and continues to resist descent.

Polly Young-Eisendrath[15] also reads the myth in terms of its relevance to the central task of mid-life, by which she means the acceptance of experiences of loss and limitation as inescapable and transformative. To understand the myth rightly, she suggests, we must see that, contra Kerenyi, it is *not* about cyclical renewal, not about raging and grieving and then getting everything back again, but about irretrievable loss, inexpungeable change. Young-Eisendrath focuses her whole analysis on one episode in the myth, Demeter's attempt to make Metanira's infant son Demophoon immortal, which Young-Eisendrath regards as an attempt to evade the reality of her loss of Persephone. This is Demeter's folly: the attempt to make time stand still, the refusal to accept that her wish to undo the abduction represents an impossible wish. As Young-Eisendrath understands it, one becomes a *person* when one has learned to renounce such impossible wishes and come to terms with finitude, with our status as mortals not gods. Some losses can be recovered but some, and this is what the myth teaches, must be suffered. Metanira here becomes the initiator: the one who knows that loss cannot be evaded or erased. Demeter shows us all the immature ways in which we are likely to respond to grief and loss, she participates in all the stages of mourning modern psychology has so carefully delineated. Young-Eisendrath focuses particularly on how in her anger at Hades Demeter identifies with the aggressor, tries to abduct Demophoon from his mother as ruthlessly as Hades had abducted Persephone. Metanira's anger frees Demeter from her identification and enables her to complete the process of mourning. This completion is expressed through the creative activity Demeter then turns to: the institution of the mysteries. Demeter herself is the first initiate. The mysteries are designed to teach what she has learned: the mysteries grant not immortality but a different understanding of loss and death.

Although most of the contemporary perspectives on the myth we have considered thus far read it in relation to the psychology of women, the myth is not just about women but also about gender issues, not just about mothers and daughters but also about the relations between women and men. Of course there are aspects that are particularly relevant to women's lives, as the all-women's ritual, the Thesmophoria, makes evident. But the Eleusinian mysteries were open to all, men and women, slave and free.

Kerenyi, noting that all initiates took names with feminine endings, says that all entered into the figure of Demeter, the first initiate, as though understanding the release from the fear of death which the mysteries provide requires entrance into a female perspective.

Catherine Keller, too, believes that the ritual made it possible for what seems like an exclusively female experience, the connection between mothers and daughters, to provide all who participated in it a glimpse of what relationships that honor both intimacy and independence might be like. The Mysteries seem to have presented the mother-daughter bond in a way that communicated to both men and women an affirmation that reconnection can triumph even over the deadening force of a rapacious separation. The Mysteries, she believes, suggested that the mother-daughter relationship can be redemptive for all. Reflection on the myth can teach us that maturation means the gradual differentiation and modulation of the original empathic continuum between mother and child, in a way that leaves us neither bound to parent figures nor severed from them.[16] Persephone, as Ovid tells us, still longed for Demeter while in the underworld but she also enjoyed her power as its queen; she rejoices in her reunion with her mother but she does not return unchanged nor to stay. She is still connected while separated, still separate when reconnected; relatedness and autonomy are not necessarily discrete developments.

Fully to allow the myth to speak today means, I believe, not trying to hold on it as just ours, as speaking only about women, only to women. The myth may today be profoundly relevant to the experiences of both women and men, as the Mysteries were felt to be in the ancient world.

I believe the myth of Demeter and Persephone might help us to imagine forward to a possible postpatriarchal world, not by interpreting what it meant *then*, but by reimagining it. Turning to the myth as a resource to support our hopes that women and men might discover forms of relationship based on our together having moved beyond the distorted and destructive forms characteristic of patriarchal society involves getting past a focus on the mother's or the daughter's, Demeter's or Persephone's perspective, as representing the only possible female perspectives. It may give us pause to recognize that in the *Hymn* great-grandmother Gaia seems to side with Zeus and Hades against Demeter, that Hecate can witness the abduction without feeling she should interfere, that Baubo can tease Demeter about how seriously she is taking what has happened, that grandmother Rhea is the one who comes up with the fertile compromise by which Demeter, Persephone, and Hades are each given their due.

We also need to begin to listen to what we might learn from the male figures in the myth. As I look at them, at Zeus, Hades, Helios, Demophoon, Hermes, Triptolemus, Brimo/Dionysos—I am struck by how many of them there are and what varied roles they play. I have come to sense that fully to understand the myth would entail a patient exploration of how each enters the tale, how it might look from his perspective, and then perhaps discovering that these so-called male perspectives are perspectives in which I participate, familiar not alien, integral not extraneous.

The "Hymn to Demeter" depicts Hades only as the dreadful god whom Demeter experiences as an intruder and despoiler; it gives us no sense of what this episode means to him, of his motives, his feelings. Ovid (though with Ovid, scholars never seem to agree about when he is being ironic and when not) writes that Hades came for Persephone after having first seen and fallen in love with her and then having received permission from her father. I am struck by how many of the gods seek to force themselves upon one woman after another and that Hades reaches only for this one—and even the hymn acknowledges the kindliness with which he sends Persephone back to her mother.

I have come to see Hades as representing the impossibility of an all-female world forever immune to intrusion by the male. Demeter had sought to keep her daughter with her forever, to protect her from all contact with the masculine. Persephone *reaches* for the narcissus as she later reaches for the pomegranate. There is some spark essential to her becoming herself, becoming the goddess of the underworld and not just Demeter's daughter, that the relation to Hades makes possible. His temple is outside the sacred precincts, his power in the underworld becomes subordinate to hers, his role is in some ways minor—and yet essential. He helps get something started that might otherwise remain barren.

Each of the other male figures also plays an essential role in the story: Helios is the only one to *see* what happened when Persephone disappeared; Zeus comes to recognize that Demeter's claim cannot be ignored; Hermes leads Persephone back up from the underworld; the birth of Iacchus marks the climax of the mysteries.

As I now review the many revisionings of this myth with which I am familiar, I find myself especially challenged by Helen Luke's reading which emphasizes the importance for women of fully experiencing their emancipation from the role of daughter—because it helped me see that in my insistent disavowal of Demeter's perspective I had been caught in an identification with Persephone's. I began to see that as a sixty year old crone it might be well past time for me to move beyond the perspectives of either Demeter or Persephone, and see the myth instead from the perspectives of Gaia and Rhea, time to take seriously again the often discredited sense in which this myth is about fertility, about the renewal of the earth. For, although we may never know exactly what the mysteries revealed that served to free those who participated from their fear of death, we do know that it was integrally connected to their apprehending an analogy between the soul's journey to the underworld and the display of a ripened ear of corn.

Unlike Demeter, Gaia is not the personal mother nor the goddess of cultivated grain but rather goddess of the earth, of all that grows, goddess of generativity, of ever renewing and changing life. In the myth she comes to Hades' aid, grows the narcissus whose plucking opens the path to the underworld; she sees what happens as part of the necessary order of things. Rhea, the mother of Demeter but also of both Hades and Zeus, appears after Persephone's return and persuades Demeter that it is time to let go of her anger at Zeus and bring an end to the barren-ness which has made this the most terrible year on earth. And at the end Demeter does seem to forgive— and straightway the fat furrows of the soil are heavy with corn and dread Hades reappears as wealth-giving Ploutos.

A postpatriarchal imagining of the myth onward involves moving to take on earth's perspective, Gaia's perspective, moving beyond our identification with male or female perspectives. Let me be clear. I am not saying that if only we were able to do this, the continuance of life would be assured, the renewal of earth established. But unless we do this, the future looks bleak, indeed.

NOTES

1. James Hillman, *ReVisioning Psychology* (New York: Harper & Row, 1975) 158.

2. Carl Kerenyi, *Eleusis: Archetypal Image of Mother and Daughter* (New York: Pantheon, 1967) 23.

3. George Mylonas, *Eleusis and The Eleusinian Mysteries* (Princeton: Princeton University Press, 1961) 285.

4. Charlene Spretnak, *Lost Goddesses of Ancient Greece* (Boston: Beacon, 1992) 105-118.

5. Herta Rosenblatt, "Three Poems," in Christine Downing, ed., *The Long Journey Home* (Boston, Shambhala, 1994) 119-122.

6. Adrienne Rich, *Of Woman Born* (New York: Norton, 1976) 240-43.

7. Carol Christ, *The Laughter of Aphrodite* (San Francisco: Harper & Row, 1987) 130-31.

8. Mary Daly, *Gyn/Ecology* (Boston: Beacon, 1978) 41.

9. Included in *Long Journey Home*, 155-160.

10. Bruce Lincoln, *Emerging from the Chrysalis* (Cambridge: Harvard University Press, 1981) 90.

11. Jennifer Barker Woolger and Roger J. Woolger, *The Goddess Within* (New York: Fawcett Columbine, 1987) 285.

12. Helen Luke, *Woman, Earth, and Spirit* (New York: Crossroad, 1981) 55-68.

13. Patricia Berry, "The Rape of Demeter/Persephone and Neurosis, *Spring 1985,* 186.

14. See James Hillman, *Dreams and the Underworld* (New York: Harper & Row, 1979) 49.

15. Polly Young-Eisendrath, "Demeter's Folly," *Psychological Perspectives* (Spring 1984) 39-63.

16. Catherine Keller, *From A Broken Web* (Boston: Beacon, 1986) 153-4.

*CHRISTINE DOWNING* is professor emeritus of Religious Studies at San Diego State University where she also served as department chair. She has also taught at the California School of Professional Psychology, the C. G. Jung Institute in Zurich, and the Pacifica Graduate Institute. She was the first woman to serve as president of the American Academy of Religion. Dr. Downing is the author of *The Goddess, Psyche's Sisters*, and *Mirrors of the Self.* Her most recent book is *The Long Journey Home: Revisioning the Myth of Demeter and Persephone for Our Time*.

This is a revised compilation of material that originally appeared in *The Long Journey Home: Revisioning the Myth of Demeter and Persephone for Our Time* (Boston: Shambhala, 1994).

# ADULT LIBERATION &
# THE MATURE TRICKSTER

### by ALLAN B. CHINEN

*from* **Transformation**

**T**HE ADULT YEARS ARE NORMALLY FILLED
with responsibilities at home, work, and in the community—obligations to one's children, spouse, ex-spouses, employers, and often to
one's aging parents. Women and men frequently feel boxed in by these
many demands. In this situation, an unexpected archetype offers inspiration and guidance: the Trickster.

Jungians usually consider the Trickster to be an immature, shadowy figure, equivalent to a juvenile delinquent or a sociopath. Such a
negative view, based on early, incomplete folklore accounts, is incor-
rect. More thorough studies reveal the Trickster to be a complex, positive, divine character who antedates patriarchal and matriarchal figures
by many millennia. A fairy tale from Italy (from Italo Calvino's *Italian
Folktales*, 1980) reveals the Trickster's positive aspects and shows how
he offers surprisingly good advice for adults. The story is typical of folktales about men and women, rather than children, and my analysis

comes from a comparative study of over five thousand fairy tales around the world.

## THE NORTH WIND'S GIFT

Once upon a time, a poor farmer lived with his wife and three children. Every harvest, the North Wind blew on the farmer's fields, spoiling the crops, so the peasant could barely feed his family. One day he had had enough, and he decided to go to the North Wind to demand justice.

The peasant journeyed for a long time before he came to the castle of the North Wind. The Wind was not home, but his wife let the farmer in. When the Wind arrived, the farmer explained his predicament and asked the North Wind to make amends.

The North Wind thought for a moment, then fetched a box and gave it to the farmer. "The box is magic," the Wind said. "It will give you food when you open it. But tell no one about the magic, otherwise you will surely lose the box."

The farmer thanked the North Wind and started back home. On the way, he wished for lunch and opened the box. Instantly, a table appeared, laden with food. The farmer ate happily, closed the box, and the food vanished. When the peasant returned home, his family asked him about his journey, and he demonstrated the magic box to them. Then he warned his family not to tell anybody about the box.

The next day, the peasant's landlord, a greedy priest, summoned the farmer's wife. The priest asked about the peasant's trip, and the wife soon mentioned the magic box. The landlord sent for the farmer and demanded the box, promising many rewards in return and threatening eviction if the peasant refused. The poor farmer handed over the magic casket. Later, the priest gave the peasant bags of rotten grain, so the farmer was soon as poor as ever.

After a time, the peasant gathered his courage and returned to the North Wind, explaining how he lost the magic box. The North Wind frowned, saying, "I told you to keep the box secret! It is your own fault you lost it!" The farmer pleaded until the North Wind relented and fetched a magnificent golden box. "This is even more magic than the last one, but do not open it," the Wind warned, "until you are starving."

The farmer thanked the North Wind and went on his way. When

he could go no farther because of hunger, he stopped, wished for a fine meal, and opened the box. Instantly a ruffian leaped out and started beating him. Only when the peasant managed to close the golden box did the thug vanish.

When the farmer returned home his family greeted him and asked what the North Wind gave him. The farmer opened the gold box and quickly stepped outside the room. Two brigands leaped out of the box and began thrashing the wife and children. After a few moments, the farmer closed the lid of the box, and the ruffians vanished. Then the farmer asked his wife to mention the golden box to the priest but not to reveal its magic.

When the greedy landlord heard about the golden box, he sent for the farmer and demanded the new casket, offering the first one in exchange. The farmer traded boxes, warning the priest not to open the golden one except when starving.

The bishop was coming to visit the priest, so the priest decided to use the golden box for a great banquet. The priest waited until everyone was famished and then opened the box. Instantly, six men with clubs leaped out and began beating the priests. The farmer was waiting by a window, and after a time he slipped into the room and closed the lid on the magic case. The thugs vanished, and the farmer returned home with his golden box. The priest never bothered the peasant from then on, and so the farmer and his family lived in ease and comfort the rest of their days.

THE STORY STARTS WITH A MAN burdened by bad weather, a greedy landlord, and a hungry family. He makes a good symbol for anyone feeling overwhelmed, trapped, or burned out at midlife. In response, the farmer goes to the North Wind to demand justice. He does not become depressed or try to distract himself with drinking, affairs, and so on. The fairy tale shows ideal development—what adults potentially can become, rather than what we commonly end up doing. The story offers us a model.

The North Wind gives the peasant a magic box which provides food. In part, this episode reflects wish-fulfillment, the dream of most overworked adults for something that will magically solve all our problems; winning big on a lottery ticket would be the modern equivalent.

A children's story might end with the magic food box, but not this tale; the peasant loses the casket, underscoring the idea that wish-fulfillment does not work for adults. Although it is a fairy story, the drama remains true to reality; it is utopian and shows ideal development, but it is not fantasy.

A plucky fellow—again providing us with a model—the peasant returns to the North Wind. The Wind plays a trick on him when he gives the poor man a beautiful golden box with the warning to open it only when very hungry. Assuming the box will provide even better food than the first one, the peasant is rudely surprised to find a violent ruffian inside.

Here the story reveals the North Wind to be a Trickster. The Wind's trick, however, has a serious purpose, for he is trying to teach the peasant about aggression and cunning, and the farmer badly needs a lesson in both. He was too meek, for instance, in giving in to the priest's threat of eviction; with the magic food box, the farmer no longer needed to work and could have defied the landlord. The ruffians in the second box symbolize the aggression and trickery—street smarts—that the peasant needs. In teaching the peasant to be a Trickster, the North Wind offers an important lesson for all adults: to survive in maturity, we must give up the role of the idealistic, innocent, virtuous hero, so prominent in children's tales, in favor of the cunning, aggressive, practical Trickster.

There is much deeper symbolism contained in the North Wind. Notice that his first gift is nurturing—the box that provides food. Across cultures, such generativity is a major function of Trickster figures. Prometheus brought fire to humankind, as did Maui, the Trickster from Polynesia; Raven from the American Northwest; and Coyote from the Southwest. The Greek god Hermes gave language to humanity, just as did the African Tricksters Eshu and Legba. Wakdjunkaga, a North American Trickster, was specifically sent by Earthmaker to clear the world of demons and make the earth safe for humanity; in Africa, Eshu had the same calling. The Trickster's ultimate mission is generative: to help humanity. He uses trickery for that end but often becomes so wrapped up in his pranks and schemes that he forgets his original calling. He falls into errors and excesses, like the peasant losing the first magic box and later unleashing the ruffians upon his family. But the Trickster also recovers from his mistakes, seen in the way the farmer goes to the North Wind for the second time, and learns to control the violent thugs so they attack the greedy priest and not the peasant's family. The Trickster offers a profoundly reassuring model here. Like him, we often forget our deepest ideals and values in the effort to survive, but we also wake up now and then to remember our divine calling.

When the peasant tricks his greedy landlord, the story pokes fun at the priest and makes a telling social criticism: instead of helping people, as he is supposed to do, the priest exploits them. The tale is subversive here, and this is another major function of Tricksters: they mock and defy authorities and convention. The Trickster's purpose is to free people from accepted traditions. Asked why he lied so much, for instance, Eshu the Yoruba Trickster, answered, "To make people think." The *heyokas* or "contraries" in American Indian tradition carry out the same function, always doing the opposite of convention. Here the Trickster offers astonishing advice for adults. Realistic responsibilities are burdensome enough without adding constricting social conventions that serve no purpose. The Trickster seeks to eliminate that unnecessary rigidity. Scandal is often the result, but once again the Trickster reminds us that it is possible to get up after an embarrassing pratfall.

In European folklore, the North Wind is usually associated with capricious, wild winter storms—a storm spirit. Storm and winds in general are unpredictable and make good Trickster figures. But in mythology, storm gods are the predecessors of patriarchal deities. Zeus, the Olympian patriarch, began as a god of storm, as did Yahweh in Hebrew tradition, Viracocha in Peru, and Nyame among the Ashanti of Africa. Storm spirits like the North Wind therefore represent a primordial, tricky divine power, antedating patriarchal deities. In fact, Trickster figures are visible in Paleolithic cave paintings, created some ten thousand years before warriors and kings appear in history. In making contact with the North Wind, therefore, the peasant gains access to a level of the psyche normally hidden by patriarchal convention.

Indeed, patriarchal condemnation and censorship explain why the Trickster has such an unfair and unsavory reputation. Like great goddesses, the Trickster has been repressed and demonized. To be sure, there is a shadowy, negative side to the Trickster. Many Trickster figures in folklore act like juvenile delinquents or sociopaths, but they appear in only a small portion of Trickster tales and are typically young. They represent immature Tricksters. The majority of Tricksters are married with children, a fact often not appreciated. These mature Tricksters represent the complete archetype and display far greater depth and complexity than their juvenile counterparts.

Interpreted psychologically, "The North Wind's Gift" suggests that even in the middle of burdensome adult responsibilities it is possible to make contact with a profoundly transformative energy, personified by the Trickster. In real life, men and women gain access to the holy Trickster, the whole Trickster, in various ways. He may come through dreams and active imagination, the way Philemon—a classic Trickster figure—appeared to Jung, introducing Jung to the mysteries of the unconscious. Or the Trickster may erupt in unconventional decisions, seen in the way Gauguin gave up his business career in his 30s, started painting, and moved to Tahiti. Yet there are no guarantees that such bold, unconventional moves will succeed; the Trickster regularly falls flat on his face. But he also gets up again and starts anew, the way the farmer goes back to the North Wind the second time. And perhaps that is the most important message from the North Wind—not just a promise of liberation but the chance to try again, as often as necessary.

A psychiatrist practicing in San Francisco, *ALLAN CHINEN*, M.D. is on the clinical faculty of the University of California. He has written extensively on adult development and aging and is the author of **In the Ever After: Fairy Tales and the Second Half of Life** and **Once Upon a Midlife**. His most recent book is **Beyond the Hero: Classic Stories of Men in Search of Soul.**

Reprinted from *Transformation*, Summer 1994, C. G. Jung Institute of Chicago, 1567 Maple Avenue, Evanston, IL 60201. (708) 475-4848.

# The Fire is in the Mind

## by David L. Miller

### from Spring

**I**NTRODUCTION: WHO IS THE TRUE DISCIPLE?

Reflection on the work of a person who is admired is fraught with an awkwardness. People of wisdom have noted the difficulty. The Hassidic master, Baal Shem Tov, said:

> No two persons have the same attributes. Each person should work in the service of god according to his or her own talents. If one person tries to imitate another, that one merely loses the opportunity to do good through his or her own merit. One cannot accomplish anything by imitation of another.

Similarly, Rabbi Messhulam Zusya of Hanipol, just before his death in 1880 said: "In the coming world they will not ask me, 'why were you not Moses?' They will ask me 'why were you not Zusya?'" the point was not lost on Rabbi Noah, who was rabbi Mordecai's son and who, like these others, stands in the line of great Hassidic leaders. When Rabbi Noah took his father's place as a Zaddik, his followers soon saw that he behaved differently from his father. They were troubled and came to ask about this. "But I do just as my father did," Rabbi Noah said. "I imitate him to the letter. He did not imitate anyone, so I do not imitate him." This wisdom is reminiscent of the advice of Nietzsche that Jung wrote to Freud on March 3, 1912, a short time before the discontinuation of their friendship. In *Thus Spake Zarathustra*, Nietzsche wrote, "One repays a teacher badly if one remains only a pupil . . . You had not sought yourselves when you found me . . . Now I bid you lose me and find yourselves, and only when you have all denied me will I return to you."

Jung himself had said, "True companionship thrives only when each individual remembers his or her individuality and does not identify with others" [*Memories, Dreams, Reflections*, p. 356. Jung wrote in a letter on January 14, 1946, "I can hope and wish that nobody becomes Jungian," and in the autobiography he said succinctly, "Don't imitate!" [p. 86].

The point of all these sayings is clear on the face of it. The seventeenth-century Zen poet, Basho, expressed it by saying, "I do not seek to follow in the footsteps of men of old: I seek the things they sought." It is a point that Joseph Campbell himself stressed, as early as 1949, at the end of *Hero with a Thousand Faces*, where he wrote that "today no meaning is in the group . . . all is in the individual," a point he was continuing to make in 1986 as he spoke to Bill Moyers on television, saying, "Follow your own bliss!"

So, as one reflects on Joseph Campbell's work, the question becomes: Who is the true follower of Joseph Campbell? Jesus preached the Kingdom and got the Church. Jung proclaimed the soul and got the Jung Institute. Campbell told us to follow our own bliss . . . it would be an extreme irony if, in attempting to follow his advice, we ended by following *his* bliss!

Who is the true student of Joseph Campbell? The question is like a Zen question. It is a bit tricky. One should not imagine too quickly, if ever, that one knows the answer to it. Is the true follower of Joseph Campbell the one who follows Joseph Campbell, or the one who follows his or her own true self? This latter may even include the possibility of following a bliss which denies that following one's own bliss is the true way! The matter is extremely awkward. But it is in the context of this awkwardness that I want to praise Joseph Campbell.

## SCHOLARSHIP: THE PLUMBER & THE ACADEMIC

Specifically, I want to praise Joseph Campbell the scholar. In doing so I bring a word from the Academy, where, as is well-known, there is considerable controversy concerning the life and work of Joseph Campbell. It is my purpose to bring some understanding to this controversy, but in order to do this I shall have to say a few words about what it means to be a scholar. In so doing, I realize that I am giving only one perspective, but I believe it is a perspective that will help to make a few things a bit clearer.

There is much misunderstanding in America today about what it means to be a scholar. On the one hand, there is an inflation of the scholar. Think of the popular attitude toward Einstein. This makes of the scholar a sort of "mana personality," as Jung called it, and turns out not to be a favor, as anyone knows who has been put up on a pedestal by another's projections. But, on the other hand, there is a devaluation of the scholar in the American context of what Albert Hofstadter has analyzed as our cultural anti-intellectualism. So to call someone an "academic" is often a sarcastic put-down, as is saying, "he's just in his head" or "she's on a head-trip and is not into her body," or in thinking universities are "ivory towers." Negative inflation is just as much an inflation as puffing one up positively. Perhaps a more modestly realistic middle ground can be reached if I say some things that may be very obvious—for which I apologize in advance—but which we often forget. And in order to say these things, I shall employ a homely metaphor.

Two weeks ago the disposal in my kitchen sink broke. I called a plumber who came with an assistant and installed a new one in less than half an hour. "Amazing," I thought as I watched! What skill he has! How easily he does it! How much he knows about wrenches and pipes and water pressure and other things about which I know nothing! "The plumber is a scholar," I thought. "And the scholar is a plumber!" This trope produced in me three or four thoughts.

First, not everyone is a plumber. It is neither good nor bad to be a plumber; it is just what that person does. It is simply a particular skill.

It is not for everyone, but it is okay for some people to be plumbers. And it is the same with scholars.

Second, plumbers both are and are not impressed with the skill and knowledge of other plumbers. They are impressed because they know what such skill and knowledge entail; but all plumbers have either that skill and knowledge or analogous skill and knowledge so it is no big deal. This point is a bit complicated and deserves further amplification.

Everyone is an intellectual. This is what Aristotle meant when he said that people are thinking animals. Nobody is not a thinker. We all think all of the time, consciously or unconsciously, always and already. Nor is it the case that ideas are in us. Rather, we are in ideas. As Jung put it, "It is true that widely accepted ideas are never the personal property of their so-called author; on the contrary, the person is the bondservant of ideas . . . A person does not make his or her ideas; we could say that a person's ideas make him or her." [4.769]

Everyone is an intellectual; everyone, a thinking type. Jung insisted that his typology not be used to put people in a box, as if some are thinking types and others feeling types, and so on. Rather, we are all of the types all of the time, but sometimes one function is working in a more differentiated way than the others.

Even though everyone is an intellectual, not every intellectual is a scholar. It is the same with plumbing: we all use it, but not all of us are plumbers. Sometimes plumbers talk to the rest of us mortals and tell us how to use the disposal; other times plumbers talk to other plumbers, and the rest of us don't know what they are talking about.

It is the same with scholars. When they talk with each other, the talk is amazing and not understandable. That's OK. They are then scholars being scholarly. But when scholars talk to the rest of us, they explain things, like plumbers do. Then they are being academic, whether they are in a college classroom, at a cocktail party, at Esalen or the Open Center. Scholars are often academic when talking to undergraduates, and scholarly when talking to graduate students, like the plumber talking to the apprentice.

A third and crucial point for proper understanding is that plumbers never prove anything. Rather, they attempt to falsify. After my plumber installed my disposal, and while still on the floor under my sink, he asked his assistant to turn on the water. Then he did an odd but important thing. He reached under the sink with his hand, and in what I thought was a slightly erotic gesture, felt the pipes fondly and sensitively and gingerly, running his hand over their every joint and turn. He was attempting to falsify his job, looking for leaks. Plumbing is never eternally true or ultimately right. It may spring a leak next week. But it can be "wrong" here and now.

Philosophers have made the same point about scholarship. It proves nothing. It is at best an hypothesis, an idea. But it can be falsified. And that is what scholars do. They look for the leaks and drips in their own work and in the work of all those that have gone before. Einstein, as Niels Bohr noted, was wrong about many things. Scholars don't love him or his work less. But scholars are amused and sometimes sad about those who dogmatically insist that someone's scholarship is "true."

This leads to a fourth point. Consistency is not a scholarly virtue any more than plumbing is expected always and forever to work. To be sure, plumbers and scholars do the best they can. And when they are being academic, rather than scholarly, they do try to be consistent and "right." But they know better when being scholarly. They know that consistency is a virtue of small-mindedness. The seminal scholar is bold enough to be wrong. "Sin bravely," said Luther. How often did Freud change his mind? Paradigms shift. Jung announced in his autobiography that after a dream of a flying saucer late in his life, he realized he was wrong about the relation of the ego to the deep Self. Korzybski said that scholars need training in non-identity. Gaston Bachelard warned that every educator who notices a lowering of his or her shifting character should be retired. The *I Ching* says that change is the only changeless. Heraclitus noted that all things flow. Now this is called deconstruction. But by whatever name and in whatever time or place, the point, as Plotinus said, is that a scholar must write "so to say" over all of his or her utterances. And more recently Wittgenstein said, "Always take back what is said." Scholars know this deep down. Socrates spent every day in dialogue seeking a new way to be wrong.

Joseph Campbell was a scholar, but he was not always scholarly. Sometimes he was academic, as when talking at the Esalen Institute or with Bill Moyers on TV. I use *Hero With a Thousand Faces* and *Masks of God* in undergraduate classes, but not in graduate seminars. In the latter, I use Campbell's 1957 Eranos lecture and the essays in *Flight of the Wild Gander.*

Like plumber's work, Campbell's ideas have in many instances sprung leaks. They are wrong. He was wrong about Hainuwele mythology because he included some of Adolf Jensen's commentary on the myth as if it were part of the people's story. This calls into question his fundamental views of planting mythology in the Pacific Area. Alan Dundes has noted that Campbell was misleading about hero-myths. And there is much controversy about the validity of a primary matriarchy lying behind patriarchal mythology. These are only a few instances.

But this does not make Campbell less a scholar. In fact, my experience of him with other scholars in the '60s, when he was being scholarly, is that he delighted in catching these leaks and drips. He changed his view of the source of myths in spontaneous parallel development in relation to historical diffusion. He corrected his mistakes about neolithic dating in the 1969 edition of *Primitive Mythology.* And one day, while he was working on *Creative Mythology,* he took delight in telling me that he had been wrong about the Arthurian Grail material. With this insight he was able to go forward and finish the book.

It is odd to say, but to the extent a scholar is bold enough to be wrong, to that degree other scholars love (and, of course, also hate) their colleague, and this happens in the very moment they are showing him or her to have faulty plumbing. If others claim that a scholar's work is "right" or "true," it simply means that those others, though no less intellectual, are not scholars. If a scholar claims "truth" for his or her idea, it just means that that person is not for the moment being scholarly. Academic, perhaps; but not scholarly. And all scholars do turn academic from time to time. After all, even plumbers have to pause and explain how to flush the toilet, turn on the hot water, and even how to dispose of garbage. And, as we all know, there is a good deal of garbage out there.

## MYTHOCLASM: HURT AND HUMOR

It is the garbage about myth that concerns contemporary scholars of myth, and this is in part what the current controversy over Joseph Campbell is all about. The postmodern academy has detected some leaks in the mythological plumbing. I will mention seven nagging drips, together with some of the names of those who have spotted them.

(1) Myths are social constructions, nurture rather than nature, learned rather than inherited (Naomi Goldenberg, Dorinne Kondo, Carlos Ginzburg). Those who argue for universal or archetypal truth in myth are authorizing a particular set of attitudes, values, and beliefs.

(2) Myth engages in objectivizing and often reifying thinking, utilizing particular concrete images and plots for abstract ideas, thereby essentializing and carrying a dominate ideology (Martin Heidegger, Jürgen Habermas, Michael Foucault, Roland Barthes). Purveyors of mythology are engaging in political ideology unwittingly, usually that of the *status quo*.

(3) Mythographers utilizing a comparative method ignore the philosophical fact that meaning is constituted by difference rather than by identity, and they thereby blur real distinction and tend to unwitting colonialization (Jacques Derrida, Emmanuel Levinas, Wendy Doniger, Charles Long).

(4) A revival of Annales School methodology has placed a new emphasis on historicism in the study of myth which works against comparative mythography and makes it seem Romanticist (Jean-Pierre Vernant, Marcel Detienne).

(5) A "Copernican" revolution in studies of violence has argued that myth is a secondary elaboration of ritual behavior which rationalizes victimage (René Girard).

(6) There is a widespread criticism of emphasis upon mythology as a perspective because it disengages and distances ideas and reality in a manner that tends to be individualistic, narcissistic, and solipsistic (sources from no. 1 and no. 2, above).

(7) Mythology—it has been argued for some time now—is anachronistic in a post-industrial time of technology and computer-theory (Rudolf Bultmann, Gabriel Vahanian, Marshall McLuhan).

These seven critiques, taken together, represent a powerful myth-bashing and bashing of scholars of myth, particularly comparativists. I call this "mythoclasm," a word I thought I had recently coined for this phenomenon, only to discover that Jerome Bruner had already used it in an essay, "Myth and Identity," published in a book edited by Henry Murray (*Myth and Mythmaking*) some thirty years ago. Bruner's and my senses of the word are a bit different. We both are using the term in analogy with the word "iconoclasm," which means "the smashing of icons or idols." But my meaning intends to lean in the direction of Roland Barthes' statement: "[There should be] no semiology which cannot, in the last analysis be acknowledged as *semioclasm*." Garbage, by whatever name, smells the same! The question has to do with the vulnerability of the works of Joseph Campbell to this mythoclastic impulse in the postmodern academy.

Lest one become defensive in the face of question, it may be well, first, to feel firmly the impulse, the mythoclasm. Is it not Native American wisdom that one walk in another's moccasins for twenty moons before attempting to engage that other? So in the case of mythoclasm, it may be well to hear deeply and feel thoroughly the hurt and wound that is being experienced which gives rise to the critique. What damage have myth and the study of myth caused, even unwittingly and without any malice aforethought?

Mythology has often, alas, functioned as (1) a repressive and oppressive stereotyping of races, religions, and genders by making stereotypes seem archetypal by way of the beauty and power of myth. Mythicizing the archetype has (2) given the *status quo* metaphysical sanction and supported political atrocity. Comparativism (3) colonializes in the name of the dominant group and (4) slights historical distinction and particularity, even (5) rationalizing scapegoating by refusing to problematize victimage and violence. Finally, the study of mythology, when being appropriated by New Age spirituality, (6) refuses moral engagement and responsibility, and it (7) becomes a defense against the realities of those suffering an apocalyptic culture and life. Much may be suffered by many in the name of mythology and the study of mythology.

But the point is not to wail and gnash the teeth or beat the breast. The point is to ask oneself to entertain thoughtfully and reflectively the postmodern mythoclastic ideas. To ask oneself without self-pity, when and where I am not sensitive to these hurts and wounds, that is, when in my myths and in my study of mythology, while following my own bliss, I without noticing keep someone else from following his or hers.

As for Joseph Campbell, this point means that the question is not primarily whether Joseph Campbell personally was anti-Semitic, racist, misogynist, or whatever. The gods will have to decide such matters.

Rather, the question is when and where and how Campbell's method, his mode of thought, without intention to be sure, nonetheless and not unlike any other, is vulnerable to such charges. Elie Wiesel has recently written, "*All* collective judgments are wrong. Only racists make them." So there is a question about the morality of the rhetoric when someone says that Jewish myths of creation are such and such or that Chinese myth is this and that. Did not Edward Said teach us all that "oriental" is a Eurocentric (perhaps Christian) notion?

Perhaps we all know this but forget it. We especially forget it when we are being academic rather than scholarly. Joseph Campbell knew it, too. He said so, when he was being scholarly. Let me give two examples of Campbell's own mythoclasm, examples of his being postmodern before the time.

In the 1959 edition of *Masks of God: Primitive* [sic] *Mythology*, Campbell forcefully argued the case that the modern study of mythology grew out of a Northern European, Romantic intuition about Aryan language and culture that was an intellectual rationale for a mythic support of the anti-Semitic politics of Nazism. At the end of this argument, Campbell mythoclastically warned: "Clearly mythology is no toy for children, nor is it a matter of archaic, merely scholarly concern, of no moment to men [*sic*] of action . . . The world is now far too small, and men's [*sic*] stake in sanity too great, for any more of those old games of Chosen Folk . . . by which tribesmen [*sic*] were sustained against their enemies in the days when the serpent still could talk." [p. 12] Campbell here is demonstrating a sensitivity to the first two critiques mentioned above.

A second example shows Campbell being equally responsive to critiques 3 through 5. Joe was not even one paragraph into his 1957 lecture at the Eranos Conference in Switzerland when the audience heard him saying: ". . . since one of the main themes of my subject is to be that of the provincial character of *all* that we are prone to regard as universal, we may let the presentation stand as an illustration of its own thesis" [*Flight of the Wild Gander*, p. 120]. I do not think that this sentence can be dismissed by calling it a "witty and ingenious . . . self-depreciation," as the biographers do in *Fire in the Mind* [p. 431]. Campbell wrestled over the question of the relation of *Elementargedanken* (archetypes) and *Volkergedanden* (stereotypes), over the difficult problem of morphological parallelism and historical diffusion. As Robert Segal and others have pointed out, he was not unaware of historical differentiation and particularity, as the *Historical Atlas* at the end of his life shows. After all, Campbell wrote about 1000 different "faces" of the hero and he called his four-volume work "masks" (plural), not "mask" (singular).

But Campbell also knew that historicism is not the way to go, at least not the literalist historicism of Von Ranke. Though he did not put it the way Derrida does, he had learned his post-Kantian lessons well enough to know that there is no *dehors texte*. One does not get rid of myth (with its mythoclastic problems) by getting rid of myth and the study of myth. By turning to literalist historicism, the myth only goes underground and is possibly more demonic for being unconscious. What, after all, is the myth of history?

Campbell's way through this garbage of myth was by way of myth. It is as if he knew that there are three possible meanings of "mythoclasm." The first is that myth can smash people. This is its repressive and violent function, which Campbell acknowledged in 1959. The second is that to some people myths are "smashing" (in the vernacular sense, meaning "terrific"). This is implicit in Campbell's Eranos speech, but is even clearer in the popular (i.e. academic, but not scholarly) Bill Moyer's interviews. But there is a third possible meaning of "mythoclasm." The term could radically refer to the fact that a myth can itself have a mythoclastic function, that is, it can smash the oppressive and repressive smashing of the first meaning, as well as the inflated mythoduly (corresponding to "iconoduly," meaning "worship of images") of the second meaning. Let me explain this in Campbell's own terms.

From the beginning of his scholarly career to the end, Campbell insisted, as he put it already in 1949 in *Hero With a Thousand Faces*, that "humor is the touchstone of the truly mythological as distinct from the more literal-minded and sentimental theological [and fairy tale] mood" [p. 180]. In the same work he spoke of "the sophistication of the humor of the imagery inflected in a skillful mythological rendition" [p. 178]. Again he said, "all great myths are humorous" [*Hero, p.* 361]. Similar remarks may be found in *Oriental Mythology* [p. 149] and in the *Historical Atlas* [2.1.111]. And To Bill Moyers he said, "The imagery of mythology is rendered with humor" [*Power of Myth*, p. 220]. The point is that the serious dogmatism in religion, the ideology in culture, and the literalism in historiography are smashed by myth, which, though dealing with powerful ideas and meanings, is after all merely myth. It is fiction, story, and hypothesis misread as biography, science and history. Myth is mythoclastic, when it is functioning truly as myth.

The presentation at Eranos in 1957 made this point even more strongly and in scholarly fashion. In that lecture entitled, "The Symbol without Meaning," Campbell argued that there are two ways of understanding mythic discourse and thinking: (1) as a symbol functioning for engagement, reference, and identification; or (2) as a symbol functioning for disengagement, transport, and differentiation. The former is especially appealing in the context of agricultural matrices and industrial civilizations, whose myths, and the religion and fairy tales and ideologies that follow from them, seem to engage people to a tribe or nation, to refer to belief systems, and to identify dogmatic and ideological meanings. The second way is more at home in the context of hunting peoples, and Campbell believed, in our time. In this perspective, it is the work of myth to disidentify, disengage, and dislocate. This is what Derrida will later deconstructively call *différance*, referring to the power of discourse to be seen and felt as forever deferring closure of meaning. Campbell appropriately used a mythic image (the wild gander flying into the void) to describe this function. He explained it this way:

> The bow, in order to function as a bow and not as a snare, must have no meaning whatsoever in itself—or in any part of itself—beyond that of being an agent for disengagement—from itself. [*Flight*, p. 178]

So it is with myth. If someone assigns a so-called "meaning" to a myth, it then serves to engage energy and consciousness to itself (mythoduly, idolatry of myth and the study of myth). For myth to work properly, "meaning" must be withdrawn, deferred, itself a catapult into the unknown and the unknowable and to be left behind. Myth is like a bow *disengaging* an arrow. So, Campbell said forcefully in conclusion at Eranos:

> The world, the entire universe, its gods and all, has become a symbol—signifying nothing: a symbol without meaning. For to attribute meaning to any part of it would be to relax its force as a bow, and the

arrow of the soul would then lodge only in the sphere of meaning . . . Our meaning is not the meaning that is no meaning; for no fixed reference can be drawn. [*Flight*, 177f, 190]

Myth is always already mythoclastic, or it has become religion or fairy tale, for believers and for innocents without real life-experience.

## CONCLUSION: DON'T MYTH JOSEPH CAMPBELL

In the '60s there was a bumper sticker celebrating the beginning of Joseph Campbell's renown and popularity. It said: "Don't myth Joseph Campbell!" Perhaps today we need another motto, one that reads: "Myth Joseph Campbell!" On his own terms it would be well to take Campbell's studies of myth, like everything else, with a bit of humor, disengaging from them at the same time that we engage them.

Surely we don't myth Joseph Campbell—rather we miss him as scholar—when we turn his work to religion or fairy tale, when we believe in it dogmatically or turn it to innocence. Would it not be more just to be truly mythic about the myth man?

The scholarly critique of Campbell is not a critique of Campbell, but of Campbell fundamentalism, its humorlessness, its over-engagement, its production of a New Age Chosen People, its lack of "fire in the *mind*." It hates talk about Campbell rather than talk about what Campbell talked about. It loves Campbell for bringing people to the study of myth and for his willingness to be bold enough to be wrong. But those participating in the controversy hate it when others present Campbell's work as "right" when what they probably mean is that it is useful, compelling, therapeutic, entertaining, engaging, and so on . . . but "right," that is another matter altogether.

I loved Campbell because he was a scholar, that is, a plumber. He plumbed the depths of myth, made it all flow, and disposed of a lot of garbage. And we—or at least some of us—might want to continue to do the same . . . but differently, of course.

DAVID L. MILLER is Watson-Ledden Professor of Religion at Syracuse University. He is the author of *The New Polytheism, The Three Faces of God, Hells and Holy Ghosts*, and other books, as well as many articles on religion, mythology, and literature. Dr. Miller has been a leading figure at the Eranos Conferences founded by Carl Jung and teaches annually at the Pacifica Graduate Institute.

Reprinted from SPRING, *A Journal of Archetypal Thought.* P.O.Box 583 Putnam, CT 06260. Subscription: $20/year.

# FACE INTO THE WIND, PROTECT THE FLAME

An interview with CLARISSA PINKOLA ESTÉS

from *Psychological Perspectives*

*Clarissa Pinkola Estés, Ph.D., diplomate Jungian analyst, and bestselling author lives in Colorado and Wyoming. She was drawn to the high country desert where her own Latina culture is integrated with that of African, Native, Asian, and European American peoples. Dr. Estés is a poet who penetrates the depths of human experience with acute intellectual, intuitive, and spiritual sight. In the following interview, Dr. Estés speaks with Charlene Sieg, managing editor of* **Psychological Perspectives.**

**Charlene Sieg (PP):** Do you view the human rights movement as a movement away from patriarchy?

**Clarissa Pinkola Estés:** I do not use the word *patriarchy* anywhere in my work because I think the overly broad use of the term does not adequately describe the etiologies of most social justice difficulties. Nowadays, *patriarchy* is used as shorthand to express or explain the legitimate pain of being caught in some sort of unrelenting Gordian knot. However, impassivity or nonresponsiveness to the suffering of others, whether by an individual or a group, usually lives on because the underlying premises are unquestioned and guarded by a significant number of men *and* women. To borrow from biology, it may be more useful to name problematical elements, part by smallest part, working one's way up to naming by "phylum" or "kingdom."

*PP:* Is your analytic work compatible with your social activist work?

*Pinkola Estés:* Yes. Jung's commentaries on the First and Second World Wars, and his brilliant diagnosis of thugs and dictators, illuminated much about the underside of social action issues in which I was involved—whether farm-workers' rights, land grant disputes, or freedom of expression for persons in prison. As an adult, the volume that drew me to depth psychology was Jung's *Civilization in Transition.* Traditionally, human rights movements in the Americas since the 1940s—those led by Dorothy Day, Martin Luther King, Los Cofrades in Guatemala, and others—have relied on the paradigm wherein valuation of inner life and that of outer action are held together as a single thought. These *together* enable one to make a potent motion in the world. *Satyagraha,* as Gandhi called it, is the power of *oldest knowing* and *just action* woven together. This world view functions with an awareness that specific grounds for injustice or imbalance arise both without and within, not just one or the other. Taken together, these constitute a trans-psychic truth that fires not just personal action, but more so, calls the soul to action; the fierce, image-making soul.

*PP:* How does one know one is being called?

*Pinkola Estés:* How? Through paradox. Persons called to such work typically feel a relentless sensation of brokenheartedness about the state of their world, or the world, but *also* carry an unshakable and inspired hope for humankind. There may be anger as well. The seemingly contradictory but powerful forces of the broken heart commingled with hope are the enduring underpinnings for effecting ongoing and positive change.

*PP:* You are saying that the social activist has a broken heart?

*Pinkola Estés:* Yes, a heart that is broken *open*—and stays broken open—a soul alert to its calling. I remember Cesar Chavez saying he knew he had to move to a certain town, else he might content himself to repeat the lives of those before him. He heard the call and went. He was one of the great brokenhearted and hope-filled activists of our time. Sometimes people think a calling is just a metaphor. Our *abueli-tas*, old women, say that being called to a certain kind of work or life has sensory features that cause nudges at shoulder, restlessness in legs, mysterious urgings that make a person move in concert with *El destino*, Destiny.

*PP:* Where did all this begin for you?

*Pinkola Estés:* It was easy in a hard kind of way . . . . I was born to it. [*Laughter.*] As a child from one of the lowest economic classes, we faced many grotesque imbalances of power. Most people of our rural community struggled mightily, sacrificed, but had pride. When did my heart break open? During the forced repatriation of Mexicanos field workers in the upper midwest . . . . The winter a toddler fell through the ice and drowned because a negligent landowner failed to fence his pond . . . . The day a faulty thresher dragged my friend's father to his death . . . . The day my aunts were tricked into working at lightning speed after being promised a small bonus; after exhausting themselves, the line man raised their daily production quotas to inhuman heights . . . . Seeing ulcerated veins on the legs of my friend's mother, lesions from ten babies in ten years while trying to follow religious proscriptions against birth control . . . . The day I saw my Magyar foster father writhe in agony as the radio broadcaster announced that Soviets had invaded Hungary with tanks while the peasants had nothing to fight with but their fists . . . . The day boys I grew up with who played "guns" in snow forts and girls who played "nurses" at the roadside, came back standing or laid down from Khe Sanh and the Tet. There were many breakings, not just one, but time and again. And still. Germans have a word for it—*Schemerzenreich*—meaning rich in sorrow, ability to bear sorrow, this essential ability for activism, and poetry, and psychoanalytic work.

*PP:* How does one avoid feeling paralyzed by witnessing such suffering?

*Pinkola Estés:* You know, because you grew up in the Dakotas, that a harsh environment spurs people to live with penetrating vitality. To be enduring, as though to shake a fist at it all. Jung said that transformation requires patience and a sense of humor. Most of the families where I grew up taught their children to value tricksterish kinds of things. There was no television, many had no telephones, many could not read or write. We were taught harmless mischiefs, practical jokes, all-night singing, dancing, betting on sleigh, dog, hen, and frog races, ice-fishing contests, harvest braggings, snipe hunts. They tried to inoculate us with an invincible sense of humor; a kind of dry wit that could shine through, no matter what. All these activities were understood as "the good life," but also, under certain conditions, as balances to grave suffering. Somewhat by osmosis, we apprenticed to the grown-ups' fierceness; that unwavering determination to stand one's ground. This gave many young northwoods children a startling kind of presence. Farther underneath that, we witnessed our elders' quietude, something completely silken and silent that ran under their words or actions, be they playful or deadly serious. These were true patriarchs, true matriarchs; many had exemplary vision, toughness, and tenderness.

*PP:* What are some of the social action issues you've been involved with?

*Pinkola Estés:* Here are some. I was initiated in the farm workers and black civil rights movements of the sixties. Also in the sixties, I worked for various Central American refugee missions. I was "detained" by *Puerto Barrios* paramilitary. It was life changing in many, many ways. Twenty-some years ago, some friends and I coordinated the first shelter for battered women in the American Southwest; learned to persuade governmental agencies that domestic assault really existed; learned to persuade grocery produce managers to donate all their mildly dead lettuce, wilted greens, and squishy fruits to the shelter. For twenty-two years I've taught writing as liberation of spirit to men and women who are in prison, especially in federal penitentiaries for so-called hard core. Along with Joanne Greenberg, (author of *I Never Promised You a Rose Garden*), I co-founded and co-direct the Colorado Authors for Gay and Lesbian Equal Rights. As straight women, we felt it was a critical time to stand up with gays and lesbians from our world family. I founded the Guadalupe Foundation, a human rights organization that, among other projects, supports broadcasting of strengthening stories, via short-wave radio, to trouble spots throughout the world.

*PP:* That's an immense amount. I know your book, *Women Who Run With the Wolves*, was written over a twenty-year period. How did you find the time and the courage to dive as deeply as your writing conveys?

*Pinkola Estés:* "Dive?" [*Laughter.*] That's where I *live.* One can raise children, run off pamphlets, write, make love, demonstrate, travel, and work from there. It is not a matter of *going* somewhere; it's a matter of cultivating where you live, at whichever level of spirit nourishes you best. Among the leaders I've lived and worked with during my life, it was their vigorous attention to their inner lives that funded their work in the world, preventing "burn-out," keeping them *fuerte y duro*, solid and strong.

*PP:* You seem to have been born to this place—no one tried to take this away from you?

*Pinkola Estés:* Yes, I think my home is there. Some have tried, a few rather vigorously, to rearrange the furniture of my psyche, so to speak. But I was raised to be like a dog with a rug. Don't give up at the first tug.

*PP:* Regarding your book, people have said to me, "How did she *do* this?" They just can't figure out how you could write such an intense work while being a mother, an activist, and an analyst.

*Pinkola Estés:* I set aside writing times; an afternoon or from midnight to 3 a.m. Also I discovered 25 years ago that, if I kept at it, I could write about two-and-a-half pages in five or six minutes. Every time I had a little space of time, I read or wrote. When demands left me not a moment to spare, I made myself write one perfectly true sentence every day. At week's end, I had seven good sentences and that felt like a great bounty. Eventually, I had a 2,500-page work about the inner life, not counting research notes and journals, on the end of the little string with the berry on the end that I had let down into the river. [*Laughter.*] Seriously, I culled 100 fairy tales from several hundred I knew, researched them, and kept going. Close to publishing I was writing and polishing 17 hours per day, seven days per week for six months, to bring all work up to the same "age," for portions of it had been written in each decade of my adult life. I brought it up to the perspective of my having lived nearly half a century.

In *curanderisma* [the old healing arts], there are certain people who dream dreams meant to guide the entire village. It seems to me that, on occasion, Jung dreamed for the world village. This dream impresses me most. Jung dreamed of moving against a great wind. A dark force bore down behind him. In the palm of his hand was a little flame. His task was not to dally with what was behind him, but to press forward into

the wind and to protect the tiny fire. This is the heart of writing,
activism, and inner life: Face into the wind. Protect the flame. Keep
going. ❧

## THE DAUGHTER OF CHILAM BILAM
by Clarissa Pinkola Estés

I dreamed that Chilam Bilam, the great jaguar priest
remembered the time his daughter saved the Mayan race.
The great floods were coming, there was war,
the necks of slaves burnt from the rope, old women
hobbled fast with tables upon their backs, fires
boiled over, the animals ran every which way,
and flame burnt the divine jungle.
The daughter of Chilam Bilam inhaled all the animals
and all the trees, and all the birds and flowers,
all the beautiful old men and women,
all the new babes, all the nursing mothers,
all the plowing men, all the sweethearts,
all the creatures of the jungle and the sea nearby
and the pine forests of the highlands
and the deserts in the lowlands.
But now she had a dilemma...
She could not let out her breath without spilling
the forests and jungles and animals and people
she had inside her. And so she began with
the dreamers of the nearest village, and breathed
some animals and flowers into their dreams
for safekeeping.
Through their mouths while they slept and
through their ears she breathed into them all
the *montañas*, all the *monigotes*, all the rivers,
all the serpents, all the old women and all
the new born and all the things which make
life what it is and good. And when she was done
there, she ventured farther and farther

across the world, filling the nights and minds
of dreamers with her enormous breath. And
that is why today, people dream monkey and
mountain and jaguar, people dream orchid and
*quetzal,* people dream old dark women and men
with long hair, even though they have never,
in real life, seen these things.
For they received the bounty, and the heart
of compassion from that divine woman long ago.
It is said that this daughter's name translated from
the Quiché Maya is in Spanish called *Esperanza.*
It is said that her name translated into English,
means Hope.

*CLARISSA PINKOLA ESTÉS* is a Jungian Analyst in Denver and author of **Women Who Run With the Wolves: Myths and Stories of the Wild Woman Archetype.** She received the Las Primeras Award (First of Her Kind) from the Latina Professional Women's Foundation in Washington, DC. She is a political activist and has testified before congress on poverty programs as a "witness for the defenseless". Her most recent book is **The Gift of Story: A Wise Tale About What is Enough.**

Reprinted from *Psychological Perspectives,* C. G. Jung Institute of Los Angeles, 10349 Pico Boulevard, Los Angeles, CA 90064. (310) 556-1193. Subscription: $22/year.

# ST. GEORGE, THE DRAGON, AND THE VIRGIN

*A sculpture made by Bernt Notke in 1489 for Stockholm Cathedral*

*by* ROBERT BLY

*from Meditations on the Insatiable Soul*

The spiny Dragon
Who lives in the rat-
Filled caves is losing.
He fights fiercely,
As when a child
Lifts his four
Feet to hold
Off the insane
Parent. The Dragon's
Hand grasps the wooden
Lance that has
Penetrated his thorny
Chest, but . . .
Too late . . .

And this girlish knight?
Oh I know him.
I read the New
Testament as I lay
Naked on my bed
As a boy. The knight
Rises up radiant
With the forehead-
Eye that sees past
The criminal's gibbet
To the mindful
Towers of the spirit city.
I hate this solar
Boy whom I have been,
Rearing with his lance above
The father. Each of us
Has been this marsh
Dragon on his back.
He is Joseph, Grandel,
What we have forgotten,
The great spirit
The alchemists knew of,
Without whom is nothing.

How long it must've taken
To temper that horse
So he agreed
To abet the solar boy.
This earth-handed, disreputable,
Hoarse-voiced one
Is dying. As children
We knew ours
Was a muddy greatness.

Did I forget to mention
The Virgin? She prays
On her knees while

This goes on,
As well she might.

I wrote this to bless
The swamp monster
And the marsh hag
Who bore him.

ROBERT BLY is author of **Iron John** and numerous volumes of poetry
including **Meditations on the Insatiable Soul** (HarperCollins).

# STORY FOOD

### by ROBERT BLY

*from* **Sacred Stories**

**O**NCE UPON A TIME, ONCE BELOW A TIME, or once inside a time there was a king with three daughters. The third daughter was especially feisty and adventurous. One day she was wandering in the woods, and she saw a white bear lying on its back playing with a golden wreath. After a while she said to the bear, "I'd love to have that wreath."

The bear said, "What are you offering?"

She said, "I will give you all of my jewels."

He said, "What good are jewels to a bear?"

She said, "I'll give you my crown."

He said, "What good is a crown to a bear?"

"Well, what can I give you for the wreath?" she asked.

"For a wreath like this, you have to pay with yourself," the bear said.

She said, "Do you mean . . ."

"I do," he said. "I'll come next Thursday (Thor's-day) to your father's castle and fetch you."

She walked home. At dinnertime she told her father about the strange event that had happened to her in the woods. "I offered him jewels and a crown, but he wouldn't accept it, so I've agreed to marry the bear."

Her father said, "It's a rash decision. What is the wreath like?"

"Oh," she said, "It's round; with golden leaves, and it's about a foot across."

Her father took careful note. Then he called his goldsmiths and said, "Start now. Melt down gold. Make a wreath of this sort. I want this wreath done by tomorrow evening." So they worked all night and all the next day, and at dinnertime the king brought his youngest daughter the wreath.

She said, "It's not quite right. It's too large." So that night the king forced his goldsmiths to stay up all night again and make a smaller wreath. He brought it to her Wednesday morning.

"The original was a little fatter," she said.

So the King ordered the goldsmiths to go to work all night again. The third wreath had leaves that looked like maple leaves instead of oak, and she rejected it too.

On Thor's-day morning, the king took all three daughters aside and said, "As you know, in our country, the oldest daughter marries first. That means, my dear oldest daughter, that you will have to marry the bear this morning. Get ready." The King then ordered his palace guards into the courtyard and said, "When a white bear comes, shoot him." When the bear arrived, they raised their guns. The bear looked at them, roared, knocked them all down, and walked straight past them into the castle. "I'm ready now to welcome the bride," he proudly announced.

When the oldest daughter came out, the bear said, "Climb on my back." She climbed on and they started for the woods. When they were about a mile away, the bear said, "Have you ever *sat* more softly than you are sitting now?" She said, "Oh yes, on my father's lap I sat more softly than I am sitting now." The bear said, "Have you ever *seen* more clearly than you are seeing now?" She said, "Yes, on top of my father's tower at the castle, I saw more clearly than I am seeing now." He said,

"Oh, hell, it's the wrong bride." He threw her off, and she had to walk home.

The next Thor's-day the king told his second daughter, "Today it's your turn. Prepare for marriage." He had meanwhile invited a number of soldiers and musketeers from the neighboring castles, so he had a small army waiting. When the white bear arrived, again he just growled, stood up on his hind legs, knocked them all down, and walked into the castle. He said, "I'm ready to welcome the bride." The second daughter came out and off they went.

About a mile away from the castle, the bear said, "Have you ever *sat* more softly than you are sitting now?" she said, "Yes, I remember in my father's lap I sat more softly than I am sitting now." The bear asked, "Have you ever *seen* more clearly than you are seeing now?" She said, "Yes, once looking out from my father's tower, I saw more clearly than I am seeing now." He said, "Oh dear, wrong one!" He threw her off, and she had to walk home, too.

By next Thor's-day, all the available soldiers in that part of Norway had arrived, plus cannons. The king said to the youngest daughter, "I grieve over this situation. I know you don't want to leave." But she was already dressed. When the bear arrived, he saw that the whole castle courtyard was full—soldiers, muskets, swords, and cannons. What did the bear do? He stood on his hind legs, growled, rushed, knocked them all down, and walked in. He said, "I'm ready to welcome the bride." The youngest daughter came out, and the bear said, "Climb on my back."

They were about a mile out of town when he said to her, "Have you ever *sat* more softly than you are sitting now?" she said, "Never." He asked, "Have you ever *seen* more clearly than you are seeing now?" She said, "Never." And the bear said, "Ah, she's the right one."

So they made their way to his castle; it turned out that he was known as the White Bear King Valemon. The odd thing about him was that at nightfall he would turn into a beautiful man and the couple would spend the night together. The princess never actually saw him, but their nights were full of joy and delight. When they would wake up in the morning, he would be a bear again and go out into the forest and do what bears do. That's how it was. Something about this life suited the princess, and three years passed in this way. Each year the princess gave birth to a child, but each time the child disappeared as soon as it was born. The disappearance of the child was only one more strange detail in a strange situation.

Then one day she said, "I want to go back and see my father and mother." The bear agreed that she could go if she wanted to, but warned her, "Listen to what your father says, not to what your mother does."

So she returned home. Her sisters were very curious and asked many pointed questions about her life with the bear. "Does he manicure his claws? Do you eat fresh-killed meat? Do you sleep in a cave all winter?"

She told them, "It's not like that. We live in a castle; it's a calm and peaceful place. At night he becomes a man, and although I've never seen him, we make beautiful love."

"You never see him at night," they replied. "How do you know he's not a monster or a dragon? What if one night he just eats you whole? That could happen. As your older sisters, we're worried about you. We certainly don't carry any grudge, but it seems clear to us that this so-called king might be dangerous."

It turns out the mother and father were listening to their conversation. "I think you should let things be as they are," the father said to his youngest daughter. But the mother said, "Take this candle back with you. One night, after he has fallen asleep, light the candle and hold it up to his body. Then you'll know one way or the other. That's my advice."

The princess brought the candle back to the Bear King's castle. The first night home they made love, and when her lover fell asleep, the princess got up, quietly lit the candle, and held it up to his body. She started with his feet; they were small and shapely and seemed beautiful to her. His shins and knees were elegant. She moved the light up over his thighs; they were strong and well-shaped, and all other things in their vicinity handsome and fine. She found his stomach flat and his chest firm. He was without a doubt a man and now that she had seen his strong body, she was even more curious about his face. But as she lifted the candle higher, one drop of hot wax fell on his shoulder and he awoke.

"Why did you do it?" he cried out. "If only you could have waited another month I could have been a human being both night and day! Now I have to leave." He became a bear and rushed out the door.

She cried out, "I don't want you to go!"

"It's too late. I don't have any choice! I cannot stay," he answered.

He rushed out of the castle, toward the forest, and she ran after him and grabbed onto his fur. He ran on all fours through trees and brush. She held on as hard and as long as she could, but the underbrush and branches tore at her, and she fell off. The bear rushed on ahead and the princess found herself on the forest floor alone.

She wandered in the forest for a long time without shelter or food. If she met anyone in the forest she would always ask them if they knew where the White Bear King Valemon might be. The answer was always the same: "I've never heard of him." One day she came upon a hut. An old woman lived there with a small girl. When the raggedy princess knocked, they took her in and gave her food. The princess spoke sweetly with the old woman. Then she got down on the floor and played with the little girl and asked her many questions about dollhouses and crickets.

When the wandering princess was about to go, the little girl said, "Mother, she's been so good to us. Could we give her the scissors?" The old woman said, "If you want to, we will." The scissors were special. Whenever a hand opened or closed the scissors, cloth appeared on its own. Whatever sort of cloth that was desired—cotton, embroidered linens, satins, lace, flannel, and plaids. The princess was glad to have the scissors. As she thanked them, she asked the old woman, "By the way, have you seen the White Bear King Valemon?"

The old woman said, "Yes, I have. He came past here about a month ago. He was traveling very fast, heading west."

The princess was glad to hear that news. She walked on in the forest, toward the west, and soon saw a second hut also inhabited by a small girl and an old woman. After the old woman had served her tea, the princess had her own little tea with the daughter and asked her questions like, "Have you learned the alphabet yet? Do you know any good stories? Do you go to school? Do you have any friends in the woods?" This went on quite a while. When she was about to leave, the daughter said, "Mother, she has been so good to us; could we give her the flask?"

The flask was strange and special—when you lifted and turned it over, any liquid that was desired poured out. If you thought "cognac,"

cognac came, or cold water, wine, or jasmine tea. "If you want to give her the flask, we will," the mother told the child. The daughter was glad to give it to the kind princess. After the princess thanked her hosts, she turned to the old woman and asked, "By the way, have you seen the White Bear King Valemon?"

The mother answered, "Actually, he rushed by about a week ago. He was going very fast toward the west. I don't know if you can catch him."

So the king's daughter kept wandering. After a while she happened on a third hut in which another old woman lived with a young girl. After tea, again the princess played with the child. She helped her make little dolls out of pine cones and asked her many questions. "What do you want to be when you grow up? Do you think animals are like people?" When the princess was about to leave, the young girl said, "Mother, could we give her the tablecloth?"

This tablecloth had magic in it. When it was spread out on the table, food appeared on its own—cheese, roast duck, salmon, sweet and sour soup, lamb stew, or chocolate mousse. Any dish that was desired. The old woman said, "If you want to give her the tablecloth, we will."

As the visitor was about to go, she turned to the old woman and said, "By the way, have you seen the White Bear King Valemon lately?"

The mother replied, "Yes! He came by here about three days ago, going west. I heard he's on his way to the glass mountain."

The glass mountain! What glass mountain? The glass mountain. So the princess set out for the glass mountain. After hours of walking she saw it looming over the trees. The sides were slippery and steep. As she approached the base she noticed the ground was covered with the bones of all the men and women who had tried to climb it and failed.

She noticed nearby yet another hut. When she knocked at the door and was invited in, she realized that it was different in several ways from the previous huts she had visited. A middle-aged woman, not young, not old, lived there with four young children. There was evidence of a man's tools. The princess saw no food anywhere; the family was obviously starving. Everyone's clothes were tattered. Soon the children confided in her. "Oftentimes we have no food. But sometimes our mother puts stones in the soup and boils them. She tells us they're apples, and the soup tastes better. That really helps."

It didn't take long for the traveler to open the tablecloth and lay it out. Soon there was lamb, good cheese, and fresh potatoes. The mother and the children ate and ate. And the flask poured orange juice and milk and hot cider. While everyone was eating the scissors made dresses, winter coats, woolen trousers, winter underwear, shawls, and socks. After they had eaten all they could, the tablecloth made salt beef, dried cod, and goat cheese to last the winter. When everyone had been provided for, the princess turned to the mother and asked, "Do you know the White Bear King Valemon?"

The woman said, "Are you the one? Are you the woman who looked at him, and whom he had to leave behind?"

The princess said yes, she was that one and explained how she had been searching for him for a long time.

"Well," the mother said, "the White Bear King is nearby, but he is going to be married in three days."

"He is?" the princess said in a low voice. "To whom?"

"Her," the mother replied.

"What do you mean, Her?"

"Her. The Great One. She lives on top of the glass mountain. No one can compare to her. She has great power and a great appetite. Fat dogs tend to disappear when they get near her. Sometimes she eats a hundred roasted songbirds for lunch. She has skeleton fingers that serve her tea and a small pine tree grows out of her nose. Many animals serve her; they bring her news from distant places. If you want to get the Bear King back, you must get to the top of the mountain soon. The wedding is in three days."

The princess thanked the woman and started out to climb the glass mountain. It was not easy. She could get no hold and slipped to the bottom again and again.

The thin woman watched her and finally came out and said, "This isn't going to work. My husband, who is a blacksmith, will be as grateful as I am for your feeding and clothing the children. Nothing could have been more wonderful. He is coming back tonight. I'll ask him to forge iron claws for your hands and feet. That's what you need. They'll get you up the mountain."

So that's how it went. The husband returned, the children told him the story, and he stayed up all night making the iron claws. Just after dawn, the princess put them on and started her climb.

When she got to the top, she found an elaborate castle, and in front of it a terrace surrounded by low walls. She had brought the flask, tablecloth, and scissors with her, and soon the fragrance of French cognac, Armagnac, Persian rose-water, dark red wine, and champagne floated over the porch. The princess laid the tablecloth out on a huge table and soon appeared roast beef, squash, and roasted turkey. The wonderful smells drew The Great One on to the terrace. When she got close, she could see oysters on the half shell, smoked salmon, baked halibut, cherry pies, and chocolate mousse. A little yellow songbird came flying by; the Great One picked it out of the air and ate it whole. Then she screamed: "Aahii! This sort of food is exactly what I want for my wedding. How did you do all this?"

The princess said, "The tablecloth you see spread here is magic, and it produces any food you would like to have."

"I want it! How much?"

"No amount of money can buy it."

"What do you want then, tell me!" A sparrow flew out of her hair.

"I want one night alone with the Bear King."

"Haaaa!" the Great One screeched. "One night you may have. Come here at ten o'clock tonight and my maid will show you where his room is. Just knock on his door. Have the tablecloth ready to give to my maid."

So that's the way it happened. The deal was made. You should know, however, that the Queen of the Glass Mountain, the Dear One with an Appetite visited the Bear King first. He was in his human form.

"The wedding is coming up, get lots of rest. Here's a little apple wine that I made especially for you. It will help you sleep," she said.

He drank it, and a sleeping potion took effect. When the princess, full of hope, knocked later in the evening, no one answered. She walked in the room and found the Bear King sound asleep. No matter how much she talked in his ear, sang to him, and shook him, he wouldn't wake up. She waited beside him all night, and he never awoke. At dawn she gave up and left.

She knew the Great One would come out for a walk on the terrace in the morning. This time the princess gathered wine glasses from the kitchen, Russian teacups, German tankards, and Czechoslovakian goblets painted with gold. She turned the flask over and filled them with black Turkish coffee, English tea, the finest champagnes, red and white wines, cherry liqueurs, vodka, and aquavit. When Bride-of-All-Beings came out, she was delighted.

"I want champagne for my wedding. Around here they produce white piss and call it wine. Where did all this come from?"

"The flask you see here is magic; when you turn it over, it pours whatever drink you want."

"All right, what's the deal? Name your price," exclaimed the great One.

"I want one more night with the White Bear King Valemon."

"That must be because you had so much fun last night." Her tusks gleamed. "Bring the flask here at ten o'clock and give it to my maid."

The princess waited impatiently all day, but that Dear Lady, the One Who Uses Boys' Bones as Toothpicks, visited the bear first. He was in human form. She offered him a goodnight drink, and he took it. When the princess knocked on the door, no one answered. She entered the room and again found him sound asleep. She spoke to him and reminded him of their old love and how dear they had been to each other. Then she told him how long she had been searching for him and how long she had suffered with the cold and the forest, but he never fluttered an eyelid. She started to cry sitting by his bed, and she cried all night until dawn.

In the morning the White Bear King awoke, knowing nothing. He opened the door to his room. As he was leaving, two carpenters who slept in the room next door stopped him and spoke to him. "Do you know that there was a woman crying in your room last night? We heard it through the walls."

He thought, "How can that be? Is it possible she is here?"

The princess guessed that the Great One would come out for her morning walk. This time the princess began work with her scissors, and soon the tables were covered with Parisian wedding gowns, velvet stoles, lace veils, bridesmaid dresses, traveling frocks, elegant black gloves, Spanish scarves, sashes, and darling jackets. Soon the Queen with Two Sets of Teeth came by carrying a rabbit she had just snatched up and saw it all. "This is perfect! It will all fit me well. I'll try them on today, and wear them tomorrow morning. How much?"

"No amount of money can buy these scissors."

"All right. What is your price?"

"I'd like a last night with the White Bear King Valemon."

"As you wish, honey. I don't know what they taught you in school. I'll take these clothes with me and you bring the scissors here at ten o'clock!"

The Queen of All the People, the One-Who-Is-Always-Hungry, visited the Bear King for a nightcap in the usual way. When she offered him the glass of wine, he turned slightly to the side, and, choosing a time when she wasn't looking, poured the drink down his shirt into a little bag he had tied around his neck. A few minutes later, he said, "Oh, I feel so sleepy!"

Now the Queen of the Glass Mountain, being of great intelligence, became suspicious. He seemed to be asleep, but she said to herself, "Something's not right in this room. I can smell it." She decided to test him, so she took a darning needle and drove it right through his arm. He didn't move. Not even a quiver crossed his face. "Ah, he's got to be asleep," she said. She was satisfied and left the room.

When the princess arrived, the Bear King was awake. How glad they were to see each other again. How they laughed and cried and told each other how terrible the waiting had been. When a time of suffering is over, it seems charming to retell it all, even while you weep. So they talked until dawn, and then they heard the carpenters stirring in the next room. They thanked them for the message they had given, and then the White Bear King asked them to make a little adjustment on the wooden bridge over which the wedding party would walk. The carpenters said, "We think that's possible."

The wedding began early the next morning. The procession started with the bride in front, as in Norwegian weddings. She started with a veil over her tusks, but the winds that rushed past her kept blowing it aside, and the fire coming from her eyes frightened the onlookers. Many people wept. They had become fond of the Bear King and felt so sorry that he had to marry The One. But nothing could be done. The Queen of the Glass Mountain ruled and no one could say no to her.

When the One Who Makes Bones Sing reached the midpoint of the wooden bridge that led over the chasm to the church, the floor gave way, and she fell through and disappeared into the river. They did not know if it was right or wrong, but it made the people of the mountain happy, especially the princess and the Bear King.

The carpenters then nailed firm boards over the bridge and the procession continued. Now the Bear King could marry his true bride. The women in the kitchen were overjoyed, and they kept bringing out food. All the farmers and their wives, and the fishermen and their wives for miles around ate food as they had never tasted before and drank wine that made them dizzy. The dancing went on until all the wine and akvavit was gone; then they danced a couple of hours more just on apple cider.

The next morning the White Bear King and the princess traveled back to her kingdom to have a second wedding at her father's castle. On the way, they picked up the tree children, one at each hut. As it turned out, these children were the ones who had disappeared each time the princess gave birth. They were so glad to be united again with their real father and mother. The wedding was the greatest ever held in the people's memory; even the two sisters danced.

ALTHOUGH I'VE AGREED TO SAY a few words about this story as a sacred story, it is presumptuous in a way to say anything, and very easy to make misleading remarks. Everything I say, therefore, is tentative; a great mystery surrounds stories this ancient.

Our story is a sacred story because the images—the white bear, the golden wreath, the lifted candle, the children nourished on stones— resonate in some holy place. The images feel like scenes from some drama long lost, carrying information we are just now remembering.

It is said that that one distinction between the folk tale and the genuine "fairy tale" or "teaching tale" lies in the nature of the main character. Johnny Appleseed is a human being and takes his part in an honorable folk tale. The Great One, the Queen of the Glass Mountain, is clearly immortal. She is closely related to the Hindu goddesses Durga and Kali, or to Rangda in Balinese culture. German, French, and Italian tales tend to overlook her. However, the great Russian, Norwegian, and Indian stories include her under many names. The Indian saint Ramakrishna, who lived in the nineteenth century, once saw a waking vision of Kali. He saw her come out of the Ganges and described her as radiant with light and joy. He watched her give birth to a baby and hold it in her arms with such tenderness and delight that he felt deep peace. Then she began to change, her face became long. In amazement, he watched her eat the child. Then she went back into the Ganges.

The story emphasizes her tremendous appetite to indicate how close she is to the biological center of life. No judgment is made on her appetite; one does not judge the divine. So this story is sacred because it makes room for two forms of the divine, the Lady of Great appetite and the God of the Bears.

There is another reason to suspect that our story is a precious survivor from ancient religion. It is a local northern European version of "Amor and Psyche," the tale central to Greek mythology. "Amor and Psyche" survived the destruction of pagan religious material because Apuleius inserted it in the center of his Latin novel, *The Golden Ass*, written in North Africa circa A.D. 155. We know from the context of that book that the tale belonged to the worship of Isis.

In Apuleius's book, the masculine hero, who has strayed too close to sorcery, gets turned into a donkey and remains so for the entire story. Only in the last pages does he become a human being when he eats rose petals that Isis has blessed. As a donkey, he hears the story of the magic castle and lifted lamp. Both Marie-Louise von Franz and Erich Neumann have written extensively on this story—von Franz in her book called *The Golden Ass*, and Erich Neumann in his book, *Amor and Psyche*. The lifting of the lamp, and the distress it causes, is famous in mythological and psychological commentary. Almost all commentators agree that the lifting of the lamp is related to the soul's intention to increase its consciousness; some relationship that has earlier been allowed to remain "in the dark" becomes illuminated. In human life this illumination often causes the relationship to end. A break occurs, which is painful in the extreme. So the story asks what the soul is willing to pay for increased consciousness. That is a proper theme for the sacred story.

We might also say a few words on the difference between the version of "Psyche and Eros" preserved by Apuleius, which has clearly been elaborated or intellectualized in the Alexandrian manner, and the northern European version you have just read. The most noticeable difference is that in the Alexandrian version the Being Who Changes at Night to a Man is the god Eros. As a Greek god, he belongs to the heavens. The bear god, by contrast, is close to earth. There is much wit around the portrayal of Eros that fits well with the Greek habit of intellectualizing the divine, perhaps so that the mind could play with the Holy. It was fashionable at that time to make gods charming. The Bear King Valemon, by contrast, is a bear, and we feel ourselves closer to the belly—to Ursa Major—and to the old bear religion of the Stone and Bronze Ages. I think the Norwegian version is closer to the root story.

In the Alexandrian version, the youngest daughter of the king is Psyche, which is a Greek word for soul. Psyche has imaginative associations with the butterfly. Souls after death, freed of the mortal cocoon, were traditionally compared to butterflies. But it seems better storytelling not to label the daughter "the soul." Those two exceptions granted, we see that the two stories proceed on a parallel path with many minor and local variations. For example, in the Alexandrian version, the parents fear the daughter is marrying Death; her parents say a tearful good-bye to her as she leaps from a cliff. But a kind wind takes her down to the valley where the mysterious castle lies. It is there where strange events occur and she makes love to the bear king. Both stories involve a divine being making love to a feminine soul.

In both stories the heroine eventually returns to her parents' home, and the mother furnishes a lamp or candle and advises her daughter to use it. The Norwegian tale retains or ads a delicate grace note, namely, the father's advice, "I think it would be best to let things remain as they are." That advice turns out to be wrong, but it catches us for a few moments, and we can all feel our own ambiguous opinions, as to whether the soul should or should not risk the candle.

In the Norwegian version, the first strong image is the golden wreath. The ancient spiritual traditions, to which the neo-Platonists such as Plotinus returned, declare that it's important that we enter this life with no memory. Therefore, at the moment of birth all the divine knowledge we possessed before we were born disappears. Sometimes an astonishing event happens to us that helps us recall what we once knew. The gold wreath and the bear shock the "soul" (the youngest daughter) into remembering that lost knowledge.

We note that the bear was playing with the wreath, so there's something playful about the whole process of remembering. The fact that the bear is white helps one understand that the knowledge we have lost is spiritual. We get a flavor here of religious ideas older than the Judeo-Christian understanding, and more wild. The scene in which the bear rolls on its back playing with the wreath seems to me a healing image.

The story is also an initiation story for women. It introduces a woman to something divine that she did not meet in her parental house. We know that in stories, youngest daughters, like Shakespeare's Cordelia, sometimes represent the soul. We can therefore say that it is also an initiation story for the soul, and so applicable to men and women. Lastly, it is an alchemical story. In alchemy, one begins with lead and depression. After a long period of self-development and inner work, something appears in the vessel that could be described as gold. So this wreath is a promise.

It seems so strange that the soul's male lover is a human being at night and a bear in the daytime. We could say that when the human soul approaches the divine, the gap is so enormous that the divine may appear as half animal. There is a chasm between human beings and animals, also. Dionysus expressed this double truth in Greece: he was a bull. Apollo was a python; Aphrodite was a dove; Demeter was a snake. Approaching the divine is a dangerous act. At the start of our story, the bear seems charming and almost ready to adapt to human ways, but as the story continues, it becomes clear that the bear, being half divine, is a little too intense for human beings. Tremendous psychic danger hovers around him. The toughening that human beings need in order to meet that intensity gives rise in the Alexandrian version to a sequence in which the heroine, in order to fit herself for the relationship, has to go through many difficult and elaborate initiatory tasks, such as separating black and white seeds or getting wool from the golden fleece. After she fulfills those tasks, the Greek heroine comes into her psychic abundance; the Bear's lover achieves her never-empty flask through deprivation, solitude, starvation, and wilderness.

There is also a psychological reading of this story as well as a mythological one. Brooding in that way over the relationship between the Bear King and the princess, we could say that their union resembles a relationship between a contemporary man and woman where neither talks. They only make love. The two are symbiotic, they merge, they don't need words. That is lovely, but the story implies that it isn't entirely right to live in such an unconscious relationship. The candle must be lighted, even if it breaks the relationship.

What the soul needs on this planet is suffering, not the success or harmonious relationships that New Age seminar leaders try to bludgeon us into. Dostoyevsky says it over and over again: Raskolnikov (which means "schizophrenic") is split—he needs a descent.

Throughout the scenes in which the bear carries each daughter on his back and asks her questions, there is a shrewd humor. The two older daughters answer that they saw the world more clearly from their father's tower, because they feel allegiance to the father's way of seeing. As Jungian analyst and author Marion Woodman would say, if that's the case, they can't be connected to the bear. A daughter like that has no right to waste the bear's time. This test is a very sharp way of intuiting which souls are ready for initiation into the sacred and which are not. The scene is meant to be psychologically disturbing.

We also feel disturbed when the princess falls off the bear's back as they rush through the forest. We gather that it's time for her to come down from her inflation. The divine moves much faster than we do. The Persian poet Hafez wrote: "The light in the hermit's cave goes out in the conventional church." Letting go of the bear's fur means returning to the normal, boring, bitter, limited, sad human state. Wandering scratched in the forest suggests a long time of loneliness, which a man or woman may experience for twenty years or so, between ages thirty-five and fifty-five perhaps. Busy in a career or not, one is alone in the forest, and not being fed. The awareness of not being fed is essential. I think the story suggests that we don't find the three huts until we know the desperation that comes with not being fed. It turns out that there is some source of abundance that we knew nothing of when we were eighteen. Once it comes, the soul can satisfy that internal craving, as represented by the starving children.

We can contrast a psychological reading and mythological reading of a sacred story in the following way. Psychologically, each of the characters in the tale are read as energies, all of which exist inside of us. For example, when a woman hears the story, she may notice that the adventuresome daughter energy is inside her, as well as the playful bear energy. She may also recognize herself in the old women, the children, and the carpenters. If she doesn't face her own dark side, she may claim that the Woman of Great Appetite, the tusked one, is a patriarchal invention. This is a fashionable habit these days. We know the patriarchal culture is perfectly capable of projecting the dark side exclusively onto women, and there is massive evidence of that chicanery. But it is a delicate matter when to act on such healthy suspicion. The evidence around this story suggests that it comes straight out of matriarchal culture in its basic outline. The tusked energy is inside a woman, as well as the so-called male bear king, the two stepsisters, the starving children, the blacksmith, and the carpenters. A woman reading the story may be struck by the awesomeness of it all, and the shocks are intentional.

A man reading the story will immediately welcome the idea that the Bear King is inside him, as are the carpenters, but he may be disturbed if he has to agree that the energy of the Queen of the Boar tusks is a part of his soul. If you ask most men about that energy, they will change the subject. It's easier for him to see it on the outside of the women he is arguing with.

So when we read a sacred story psychologically, we often find ourselves astonished at the leaps of inclusiveness asked of us, particularly in consciously admitting our weaknesses.

When read mythologically, the story requires steps even more difficult to take. Mythologically, the Awesome Lady of Vast Appetite and the Bear King belong to a wild side of the universe. The rituals around Dionysus always spoke of a wilderness beyond the human, which could easily tear and destroy the human. The Bear King is related to the Wild Man, who is a god, not a man. Clarissa Pinkola Estés calls this being a "wild god." It's possible that in some preindustrial, preagricultural time, a woman and a man might have been able to sustain a long, or longer, union with the "wild force." But the more emphasis we put on morality, intellect and light, that is, the more civilized we become, the more we are separated from the Bear King, who represents our instincts. Deconstruction and logical analysis are just two more steps in the long series of intellectual maneuvers that separate us from the animal and the divine. The trouble with them is that they provide no way by which the soul can reconcile with the wild god.

Mythological themes often concentrate on ways in which the animal soul and the spiritual soul become rejoined. The fear that the wild god is within days of remarrying All the Appetite in the World is a mythological theme. The glass mountain is a mythological theme. That we may not find the mysterious source of abundance inside of us until we meet the wild god is a mythological theme. That there is a god or goddess of astounding appetite that we can distract with our abundance is a mythological theme.

This abundance, suggested at the earliest moment of the story by the golden wreath, shows how high the stakes are in a mythological reading; far higher than in a psychological reading. The golden wreath asks how much "gold" or greatness we allow ourselves to see in our own souls. Beyond "infantile grandiosity," which we make fun of in psychology, there is true grandness, the fragrance of greatness in us, the true gold of grandiosity.

What is amazing to me in this story is the amount of genuine grandness it allows and even encourages in us. Heinz Kohut, the Austrian-born psychoanalyst, believes that without genuine grandiosity, personalities fragment. In many contemporary personalities, there just isn't enough gold to hold the pieces together.

The sacred story tries to protect our grandness from belittlers, whether those belittlers are fathers who want to manufacture a golden wreath so we will remain domestic, or "stepsisters" inside us jealous of our association with a wild god. Secular stories talk of who you are; sacred stories playfully explore who you aren't. Antonio Machado, speaking to both men and women, says:

> Don't trace out your profile,
> forget your side view—
> all that is outer stuff.
>
> Look for your other half
> who walks always next to you
> and tends to be who you aren't.

*ROBERT BLY* is a poet who has won the National Book Award, a translator of great world poets, and the most prominent figure in the men's movement. He is the author of *Iron John,* and many books of poetry, including *The Light Around the Body, Gratitude to Old Teachers, News of the Universe, Loving a Woman in Two Worlds,* and *Meditations on the Insatiable Soul.*

Reprinted from *Sacred Stories,* edited by Charles Simpkinson and Anne Simpkinson (New York: HarperCollins, 1993). Used by permission of the author.

# Stepping Over the Threshold

## Into the 'Black Hole' at the Center of Self

*by* Marion Woodman

*from Noetic Science Review*

**M**ARION WOODMAN IS AN INTERNATIONALLY *known Jungian psychotherapist, and the author of several books on the emerging balance between masculine/feminine energies. As part of her work, she approaches "addictions" as symptoms of psychospiritual yearnings which most, if not all, people in our culture experience. These addictions may manifest in a wide variety of symptoms, ranging from alcoholism and drug dependency, to diet disorders, "workaholism," dependent relationships, and even to certain styles of thinking. "Addiction" in this sense is any habituated attempt, often unconscious, to fill a spiritual void at the center of our lives with inappropriate "remedies."*

*By becoming more conscious of our addictions, Woodman maintains, we confront our "shadow selves," and can learn their deeper spiritual meanings. This process, however, often requires courage to step over the threshold into the void and to make contact with our inner angels and devils. It is a process that can be both creative and healing.*

*This article is adapted from a presentation given at Institute of Noetic Sciences' Heart of Healing conference in June 1993.*

As a culture, we are moving into the new millennium shadowed by a specter of addiction. It is a common response by many to a growing sense of despair and alienation. We fear a black void at the center of our lives, buried deep somewhere inside us. This image can ring true for any of us, for we are all touched by the emptiness of the soul that underlies addiction.

Which of us does not know the alcoholic's feeling of emptiness and aloneness? Or how many of us have successfully avoided an addiction to speed, or an addiction to the compulsion of getting and spending? Most people that I know, if given three months to do nothing, just might catch up a little with where they're supposed to be. Their energy is traveling weeks ahead of their bodies in an effort to keep up. An addiction to speed, an addiction to materialism, is rampant in our culture. It is so rampant that we are putting our garbage in any possible fill we can find, or putting it on ships to sail it around the world; and do we ever stop to wonder who is going to take care of all this detritus?

The image of garbage landfills is also an apt metaphor for how we deal with our internal lives. Our culture worships the gods of progress and efficiency in a blind struggle to fill in the black hole at the center of our selves. Without imagination, we unconsciously attempt to concretize the world around us, turning it into objects we hope will fill up the void. But these efforts to replace something missing cannot substitute for what we really seek. For example, if we have not experienced the nurturing, cherishing love of a positive mother, someone who loves her own feminine body, we tend to project it on to a concrete object—in many cases this will be food. Chocolate or honey granola or muffins become our sweetness, our love, our nourishing—we project that goddess and then we want to eat her. We want the communion of eating that which we have projected out.

Too often, when we want to get out of the mire of matter, when we want to fly with the spirit and be free, we turn to bottled spirit, and instead of flying with the genuine spirit, we get drunk on alcohol. Or we may want light, so we turn to cocaine. Or perhaps we want the union of masculine and feminine that is supposed to bring joy, and we get into compulsive sexuality. Or maybe we want union with the beloved, so we project our own inner beloved onto someone out there; we fall in love with our own image, and find ourselves enmeshed in a compulsive relationship. By continually projecting the god or goddess within onto external objects, we entangle ourselves deeper and deeper into matter, into what Karl Marx deified as "dialectical materialism". And the tragedy is that in the process we are rejecting ourselves as human beings.

In another sense, our entanglement with matter, with the body, is part of a deeper movement to embrace the feminine principle. When this drive is misdirected, the consequences may be one or more of the many addictions that ensnare us. But we may also open up to the rising surge of the feminine, and use its force to transform our relationship to matter. The feminine wants to live in the body; it wants to experience the consciousness of the body.

When I use the word "feminine" I'm talking about a principle active in men as well as in women. Masculinity and femininity are complementary energies operating in all of us. The feminine principle is experienced as an attraction to matter, to the concrete, to the tangible stuff of the Earth. The masculine principle is an attraction to the rarefied realms of spirit. Falling into addiction is an attempt to escape from our relationship to the feminine, to Mother Earth, to reach for ideals of perfection with such intensity that the spirit flies away from the Earth, away from life.

Another way to escape is to go deeper into blind instinct, to turn away from consciousness and hand over responsibility to the darker, more basic instincts populating the unconscious. But sooner or later we discover we cannot run away forever, and there is a price to pay for repression.

## RUNNING AROUND A CORE OF EMPTINESS

Many people are running as fast as they can around the outside of the black hole at the center of their being. It is the core of emptiness that poets have spoken of—a gaping loneliness and impermeable isolation. Emily Dickinson said it well:

There is a pain—so utter—
It swallows substance up—
Then covers the Abyss with Trance—
So Memory can step
Around—across—upon it—
As one within a Swoon—
Goes safely—where an open eye
*Would drop him—Bone by Bone.*

As long as we stay in the unconscious we can walk in a trance. If we open our eyes we would experience the death of what we are in. It seems to me that many addicts—and that includes most of us, for who in this culture is not an addict?—know at some level that we have to go into that hole. In dreams, repeatedly the dreamer is told there is a black hole; frightening, forbidding, but nevertheless we have to walk over the threshold and go into that hole. And often we say "No, I can't do it." Sometimes it takes years before the dream says "Okay, now's the time, move!" And when it does, sometimes, as in a fairy tale, the dream takes us to a door or to a threshold. Sometimes, instead of following the dream, we back off and start running around the hole again.

If we ever get the courage to go into that hole, what do we find? Sometimes it's a starving child with huge eyes like a little Somali, and the dreamer asks "Why are you here?" And the child says "You would have killed me if I came out." The dreamer has then to recognize the soul he or she left behind as a little child. It happened around the time when we began to perform for other people—began to try to be the best little student, the best little scholar, the best little athlete, the best musician. When the central task became a performance to please someone else, the one at the center—the soul—was left behind in the basement, under the basement, cut off from the nourishment of life and spirit. And with that the feelings, the connection to the heart, the connection to the body, the connection to the feminine, were all left behind.

To go into that hole at the center—which is really the creative matrix—is to venture to find our own angels and our own devils. It is to face the truth of ourselves, to find the fire in our bodies, to ignite our real sexuality, to bring the sweetness of the body to life. That is where life is.

People who work with the body know how hard it tries to please and to be a part of us. Its sweetness makes us cry. Even more so, when we connect with the heart we no longer want to have power over other people, we no longer take our identity by controlling ourself, controlling our weight, controlling this, controlling that. We are no longer interested in controlling other people because our heart is cracked open, and through that cracking, through that suffering of going into our own demons, into our own angels, we find a love that opens us to the beauty of life.

## METAPHOR AS TRANSFORMER

What I'm suggesting is that to make the transition into the new millennium, we are going to have to move into our bodies in a totally new way. We are going to have to find the images that live in our bodies. Something has happened in the world. We are in chaos, and no one has the vision to guide and direct. It seems to me that as individuals we are on our own, and need to find our own direction. Many people are still projecting onto gurus, onto teachers, onto whatever their addictive image is, and hoping, even believing, that it's going to help them. Inevitably, they end up with an empty hole inside. However, if they took the time to allow the images to come from the musculature of the body, they would be full of their own images, they would have their own guidance, and would gain sustenance from their own well of life.

What I'm talking about here is recognizing and using image or metaphor as a transformer. Metaphor means transformer. The image, the metaphor, comes in one way, moves through the transformer, is changed and comes out at another level. To me this is where healing lies—within ourselves.

This is not to rule out medical science, but rather suggests cooperating with medical science in finding our own soul in our own body. Jung saw the body and mind as two cones—spirit as one cone, body as another—two cones that meet and do not meet at their apexes. He meant by this that we don't know where chemistry turns into psyche and where psyche turns into chemistry. We know that depression causes a shift in the chemistry of the body. Similarly, the chemistry of the body can change the imagery of the body.

Fifty years ago, Jung could not see where the psyche-soma connector was, but he knew there was a connector. He called the energy that ran between them the "subtle body"—a metaphorical body. This is the world of the dream. This is the world where we get a picture of what is going on in our instincts. It is a picture that gives us a spiritual message. In our dreams, we can see our spiritual condition in the images our dreams unfold.

Since Jung's time, we have begun to narrow the gap in our understanding of the interactions between mind and body. At least we have isolated some of the chemical intermediaries—neurotransmitters and neuroreceptors. We now know that when an image comes in, especially one that is emotionally charged, there is a correlative shift matching the action of neuroreceptors and changes in the body's chemistry. I think this is incredible. It tells us a lot about the connection between psychology and medical science, and points to a remarkable future in the science of psychoneuroimmunology (PNI).

Jung had a lot to say about psychology and the body; in fact, he anticipated the idea of PNI when he said not only is it possible, but it's even probable, that psyche and soma are aspects of the same thing. Jung was profoundly interested in the body because he knew that the "shadow" was in the body. Our culture, our science and our medicine, not to mention our psychology, have yet to catch up with his vision. And that's where our culture is off the rails: We don't accept the huge energy lying dormant in the body. If we don't pay attention to this energy when it starts to move, it turns against the body, and the results are different forms of addictions and other illnesses.

When the energy starts to move us toward a psycho-spiritual shift, the addict in us becomes frightened, terrified to go with it, then backs off, and soon there are no dreams. Next, there is a symptom. What I'm getting at is the need to recognize that these two elements—psyche and soma—are joined by the dream, as Jung argued. Our dreams are a medium through which the archetypes of the collective unconscious make themselves known to us. The archetype is that unknowable entity which lies behind the dynamics of psyche and matter, which gives form to our dual-natured being. Just as there is an organizing pattern in nature, responsible for all detectable forms, Jung believed that we have organizing, potential patterns within us—the archetypes. We give these archetypes, these potential patterns, specific forms and images by projecting our own personal idiosyncrasies onto them. What we project is our own stuff. But there are also inherent images which the archetypes can bring to us—images from the depths of nature rather than our own projections—and these are the images that heal.

If, therefore, we find our rational world in chaos, our solution may be to take the time to drop into the unconscious, into the non-rational world, into the "black void" as William Blake did. There we will find the order that is available in the spaceless-timeless world of the archetypes, the order that may replenish the entropy and chaos of the over-inflated rational intellect. As Jung pointed out, that's the source of the healing power. Without the archetypal energy, there is no healing. Anything else is bandaids. If, however, the archetypal image moves in, it changes the energy of the system, and that image changes the neurotransmitter system, changes the immune system and the healing begins.

## THE HEALING POWER OF DREAMS

Let me give some examples of this. At a conference on schizophrenia last year I spoke of the healing power of archetypes and dreams, and I was told that dreams are just mental anecdotes, that nothing can be healed by dreams. Well, of course, I cannot believe that because I work with people eight hours a day and see dramatic effects from dreams. I see people come into the office bloated, with faces big and puffed, their eyes squinting, their bodies uptight. They sit down in the chair and I say "Did you have any dreams?" Their response is often anger at such a "trivial" question, unworthy of their serious issues. They are not present, they are trapped in their own memories, and their old complexes. But eventually they start to recount their dreams, and invariably become interested in their own images. In the end, they may even dance the image or draw it and, as they talk, the face loses its bloat. The shoulders go down, the complex moves through the body and is sometimes released.

I once had a patient who dreamed an image something like a great "Y". There was a terrible black bird's nest right on the "Y". She said "That's my mother sitting on my sexuality." I immediately saw what it was: She was drawing her ovarian tubes. About a month later, she came in with a purple hand splattered on top of the nest. The hand was so ugly my whole body just cringed back from it. I said "You know, if I were you I'd go to a doctor." And she did. The doctor didn't find anything at first, so he gave her an ultrasound. He was astonished. "How did you have any suspicion so early?" he asked. It turned out to be a cancer.

In another dream, the woman drew her torso. A spider had wound its way inside her, and spun a mass of black web. Very shortly, she came down with severe candida. A young boy dreamed he was bitten by a wolf right in the face, and within six months he was diagnosed with lupus. Lupus, of course, means wolf. One of the symptoms are marks as if the sufferer had been bitten by a wolf.

Another woman described how she was told to go down an ancient staircase that she didn't know existed. When she reached the bottom, she found there an old lagoon, full of stale, stagnant water. She found a huge black snake in this filthy pond, and a wheel meant to take the water up to the upper part of the building. The snake's task was to turn the wheel, but it couldn't reach it. The water which should have been feeding the upper part of the building was stuck in the lagoon. The snake energy, the life energy, that should be driving the wheel was incapacitated. The snake was angry. It knew what it should have been doing but couldn't. That woman was suffering from a severe kidney disorder.

These dreams functioned diagnostically. Sometimes dream images are metaphors, sometimes they present something literal. It takes practice, training and attention to images and associations to learn how to listen to the messages inherent in our dreams. But, literal or metaphorical, dreams do bring us messages from deeper levels of our being, and even when they're functioning as diagnosis, they are leading us towards wholeness. Some dreams, however, go right beyond diagnosis, and have the power to heal directly. My own experience of healing through an archetype illustrates this.

In 1968, I was in a car accident which badly damaged the left side of my head. It healed quite well. The doctors were marvelous with their plastic surgery, but I was left with tinnitus in the ear—a constant ringing that never ceases, and drives you crazy. The more tired you become the louder it rings. Specialist doctors in England told me I'd just have to get used to it, that it would be with me for the rest of my life. Then I had a dream of working a machine—a "metaphor machine" for transformation. Energy came in on one level, the instinctual level, went through the machine, and came out at the spiritual level. I couldn't figure out how to work the switches. However, there was a presence there with me, and I knew that the presence did understand the switches. So I let the presence do the work. He said to me "How does it feel on the eve of becoming everything you have fought against all your life?" That threw me into panic. It was propositioning me to jump into the black hole, to go deep into my body. I said "No way!" Anorexia had kept me very safely *out* of my body; I wasn't going to have anything to do with what I imagined was *in* my body.

I went out to the kitchen and, of course, my head was shrieking with the tinnitus. I knelt down on the kitchen floor and said "Dear God, take this away or let me die. One or the other, I can't stand it." And with that, an incredible mock orange bush appeared before me, full of glorious ivory-colored blossoms that come out in the month of June, filling summer evenings with an exquisite perfume. I was so enthralled with the bush I just took the perfume in, not realizing that it was coming through my feet. Then I sensed that the cells of my body were being opened by the fragrance, and the perfume was very slowly coming up my legs. It came through my thighs, into my torso. At some point, I was up on my feet, lifting up my hands and my head, and my whole body was perfume. *I became the metaphor.* When the vision was over, the tinnitus was gone and it never returned. I went to the kitchen and was fed, my body was ensouled.

This, of course, changed my life. I realized that if I could concentrate sufficiently on an image given by the unconscious that the chaos in my rational mind could be met by the order in my unconscious. The archetypal image coming from the deep unconscious—from the black hole—could bring order to the conscious and unconscious, and I could be whole. The h-o-l-e became the source of wholeness, what I call the "ensoulment of matter."

## A METAPHOR FOR THE NEXT MILLENNIUM

Now why is that? Why, as Jung says, is the symbol a healer? Why is the symbol in your dream a gift from God? The reason is this: The image works on your imagination, it works on your emotional body, it works on your thinking, and on your intellect. So for a moment your intellect, emotion, imagination are one. You are whole. The image clicks, and at that instant your whole being says "Yes!"

When I do dream interpretation in the office I wait for that moment when I can feel the "Yes". That's where the healing is. The patient can take that out of the office for at least a week, and that's the touchstone to come back to and say "This is what it means to be whole." Without that moment of recognition, the session is incomplete. It often happens in silence. Of course, the images change every week; I must emphasize that. They do not stay stagnant. They change every day in fact. They move, they guide us to be whole.

The images from the body are also a metaphor for where we are today and where we are headed. I would say that as we move toward the threshold of the new millennium, we have ourselves to look to, to guide us. We have access to the images we need. We can embody our souls if we work hard at bringing our body to consciousness. As long as the dream is imprisoned in the body, and not lived, we are not taking the energy of the image into life. But if we can take the energy of the image and live it as Blake did, dance it, make up music, work in the garden— engage in some form of creative expression—we are living our own life.

To know what it is to feel your heart, to feel your kidneys, to feel your embodiment and your ensoulment, to experience yourself as a container open and flexible, you will be strong enough to receive the kiss of the spirit. The penetration of the spirit that comes into soul and lifts it changes consciousness forever. This is the only way I see to break from the domination of power into the kingdom of love.

William Stafford said it well in a poem, "A Ritual We Read to Each Other":

It is important that awake people be awake,
or a breaking line may discourage them back to sleep;
the signals we give—yes and no, or maybe—
should be clear: the darkness around us is deep.

*MARION WOODMAN* is a Jungian Analyst in Toronto who includes somatic and spiritual approaches in work on addictive behaviors. She is the author of *The Owl Was a Baker's Daughter*, *Addiction to Perfection*, *The Ravaged Bridegroom*, *Leaving My Father's House*, and *Conscious Femininity*.

Reprinted from the *Noetic Sciences Review*, Winter 1993, 475 Gate Five Road, Suite 300, Sausalito, CA 94965. Membership: $35/year.

# BEAD WOMAN'S DRESS

### by ALEXANDER ELIOT

### from *Global Myths*

**W**HAT MEANS THE DISTANT PAST, THE far future, the divine in nature, the inner existence of plants, the emotions of animals, and the beginnings of mankind? What means our life, our death? And is any sort of immortality in store for us? Tales which purported to convey the truth about such matters were once accepted by whole tribes, cities, and nations, all around the globe. People not only believed in myth, they lived by it. That is, they revered, and were guided by, the central images of their myths. Isn't it the same with us?

Largely unexamined belief-systems provide the basic context of human life in general. We hardly know what myth is all about; that's so, and yet—whether we think we can or not—nobody lives a happy life without the assurances that myth provides. We all trust in science, and most of us practice some religion as well. In short, we live by faith, as human beings must. Spiritually speaking we can't swim; there is no way to breast the unknown on our own. So we are in the same boat with our ancestors!

There was a time when one's own inherited belief system, plus what one learned in school, sufficed throughout life. We have passed that point. Today, our faiths are frayed and our knowledge is discounted. Insistent clamors arise all around. Racial, religious, economic, and political wars abound. Under these conditions, our normal self-assurance ebbs. Society seems in bitter turmoil, by and large. We come to feel that little is certain. Yet some things do comfort our minds and pull us together still. Some things help us to maintain our brotherhood, and sisterhood, under the skin. And among all such positive forces, living myth stands first.

Myth used to be regarded as a matter of academic, rather than personal, interest. It was presented in the past tense, as though mythology concerned outmoded accounts of dreamlike and half-miraculous events. In fact, myth is alive and well; it influences all our lives, here and now. That's one thing which psychology has clarified. But myth is not a province of psychology: that doesn't follow. It's true that some psychologists claim professional understanding of myth, on the grounds that it belongs to their particular realm of expertise. Namely the human soul; in Greek: psyche. However, most psyches prove to be so bitter, and/or sweet as the case may be, that the forked, probing tongue of psychoanalysis recoils—numb.

There's nothing wrong with extracting "dream-wishes" or "archetypes" from mythic material. But to dissect and categorize such things with one eye shut, and force the abstruse results to some theoretical conclusion, is useless. Codify myth and in effect you deny it. Accept someone else's codification, and you're in the position of a person who looks up his dreams in a dream-book, hoping to discover what they "signify."

"I do not know what I may appear to the world," sir Isaac Newton once remarked, "but to myself I appear to have been only like a boy playing on the seashore, and diverting myself in now and then finding a smoother pebble or a prettier shell than ordinary, whilst the great ocean of truth lay all undiscovered before me."

When I was a child I thought as a child, I felt as a child, and so on. I saw things from the corners of my eyes as well as face to face. But now that I've become a man, I find myself peering through dark sunglasses much of the time.

Among my friends in the old days were some red-lettered blocks which I would pile up and then send crashing to the floor again: great fun. And I'm still playing with lettered blocks, in my own fashion. I've never put away childish things, simply transformed them: piling letters into words and words into books. Yet now and then I fear I've lost my way. Worse, that I'll never know the place where I began!

Childhood was more a time of learning than of bafflement. Adulthood is the opposite. Diligently, even angrily, we express, discuss, and defend our ostensibly knowledgeable positions. But little can be decided in this way. Advances are tiny, for two reasons. First, because "my opinion is as good as yours." Second, because under the rules it's possible for me (or anyone) to claim some sort of "expertise," and with it the right to marshal a mind-numbing succession of facts in support of my case. The road to hell is paved with expertise; the life goes out of the party. We come away well-pleased with ourselves, perhaps, but seldom have we taken the least delight in others' efforts. In retrospect, we may complain of having learned nothing new or exciting, nothing that passed beyond mere facts and opinion. We've been chasing our own tales, as Aesop might say.

"In the beginning, was the Word, and the Word was with God, and the Word was God." So opens the Gospel According to Saint John. But the poet Goethe roundly rejected that idea. Goethe's *Faust* says this (in Albert Latham's translation):

Tis written: 'In the beginning was the word.'
Already I stick, and who shall help afford?
The 'word' at such high rate I may not tender;
The passage I must elsewhere render,
If rightly by the Spirit I am taught,
'Tis written: 'In the beginning was the Thought.'
by the first line a moment tarry,
Let not thine eager pen itself o'er-hurry!
Does 'thought' work all the fashion all outright?
It should stand: 'In the beginning was the Might.'
Yet even as my pen the sentence traces,

A warning hint the half-writ word effaces.
The Spirit helps me—from all doubting freed,
Thus write I: 'In the beginning was the Deed.'

That's perfectly in character for Faust. What's more, it fits the modern—scientific—view of things. At the beginning of time, according to cosmologist Stephen Hawking, the entire universe resided in a sort of nutshell. When it cracked wide open to pour forth billion-mile plumes of blazing light, the mother of all shouts must also have occurred. Scientists blithely refer to that as the "Big Bang," and they believe its echo still resounds.

The Yoruba people of Africa tell us that the "Word of Mawu-Lesa" sprayed forth from the Creator's lips to become "The Sons of Fa." The Hindus of India have a different idea. They say the golden vowel "Om" is the immaterial womb of all and everything.

"In the beginning was the Word." The blind Puritan poet John Milton found his voice by listening—in alert uncertainty—for after-tones of the divine. Witness these deathless lines:

Sweet Echo, sweetest Nymph that liv'st unseen
Within thy airy shell
By slow Meander's margent green
And in the violet embroidered vale
—
Sweet Queen of Parley, daughter of the Sphere!

Only if the billion-times-fragmented Word remains part of our human charge—only if we still have a say in it—can we call our souls our own. But sweet Echo has long fled, and the din of present opinion deafens us. Our trouble is not that we "know nothing," it's that we think we know so much. Suddenly the earth swarms with hot information. The intellectual atmosphere turns searingly dry, divisive as hell. Strictly analytical thinking pays off. Wandering, dreaming, and "inviting one's soul" are frowned upon. Too bad.

The gates to the City of Knowledge stand wide indeed, but knowledge isn't everything. If you're looking for inspiration and spiritual elbow-room, then feel along the wall nearby. There you'll discover a low, ivy-covered door. It's unguarded, barely big enough for one person to squeeze through alone. This leads out onto a solitary cliff which overlooks an ocean whose ceaselessly churning depths vibrate with phosphorescent monsters, children of Triton: myths.

The ancient Greeks maintained that although Herakles was dead, he lived. His human body had been burned to ashes, true, but now he was a god. I regard mythology the same way. It's a Triton whose ashes are literature. The godly beast of half-forgotten lore still swims, dives, copulates, and cavorts with his phosphorescent progeny in the timelessness of the sea.

If that sounds metaphysical, it's meant to be. We are bodies, but how much more besides! The same mythic wind and water, the same mythic darkness and light, the same mythic people and animals, live on, ever changing, always reborn. The myths are in the depths, and then again the depths are in the myths. They surface unexpectedly, like fine spume or sparkles on a human soul-wave which comes hissing, lifting, curling under and passing, thousands of years wide.

In his introduction to *The History of English Literature* (1863) Hippolyte Taine observed that "art everywhere is a sort of philosophy made palpable; religion is a sort of poem regarded as true; and philosophy is a sort of art and religion, dessicated and reduced to pure abstractions. Each of these groups centers upon a common element: conception of the world and its origins." thus, in elegantly gallic style, Taine made the point that art, religion, and philosophy, all three, hark back to the same oceanic murmur. I agree.

## THE EAST WIND: BEAD WOMAN'S DRESS

What is the power of primitive myth? Bronislaw Malinowski, a pioneering anthropologist, called it "The rearising of primordial reality in narrative form." This class of legend largely concerns human beings in nature, rather than the nature of human beings. It's unanalytical, intuitive, and often wonderfully bold—as dreams are bold.

Primitive myth comes to us through the kindness of shamans, village elders, witches, warlocks, and medicine men. Over the past hundred years and more, such sources have retold their holy legends, at least in part, to thousands upon thousands of anthropological field-workers. The resulting literature expands at such a pace that no single scholar knows more than a small portion of it. But one can easily cull and re-present this material in such a matter as to "prove" whatever one pleases concerning human society and the human spirit.

Whether for career purposes or to promote preconceived ideas, or simply to make a sharper, more effective impression, specialists often oversimplify and skew the evidence which mythology offers. Suffice it to note that Sir James Frazer, the titanic author of *The Golden Bough*, expressed regret for having led people astray. He'd never meant to imply that tree-worship and human sacrifice were all that central to primitive social practice. "Fear of the Dead," he decided, shaking his snowy locks and scratching his venerable head, was far more important!

Another thing that interferes with our understanding is this: when primitive myth is transferred from rhythmic oral transmission to words on paper, it suffers extreme diminishment. Some fur-clad shaman's chant, performed beside the campfire on a cold starry night in a remote region of Turkestan, with drumming and dancing to boot, might well sweep the soul with its cumulative, rhythmic rush. We're not positioned to share in such experience.

If the written record leaves us relatively cold, that doesn't make primitive myths any less holy to the scattered and steadily dwindling peoples who participate in them. And such tribes doubtless keep their profoundest secrets to this day.

It's a little inhuman, I think, to view primitive myth as having merely academic or anthropological interest. If, on the other hand, we approach this subject warmly, in a seeking way, we're practically certain to come upon stories which reconnect us with our ancestors. Wherever one may find them, some few primitive myths appear especially designed to mesh with one's particular psyche. These deepen the world for us. They seem to speak directly out of the dark into your ears or mine alone.

This primitive myth is part of the very rarely performed "Bead Woman Way," a Navajo Indian ceremony. It seems to prefigure Greek tragedy, and science fiction as well. I find the story far and away too subtle to follow, utterly unanalyzable. For that very reason perhaps, it happens to touch my heart:

BEAD WOMAN MARRIED A STRANGER who came from west of the Grand Canyon. They had two sons. One day the elder of the two went out hunting, and disappeared. One year later, to the day, three strangers came to call on Bead Woman's younger son. They'd journeyed all the way from White House Pueblo at Mesa Verde. Their entire tribe, they told the youth, was suffering from acne to an excruciating degree. "It has been whispered that you possess magic powers," they said. "Please come and heal our people. We'll pay you well."

Bead Woman's younger son possessed no magic powers. However, he promised to visit White House during the next full moon. After the emissaries had gone, he sat thinking for a long time. Finally, his elder brother appeared before him and told the following tale:

"When I vanished, it was because the White House People had captured me. For twelve days and nights they kept me tightly bound in their council house. I got nothing but scraps to eat. Then Talking God came to me in dream.

"'Tomorrow,' Talking God said, 'you'll be lowered by rope to an inaccessible rock ledge. There you'll find a nest containing two eaglets, one male and one female. On the plain far below, other White House People will stand looking up, waiting for you to toss down the eaglets. Once you've obeyed, you're finished. You'll be abandoned to starve on the ledge.'

"'Grandfather, this is terrible,' I said. 'What shall I do?'

"'Nothing. Just protect the eaglets.'

"Things happened as Talking God had predicted. Having been lowered to the ledge, I first introduced myself to the eaglets. Fortunately, a Big Fly whispered their names in my ear. All day the White House People on the plain below coaxed me to toss down my new friends. At sunset, the tribe trailed away home, leaving me stranded halfway between earth and heaven. All night the eaglets perched at my sides, warming me with their wings.

"On the second morning, the White House People came streaming back across the plain below. At the foot of the sheer cliff they spread various bribes, including food and drink, in order to induce me to obey. When I still refused, they gave their war cry and began dancing about to frighten me. But my predicament was frightening enough already. On the third morning, the White House People returned again, armed with bows and arrows. Since we were so high up, they shot at us in vain. By now the eaglets had developed to the point where they could fly a little. Circling out from the cliff and back again, they shed a few feathers on our tormentors. Mind you, those eaglet feathers are what spread acne among the White House People.

"Very early on the fourth morning, forty-eight eagles and hawks arrived at our ledge. They'd brought along a turquoise basket and a basket of whiteshell in which to carry the eaglets. Having painted my face with white clay, they gave me a crystal and a hollow reed. Then they wrapped me in a dark cloud, which the crystal lit from inside. When I breathed through the reed it made a whistling sound. The forty-eight hawks and eagles attached three lightning bands and three rainbows to the cloud. They all caught hold of these in their claws. Then, dropping free of the ledge, the forty-eight hawks and eagles soared out and up along the sunrise updraft, bearing me in my dark cloud aloft. Unfortunately, the cloud had a dampening effect upon their beating wings. Four times, the birds were forced to stop and rest upon the air. Finally, feathered serpents looped down from overhead and helped to hoist me up. I found myself drawn through a hole in the sky, to spiritland."

The elder brother had finished his story. He waited politely, but while he was waiting his aspect slowly changed. He became Talking God! This development astonished Bead Woman's surviving son, who nonetheless succeeded in maintaining a semblance of calm. Finally, in a soft voice which shook only a little, the youth spoke up:

"Grandfather, this is terrible. What shall I do?"

"Nothing. Just visit the White House, as you said you would, and heal those people. Now that you know what they did to deserve their acne, it should be easy. Only make sure they pay you as promised. Bead Woman needs a new dress!"

*ALEXANDER ELIOT* is the author of a classic work on the world traditions, *The Universal Myths*, a cousin of T. S.Eliot, a Guggenheim Fellow, a Japan Foundation Senior Fellow, a distinguished lecturer, and a world traveler. His most recent book is *The Timeless Myths*.

This is a slightly revised version of the articles "In the Beginning", and "The East Wind: Bead Woman's Dress" from *The Global Myths*, copyright © 1993 by Alexander Eliot. Used by permission of Dutton Signet, a division of Penguin Books USA Inc.

# PSYCHO-EROTICA:
# PURSUING THE PERVERSE WITH MADONNA

## by PATRICIA REIS

*from* The San Francisco Jung Institute Library Journal

**O**NE NIGHT DURING THE SUMMER OF 1991 after yet another program featuring the desperate plight of Kurdish refugees, a short editorial clip was tagged onto the evening news. Newscaster Bruce Morton asked a rhetorical question about how far women have come in their quest for liberation. In answer, he presented his idea of progress in the guise of two female icons, Marilyn and Madonna. As sex goddesses, they both portray (betray?) the sexual fantasies, myths, and mores of our time and, Morton would have us believe, they are markers for measuring the distance women have travelled in their desires for sexual equality. Morton gives the standard canonical interpretation of Marilyn as the quintessential image of feminine sexual vulnerability while Madonna on the other hand is presented as a new and revolutionary image of women's suddenly triumphant sexuality, the ultimate take-charge woman. Are these two icons a true representation of the changes women have been working for? Are they accurate markers for the changes in women's desire, the changes in women's experience of their sexuality? Or do they represent men's desire for and fear of what women have become? Is Madonna and all she represents truly an image of a woman in charge of her life, outside the domination of men's fantasies, or is she operating as much as anyone within the old ethos of domination and submission different only because she is occupying the other side of the split—exciting and disturbing because she is in the driver's seat? These questions perplexed me.

During this same period of time, I came upon a weighty book with a compelling title, "Female Perversions: The Temptations of Emma Bovary" by psychoanalyst Louise J. Kaplan.[1] The jacket cover was tastefully illustrated with a rather undistinguished nineteenth-century painting of a reclining nude, her backside gracefully draped with a swath of silk. It was the title not the illustration that grabbed my attention: the word "perversion" made me buy the big ticket, 580 page book. Narcissism was all the rage in the eighties; are perversions the thing for the nineties I wondered? And is female perversion something new? Will this book help me understand something about Madonna and Marilyn? About the women in my practice? About myself?

Psychoanalytic discourse on "perversions" has been around as a topic since Freud first theorized perversion as "the negative of neurosis." As one of his earliest analytic concepts, Freud understood perversions as a "disorder of sexual aim" arising out of constitutional (biological) and/or accidental (interpersonal) circumstances and events. Krafft-Ebing's classifications of the sexual perversions still stands more or less complete despite the DSM III R decision to elide "Perversions" as a diagnostic and clinical category in favor of "a less morally charged word (the main and most important difference being the exclusion of homosexuality from the category). Despite the attempt to rename and thus defuse the concept of its perjorative connotations, perversion continues to be discussed and analyzed with a new fervor of interest, replacing in some way the recent attention focused on "the borderline personality" and "narcissism." Although Kaplan's book is rooted in Freud and looks hard at past analytic work (she does a particularly heavy critique of Karl Abraham) her interest is focused on more recent texts. She concentrates primarily on the late Robert J. Stoller's work: *Perversion* (1975), *Sexual*

*Excitement* (1979) and *Observing the Erotic Imagination* (1985).

Stoller stands out as one of the few analysts who made his mark in psychoanalytic literature by focusing on the classic psychoanalytic subjects of sexuality, erotics, and perversions, extending these into the modern themes of obscenity and pornography. His work is refreshingly direct and frequently irreverent. He energetically engages with both his material and the reader—and he is funny. Stoller makes a strong argument for keeping the word perversion in analytic discourse because he insists that analysts, although they would like to believe they are going about the business of science, do have a vested interest in moral matters. His main hypothesis about what he sees as the continuum of sexual aberrations from perversions (enactments), daydreams (fantasies), to pornography (fantasy productions) and obscenity is that hidden within all of these forms is revenge, hatred, hostility, and a desire to do harm. For Stoller, variations along these continua of sublimated aggressivity provide the identifying factors, the distinguishing marks between interesting or even bizarre sexual behaviors and sexual perversions.

Although Stoller acknowledges the lack of female perversions in analytical literature ("women practice almost none of the official diagnoses"[2]), he does not think that women are not perverse nor that they are innocent of pornographic imagination; citing for instance, "bodice-buster" romances, and he frequently includes women in his exploration of perversions. Stoller understands perversion, as did Freud, to be a "gender (anxiety) disorder," ("I.e., perversion result(s) from the attempt either to prevent castration or, in females, to make reparation for the 'fact' of castration")[3] but he does not heavily theorize about the different nature of female perversions because, as he says in his later work, "the issues are too politically loaded"[4] for a reasonable discussion. At the time he wrote this, in the early 1980s, he was probably right, or certainly savvy enough to know it might be "dangerous" to try to say why.

Writing almost ten years later Louise Kaplan also notes that analytic literature has left women out of the realm of perversions but is more ready to theorize. She says women are left out of the literature because analysts (and others) are looking in the wrong place. Female perversions are not just male perversions with a difference. Armed with insights gained from feminist examination of our current sex/gender system she sees that what makes a perversion a perversion is not sexual activity per se, nor even Stoller's criterion of hostility, but rather a *perverse strategy*—a mental strategy that uses normative stereotypes of masculinity and femininity in a way that disguises the unconscious meanings of the behaviors. Perversions, in general, derive their emotional force from socially accepted and promoted gender stereotypes and are, Kaplan says, "as much pathologies of gender role identity as they are pathologies of sexuality." [5]

For Kaplan, perversions are not "gender disorders" as much as they are "disorders of gender." Here gender is understood, not as Freud or Stoller construe it, but as feminist analysis has exposed it—as a socially constructed ideal with normative behavioral proscriptions. "What makes all the difference between the male and female perversions is the social gender stereotype that is brought into the foreground of the (perverse) enactment."[6] For instance, male perversions permit a man "to express his forbidden and shameful feminine wishes by disguising them in an ideal of masculinity.[7] Although a man's perverse strategy is ultimately aimed at achieving a socially expected and acceptable virility—sustaining an erection, penetration, and orgasm: "Macho genital prowess and the impersonation of fantasized, idealized males are, Kaplan says, "hiding places for the man's humiliating feminine strivings."[8] So, the vehicle used in his perverse strategy could include fetishizing certain "feminine" objects, wearing a woman's lacey underwear, having fantasies of being sexually dominated or humiliated by a woman, choosing as a partner a younger, vulnerable, "feminine" male. The classic perversions, Kaplan says, belong to men and their struggle with our culture's gender ideals of masculinity. Fetishism, transvestism, sexual masochism (in Kaplan's ratio men comprise a surprising twenty to one female for seeking out masochism which is usually thought of as a woman's disorder) and sadism, exhibitionism, voyeurism, pedophilia, necrophilia to name just a few of the better known perversions don't translate into female behaviors. For a woman's behavior to be perverse, Kaplan points out, a completely separate group of behaviors, usually not even thought of as sexual, must be brought to light. Included in her listing of female perversions are (among others) kleptomania, homovestism, extreme submissiveness, mutilations (delicate self-cutting, addictive surgeries, hair pulling), anorexia, and (one which we shall return to later) female impersonation.

What has thrown analysts off the track of female perversions, Kaplan says, is that they have been looking for a *sine qua non* of perversion envisioned from a male perspective—evident sexual excitement and sexual arousal. Female perversions, unexpectedly, are not so obviously sexual. According to Kaplan's view, they are embedded in the socially accepted, stereotypically gender proscriptions for femininity which "serve as screens or disguises for a woman's forbidden and frightening masculine wishes." If cultural constraints deprive men of enacting feminine attributes of softness and receptivity, women through the gender ideals of purity, cleanliness, modesty, and submissiveness are deprived of expressions of power and active sexuality. Whereas male perversions in their obsessive pursuit of idealized male behavior eventually end up outside acceptable social and psychological norms, female perversions are centered in the normative from start to finish. To find the locus of female perversion, Kaplan says, we must look "to our most revered social institutions—the family, the church, the fashion and cosmetic industries, the pornography industry, the department store and, not the least perverse among them, the medical profession."[9] In either case, Kaplan says, our society's gender stereotypes are "the crucibles of perversion."[10]

Beginning with descriptions of the standard canon of male perversions and their hidden agenda of feminine strivings, Kaplan moves on to the female perversions through an exploration of Gustave Flaubert's 19th century novel, *Madame Bovary.* Here Kaplan finds displayed a wide array of perverse female activity stemming from the social constraints placed on Emma's ambition, intelligence and creativity. Bound by the strictures of her time and in desperate pursuit of her lost power (the missing phallus) Emma becomes, variously: a woman who loves too much; a woman driven and consumed by her excessive desires for the compensatory pleasures of the material world; an inconsistent, erratic and abusive mother; a romance addict given to exaggerated moods and flagrant desires. Using Emma as her model, Kaplan shows how the culture's denial and rejection of a healthy female identity colludes with the culturally supported pursuit of phallic trophies from the male world giving the true identifying mark of a female perversion: It is the fetishizing of the material world, or the lover's penis, or one's own body, that distinguishes women's erotomania.

As I was reading Kaplan's book I came upon, quite synchronisti cally, the June 1991 issue of *Rolling Stone* magazine in which Carrie Fisher did an interview with Madonna, billed as "Big Time Girl Talk" on the cover and "True Confessions: The Rolling Stone Interview with Madonna"[11] as the article title itself. Reading Fisher's interview simultaneously with Kaplan's book, I became eager to investigate Madonna in the light of Louise Kaplan's notion of female perversions. If Kaplan was right about the areas where female perversions reside—the family, the church, the fashion and cosmetic industries, the pornography industry, the department store and the medical profession, shouldn't these be the very places Madonna situates herself? Don't each of these arenas provide Madonna with the very stuff for her visual and musical narratives? Is she enacting female perversion scenarios I wondered. Is her obvious erotization of power and materialism a co-optation of or a challenge to gender stereotypes? Is the instrumental use of her body freeing or dehumanizing? Is she pushing us to consider a wider definition of female sexuality or is she serving up the same old hash on a different plate? And why is it all so appealing to so many people, particularly young women? What is it about her image—is it perverse, liberating, decadent, revolutionary, conservative?

Obviously, many people with varying perspectives and concerns have tried to take the measure of Madonna and her popularity. My own take focuses on the connections I see between Madonna's self-presentation in her *Rolling Stone* "confessions" and her artistic productions, particularly *Truth or Dare*,[12] and *Sex*,[13] and Louise Kaplan's (along with Robert Stoller's) view of the perverse. Later, I will add into the mix, Susan Bordo, a feminist philosopher, whose understanding of "postmodernism" and Madonna's place in the postmodern conversation has led me to some provocative insights from outside the rather repetitive purview of analytic discourse.

## TRUE CONFESSIONS

The inset cartoon illustration in the first Rolling Stone article shows a blonde Madonna, cross dangling from her neck, rosary in hand, inside a confessional, pouring her heart out in the direction of a curtained-off window where one would expect the priest to sit. This is not exactly shocking; Madonna is notorious for her use of religious ritual and imagery in her performances. Exorcising Catholicism and its libidinally deleterious effects of guilt and sexual repression provides much of Madonna's artistic material and accounts for much of her appeal. As she says, "Rebelling against the church and rebelling against the laws decreed by my father, which were dictated through the church," is an important activity for her. This situates her work as a particularly "adolescent strategy" where resistance to the cultural institutions that regulate sexual behavior are mocked and debunked while she pushes with youthful energy and charisma for the exciting and entrancing boundaries and edges of a deregulated sexuality.

Yet there must be something about the adolescent confessional mode that still appeals to an adult woman's erotic imagination. As an adolescent, I remember well the mingling of guilt and excitement as I entered the sweaty darkness of the confessional, whispering the words of my "impure thoughts and deeds" into the waiting ear of our local pastor, a man my father's age. Making a "full" confession was the ideal. "How many times?" the priest would always ask. Only now do I understand how this ritual amplified the original "impure" act or idea by pushing it into a further erotic adventure through the process of concealing and revealing within the confessional. Although there is always the rule about "full" confession—going all the way—and we are tantalized by the promise of exactly that in confessional pieces, the confession, like some kinds of sex, seems to depend on some aspect of withholding for its excitement.

The psychoanalyst, Masud Kahn, describes "confession" as having a basic function in perversion. Being expert at what he calls "the technique of intimacy," Kahn notes the "singular unrestraint, lack of shame and guilt" with which a perverse individual "confesses" what is perverse both through the acting out of body-intimacies and then through their retrospective verbalizations. Pornographic material frequently uses the trope of confession; Kahn notes such confessional technicians as Henry Miller, Andre Gide, and Jean Genet. But women also use the confessional mode with each other, and it seems that confessions between women, who are steeped in the knowledge of intimacy while being simultaneously sanctioned against speaking about it, are often even more seductive in their effect than confession by women to men. Thus, the Regine Deforges interview with Pauline Reage, author of the infamous porno- graphic *Story of O*, is called "Confessions of O: Conversations with Pauline Reage"[14] indicating a further titillation.

Back in the following *Rolling Stone* article, "Girl Talk, Part Two,"[15] Madonna is shown again in the confessional and this time Carrie Fisher appears as her confessor wearing an unmistakable white collar. In confessional interviews between two women the confessional hierarchy breaks down. The confessor is equally confessing. Where Regine Deforges merely confessed herself to Pauline Reage, Madonna and Carrie Fisher, in a version of truth or dare, provoke each other to divulge more and more classified and titillating information about themselves. Eavesdropping on their confessions, we become voyeurs to these technicians of the confessional, implicating ourselves by our curiosity.

The confessional is a uniquely Catholic experience where sin and forgiveness are supposed to meet through the process of self-examination, telling, and forgiving. In confession one must know "the laws decreed by the father" in order to fully know and understand one's transgressions. Stoller says that a necessary ingredient in perversion, (contained even in the word itself) is the sense of sin and sinning. "The activity is perverse if the erotic excitement depends on one's feeling that one is sinning."[16] The desire to sin is an essential ingredient for being turned on while the sin is "the desire to hurt, harm, be cruel to, degrade, humiliate someone."[17] But, the "sins" in Madonna's confession are about her transgressions against prescribed gender roles, sins against the tyrannizing ideal of "femininity." So, one could ask, who is being hurt or harmed, who is being degraded and humiliated—women or those who create this representation of women? Isn't this what we want her to do? Expose the patriarchally inspired "feminine" ideals as perverse?

In her road show "Blonde Ambition," Madonna enacts another confessional scenario: a woman on her knees "examining her conscience," is in the throes of guilt-ridden, erotic agonizing when she is overtaken by a rather demonic, sexually-intentioned "priest" who sweeps her off her prie-deu. Is Madonna engaged in critiquing the Church by showing how perverse this sacrosanct religious ritual is, mocking its holy pretensions by revealing the erotic suspense inherent in its structure? Or, is she exposing a quintessentially female perversion that Kaplan failed to note—revealing how women cultivate religious obsessions, combine devotional piety with erotic fantasy, and thereby keep themselves in a perpetually overheated state? Certainly she is not the first to play on that theme—pornography, especially of the "classical" or "literary" kind frequently exploits the repressed eroticism contained in religious fervor. But, Madonna does it with a difference in that she is a woman who *knows* she is exploiting this image because of its gendered implications. Here Kaplan is helpful: women who are pressed into non-sexual models of feminine purity, are most apt to fall prey to "perverse strategies" in order to gain their power. Madonna simply shows us more clearly than anyone else has how its done.

As Fisher says to Madonna, "Being controversial used to mean talking about things that were never talked about. Now, it seems controversy is just a diluted form of pornography or obscenity. I'm not suggesting you do pornography but you do obscenity." At first, I thought Fisher's distinction was a good one but then I began wondering what she thinks the difference is.

Stoller defines obscenity as "a political act, a declaration, an engine of separation (rupture of symbiosis), an accusation, an excuse, a renovation. It is to be revolting—*revolt but not revolution* . . . . Obscenity has no point unless we can entice others into opposing us—audiences that judge our naughtiness . . . . (It) is a planned assault on an audience. It is exhibition, theater. So we are not surprised that, like perverse exhibitionists, those using obscenity are titrating danger against safety in a social arena and may also be prone to see punishment. [18]

IN HER FILMED DOCUMENTARY *Truth or Dare,* Madonna risks being thrown in jail in Toronto or evicted by the Pope from Italy for her masturbation scene in her show "Blonde Ambition"—and we cheer her on, thinking we are on her side. Her manifesto on artistic freedom of expression in the face of those absurdly stern male authorities justifies all and we love it. The audiences go crazy for her and call out her name over and over again outside her hotel. She is a heroine and, watching it all, we think she is courageous as well as outrageous. She appeals to the rebellious adolescent in us. As Stoller says and Madonna shows, "Obscenity is part of the oldest game of all—the children against the parents."[19] Again, none of this is exactly new—Lenny Bruce stands as a monument to this kind of use of obscenity—the only thing that has changed is that a woman is doing it. And that seems to change everything.

But does it? Societies, Stoller says, need obscenity for various and varying reasons: "to improve moral tone, to keep evil hidden but alive inside ourself, to maintain within us the tensions between the allowed and the forbidden, that is, to relieve boredom; to provide scapegoats, to keep rebellions alive; to exteriorize, a bit disguised, what we think— consciously, preconsciously, and unconsciously— about our interior, to shame others as a way to avoid feeling shame ourself."[20] Mostly, he says, "Those who hate need obscenity." And either you are disposed toward judging and punishing it or doing it and being punished for it. Madonna responds to Fisher's suggestion of obscenity by saying, "To me, a lot of obscene things happen to people in their lives. I just don't happen to cut it out of my movies."

As an example, Madonna relates an incident that documents the early beginnings of her rebellion against family and church. Her stepmother (who apparently slapped her a lot) in an attempt to be frugal, made dresses alike for Madonna and her three sisters—dresses which Madonna hated. One Sunday, as her large family packed in the station-wagon to go off to church, Madonna made some negative comment about the hated dress: her stepmother slapped her, causing her nose to bleed. "Even though I was in agony," Madonna says, "I was thrilled. Not only did I not have to wear the dress, but I didn't have to go to church. My nose wouldn't stop bleeding, so everyone left and I got to stay home." The blood, although purchased through pain, destroyed the hated dress and left her with the satisfaction that she accomplished her desire to be unique and could therefore forego the collective ritual of religious indoctrination. She does not mention the perverse delight she must have felt in enlisting her step-mother's rage to accomplish her goal. In this family scenario, all the attributes Stoller assigns to "obscenity" are present—undoing of childhood frustrations and traumas, revenge, triumph, victim becoming victor, rebellion, evocation, performance and illusion. Obscenity, according to Stoller, starts early in life and can become a lifelong theme in the search for autonomy.

One can also find in this telling teen-age scene evidence for Kaplan's thesis regarding the origins and purpose of perversion: Madonna's rebellion is against her step-mother's attempts to make her a good girl, conforming to the traditional Catholic ideals of feminine purity, religiosity, and submissiveness. These are countered by the star's later facility for becoming obscene, "dirty," irreverently mocking and, most important of all successful on the basis of these tactics. It's hard not to like Madonna for winning the adolescent battle. And its hard not to feel some compassion for her early struggles.

Yet it's also hard to go all the way with her. In the *Rolling Stone* interview, Fisher interrogates Madonna about her use, in the road show and videos, of demeaning images of women, such as getting spanked, wearing a dog collar, and engaging with other degrading behaviors. Does she like getting spanked? Is this for real?

Madonna replies that "These are traditional roles that women play, and here I am doing them, but that's not really what I'm doing." In other words, she is not "doing" these traditional roles as they would be done in pornographic material produced by men. So, what *is* she doing? She says she is showing "Extreme images of women: One is in charge, in control, dominating; the other is chained to a bed, taking care of the procreation responsibilities. " Is Madonna exposing women's perverse scenarios by juxtaposing them in a pairing of female "tops and bottoms," thus making all of them visible?

Kaplan says that women "employ social gender stereotypes to express the desires and ambitions that are forbidden to them, and in those stereotypes of normal femininity we will discover the female perversions."[21] Is Madonna's artistry successful because she is so exact in displaying our perverse desires? Certainly she follows Kaplan's notion when she shows both the inverse and the obverse of women's perverse strategies as they are enacted in our male/female relationships. I personally don't find Madonna's work either pornographic or erotic; rather it is somehow clinical. I am beginning to see it in Kaplan's terms as an accurate portrayal of female perversions as they exist in our culture. But I don't think Madonna, despite her protofeminist declarations, really comprehends or cares to comprehend where her material is situated. Despite her manifesto for artistic freedom, she is not a theorizer: she is more like a cultural "sex-worker" "doing" obscenity in the guerilla theater of the sex/gender battlefield.

From this position, Madonna does have much to say about gender relations. Although her discourse is encoded in the symbolic terms of penis and vagina in the interview Madonna disavows any overt penis envy. Glad to have a vagina she can relate to, she can "barely relate to a dick now," and she "can't imagine having a third thing hanging off my body. How dreadful!" She rejects what she sees as demeaning oral sex— fellatio is out (of the question), too humiliating, cunnilingus is in (but not really in). Feeling the need to reaffirm her image of a girl who is in charge of the (hetero)sexual scenario, she says, "Let me put it this way: I've certainly had fantasies of fucking women, but I'm not a lesbian." As a dogged "sex-worker" acting out the stereotypes of femininity, she finds more pleasure in pursuing what Kaplan calls the "social trophies."

The penis is a rather puny and insignificant signifier in Madonna's world, other trophies are of more consequence—fame, money, and power, for instance. Forewarned by Kaplan's theory about restitution of phallic powers, we are not deceived by Madonna's disdain for penises. Kaplan says it is anyway no longer the *literal* penis a woman seeks in a perversion scenario, but rather its substitutes; it is these a woman will try to co-opt in a deceptive way.

Penis envy is the classic analytical concept used for the most part by men to understand female perversions, Kaplan's strategy is not to reject it, but to refocus it from within a feminist perspective to achieve greater empathy for women's struggles. In resolving her oedipal complex, Kaplan says, a small girl may suffer the vicissitudes of her "castration" and come to terms with her female identity. But, for many women, there remains a feeling of loss. If a woman has had to renounce her ambitions and sexual strivings in order to conform to a gender stereotype of femininity she will rightly feel that something has been stolen from her. The longing for the missing aspects of her self may well be symbolized in what Freud observed—an envy of an idealized phallus which can be projected onto a man and result in scenarios of abject submission. Or, she may find ways of stealing back what has been taken from her. For Kaplan, reappropriating the stolen phallus (that detachable fictitious genital) is the premier female perverse strategy. The stolen phallus can appear, she says, in such desirable social trophies as cars, fur coats, clothes, jewels, and even the actual penis of a lover, all of which can become fetishized emblems of phallic overcompensation and restless, rebellious masculinity.

Madonna's capacity for reappropriation is legendary: she can command penises to appear anywhere, on a girlfriend (as a dildo), on her gay male dancers (as elongated phallic breasts), or in piles of money spent on a buying spree at Chanel's—an activity that the self-named material girl, rightly claims can really "cheer a girl up." Although the documentary *Truth or Dare* supposes itself to be a paean to self-exposure, as in the confessional there is much that remains concealed. One thing that goes on behind closed doors, hidden from the omniscient eye of the documentary camera, is the money talk: the most obvious phallic trophy is kept a secret. (The star coyly pulls the door shut as she is about to make her big-time financial deals.) One begins to wonder if money deals are not the ultimate hiding place for the truly perverse strategies of women in our culture.

All the social trophies, Kaplan says, serve as symbolic equivalents to social power; they cover and "compensate for devastating disappointments and losses commonly suffered by females. Paramount among these painful losses would be the loss of the soothing, protecting mother of infancy and the loss of the mother's positive value in a social order that denigrates females."[22] In *Truth or Dare*, Madonna takes us to her mother's grave site while she is on tour in Detroit. Her mother (also named Madonna) died of breast cancer when Madonna was six. In the cemetery she uses the granite stone marker on her mother's grave as a pillow for her head as she lies down on the family plot. The scene is surreal, with few words and little emotion conveyed, a strange and eerie interlude in the midst of all the frenetic action of the tour. Madonna seems vague and dissociated, and there is a palpable absence of mourning. Viewing her, one feels unsettled, our feelings of sympathy for this "motherless child" somehow exploited by the scene. Is it possible that Madonna is cashing in even on this loss, extracting profit from her pain, and in effect emotionally manipulating her audience by taking advantage of our willingness to feel for her?

In the interview with Fisher, Madonna freely talks about her "mother complex." She explains how she "mothers" the people in her entourage, especially the gay men, whom she perceives as innocent and vulnerable. She also explains how she early turned her need for love and attention to the world, though she admits "I'm always looking for someone to fill up my hole—no pun intended." Conflating emotional emptiness with vaginal space, she says, "That's what makes women vulnerable, that extra hole."

Olympia, a Raunch magazine and centerfold model interviewed by Stoller and quoted by Kaplan, also talks about the "hole." She says, "The biggest part of female sex organs, the most important and best part, isn't what's there, but what isn't. It's the space, the void . . . it's what's not there that counts, not what is there."[23] It is this empty imaginal space that creates what Kahn refers to as "the conjuring void" of pornography. Stoller tells us how this acute awareness of "the void" translates into the need to be seen: A person engaged in obscenities, he says, "has goaded the authorities, forcing them to admit that one really exists."[24] As Olympia tells Stoller, "I'm on camera twenty-four hours a day."

It becomes obvious in the *Rolling Stone* confessional, in *Truth or Dare*, and especially in *Sex*, that Madonna is also endlessly seeking to be "on camera," filmed, watched, interviewed, and documented—the continual mirroring apparently needed simply to remind her that she exists. In the film she is constantly being "worked on." Surrounded by her support people who massage her shoulders, give her neck a chiropractic "pop," make her up, touch her up, comb her hair, and film her. (The level of attention causes a rather bewildered, testy, and possibly envious Warren Beatty to ask the all-seeing camera eye of the documentary filmer "Does she [Madonna] even exist off camera?" Madonna's movie revenge manages to reduce this top male star to a simpering, bespectacled puppy dog).

Although she is, by her own proclamation, not "attached to her body," Olympia confided to Stoller that her body is an "instrument" or a "container" keeping her from being dispersed "in a billion places all over the universe at the same time."[25] A *femme evaporee*? Olympia, like Madonna, uses her body instrumentally as a fetish. Claiming that it takes many people to create her—a choreographer, dancing teacher, singing teacher, songwriter, the costume maker, biographer, photographer, "Oh—and a financial backer"—they are all involved in "creating a certain sexual image." "Without them, I would be nothing." And, she says, (before we can even think it) "I see myself as a commodity."[26]

One begins to wonder what is the difference between Olympia the centerfold and Madonna the superstar. Using the female body in a fetishistic way for enactment of sexual fantasy is not so unique, in fact it is rather banal. What makes Madonna appear to be so revolutionary?

Lacanians would say that she is a woman who has appropriated male fantasy, the male gaze, and the male prerogative of domination. If so, what do we, as women, learn from this contemporary star about the perquisites of this privilege?

Following part one of the *Rolling Stone* interview are some photographs of Madonna taken by Steven Meisel, (a collaborator in her later work, *Sex*) a series he calls "Flesh and Fantasy." These were inspired by the work of the notorious Brassai who photographed the demimonde of "the secret Paris" of the '20s and '30s. Like Brassai's Meisel's erotica are not the crude and brutal images that we have come to expect from contemporary pornography. There is no exposure of genitals, or even of bare breasts. The images are of whole people, not assemblages of fragmented body parts. Yet there are evocations of sado-masochism with scenes of potentially sinister domination, and they depend on the imagination for activation. These scenes are potent fantasy inducers: they are nostalgic daydreams made up of a world of images that intimate sexual obsessions. A smooth, silk-stockinged leg exposes the soft skin of a woman's upper thigh, and we experience the luxurious sensuality of women's flesh against women's flesh. Madonna, with a cigarette dangling from her lips, dressed in a man's trousers and vest, stands in a mannish pose amidst a bevy of young men posed like mannikins in black stockings, garter belts and heels. Three women pose together in a languid display of silk slips, stockings and garter belts, all of which (again) expose the tantalizing piece of bare thigh. The images are psychological in that they turn on the erotic edge of bi- and homo-sexuality, gender crossing, and the gender re-location of domination and submission. Men's bodies suddenly become vulnerable in black garter belts and stockings, with their vacant stares and mannikin bodies, and the effect is compounded when there is more than one man in the picture, their gazes averted, while Madonna stands, legs astride in a posture of domination, staring directly at the viewer.

The sixties and seventies brought pornography up to white heat with the additional fuel of sexual violence. Culminating in "snuff" films in which porn actors were actually murdered on camera, pornographic images, like drugs, needed to be taken to greater and greater extremes in order to achieve their desired effect. And feminists, at least one— Catherine MacKinnon—has argued compellingly against pornography as an addiction to sexism. But Madonna's "Flesh and Fantasy" photos seem to put us back into a genre that is less disturbing, more innocent. Conservative, these photos take us back to the time of the early 1930s, the time of *The Blue Angel,* a time for which we can safely be nostalgic, when the pornographic image could still tease and titillate us.

But are the pictures themselves safe? In the first photograph, Madonna is shown with head lowered, eyes seductively raised, in the act of slipping on or off a delicate gold chain with a pendant Star of David. One could ask what that particular icon is doing here. Everyone knows Madonna is notorious for flaunting religious symbols. But the Star of David in a scene evocative of the 1930s insures that we locate these images in a deeper and more sinister scenario of the time. The prelude to that ultimate of obscenities, the man-made death events of the holocaust, lurks in the background, fueling the sexual imaginary with the unrepresentable pornography of death.

Masud Kahn points out, in *Alienation in Perversions,*[27] the nostalgic atmosphere that appears in pornography. Time is encapsulated in the perpetual and static present. The appropriation of static images—unsituated, out of human context, ahistorical—is necessary to stimulate the pornographic imagination. To be sure, pornographic events can only "happen" in the mind. But, Kahn tells us in no uncertain terms, "the politics of pornography are inherently fascistic." Is this Madonna's message? Does she have the depth of knowledge to know what she is evoking? I don't think so. Does she care? Probably not. In looking through her latest work, *Sex,* further questions arise. What is an artist's relationship to her images? Where does an artist's responsibility *to* and *for* her images reside? Is it acceptable to present any image, in the name of art or fantasy, without taking and acknowledging the weight of responsibility for the impact of that image on others? Can one ever be responsible or "in charge of" (in control of) images that tap so deeply into the powers of the unconscious?

Undoubtedly one cannot, but surely an artist ought to have a relationship to her images that involves more than just using them because they are potent, disturbing and make big money. This is where, for me, Madonna's "adolescent strategy" breaks down—because she profits from her imagery. Unlike the punk on the street she is not innocent of complicity in the system she satirizes.

The original Brassai literally risked his life to photograph the Parisian underworld. He lived and ate and drank with the people he photographed. He made friends with them, probably slept with some of them, and, at least on one occasion, had to escape from them to save his life. The only way he could accomplish his work was to become intimate with his subjects, and he took that risk. What was critical to the pictures, he said, "was for the suggestion to take photographs not to seem to come from me but from them."[28] Brassai's work is authentic and moving because he photographed real people within their real life context. Brassai is re-presented by Madonna with none of the personal passion and without the force of history. She is truly "shameless" in her willingness to skim off the cream of any historical event—her mother's death, the prelude to the holocaust, or the pornography of S and M in the age of AIDS—when she thinks it will fit her needs. This postmodern star will also appropriate other star's names and images to embezzle their autobiographical energy.

Madonna has kept her mother's name and effaced her father's and she revels in taking on the names of various defiant women who have an historical or fictive past, Daisy (Miller), Lulu (Louise Brooks), Kit (Kit Moresby/Jane Bowles), Dita (Dita Parlo), the actress from the thirties, whose name Madonna uses for her "good-time girl," fantasy self in *Sex*). Frida (Kahlo) was discarded only because she has become too popular. As Fisher wryly comments, "they are all dead women." Madonna has a whole wardrobe of sexual personae: Marilyn Monroe is one of her favorites. This appropriation and diffusion of identities is part of the Madonna masquerade. Without a unified self-image she can disturb and disrupt, but there is no one to be held responsible. Because of this she is seen by some as the quintessential postmodern culture heroine. And this makes us re-think the postmodern.

Feminist philosopher, Susan Bordo, in a piece which draws inspiration from Madonna, defines the postmodern conversation as containing elements such as "intoxication with individual choice and creative jouissance, delight with the piquancy of particularity and mistrust of pattern and seeming coherence . . . suspicion of the totalitarian nature of generalization along with a rush to protect difference from its homogenizing abuses."[29] These elements produce, Bordo says, a new concept of the self, "one no longer caught in the mythology of the unified subject,

embracing of multiplicity, challenging the dreary and moralizing gener-
alizations about gender, race, and so forth that have so preoccupied
liberal and left humanism. "[30]

Whereas Kaplan shows how gender norms foment female perversions, Bordo's primary focus is how the culture works to press women
into normative prescriptions for their (our) bodies. Bordo points out
that it has become *de classe* to talk about "the grip of culture on the
body" since, in postmodern thinking there is no such thing as a monolithic entity called "culture" which exercises its will on passive subjects.
Postmodernists, she says, prefer to view individuals as fragmented and
nomadic yet nonetheless disruptive of dominant culture. However, the
pursuit of a body which meets what can only be called the brutal
standards of a cultural ideal is, as Kaplan and Bordo both demonstrate,
a major (and often perverse) female occupation. Kaplan tells us that the
medical profession is a hiding place for female perversions. And Bordo
notes, "Medical science has now designated a new category of "polysur-
gical addicts" (more casually referred to as "scalpel slaves") who return
for operation after operation in perpetual quest of the elusive yet ruthlessly normalizing goal, the "perfect" body."[31] And as Bordo correctly
acknowledges, the availability of this pursuit of the perfect body, as
usual, lands in the hands of people who have the money and time to
enjoy such "pleasures."

Like Kaplan, Bordo is concerned with "the hegemonic power of
normalizing imagery." Resistance to this power is, Bordo says, a serious
and embodied struggle: and it is within and through our bodies that we
define the discourse of our struggle.

Postmodern resistance is imagined, however, as "the refusal to
embody any positioned subjectivity at all: what is celebrated is continual creative escape from location, containment and definition . . . From
this perspective the truly resistant female body is not the body that
wages war against feminine sexualization and objectification, but the
body that, (Bordo quoting Cathy Schwictenberg) "uses *simulation* stra-
tegically in ways that challenge the stable notion of gender as the edifice
of sexual difference . . . (in) an erotic politics in which the female body
can be refashioned in the flux of identities that speak in plural styles."[32]

Kaplan states "that in the female perversions a display of stereotyp-
ical femininity acts as the disguise for what a woman experiences as a

forbidden masculine striving."[33] Madonna reverses this scenario. In *Truth or Dare*, Madonna cultivates a look that visually simulates Marilyn Monroe, thus encoding the kind of femininity Kaplan talks about which relies on blondness, vulnerability, sexual submissiveness. By forcefully subjecting that image to an inversion, through sexually muscular scenarios of female domination, Madonna turns feminine sexuality as it is conventionally defined inside out: she reveals the hidden fantasy within women's sexuality—a desire to dominate and control. Dislodging the visual rhetoric of gender gives her work its look of revolution. But, as Gloria Steinem has remarked, Marilyn Monroe was a female impersonator. Does that not make Madonna a female impersonator impersonating a female impersonator? How perverse do we want to get?

Onstage as the "postmodern heroine" who uses her body subversively as the point of resistance, Madonna appears to be steadily de-constructing traditional gender stereotypes. Her refusal to enact a passive feminine sexuality, her active defiance and rebellious sexuality, her self-defined images and her "defiance of the cultural gaze" all give her the look, of a female sexual liberator. But is Madonna truly revolutionary? Is she giving us anything new? Or is she just one more female show business trickster in a long tradition that goes back further in American show business than Mae West and Marlene Dietrich—at least as far as Fanny Brice. Granted, she destabilizes the notion that masculinity is the only domain of power and domination. She eroticizes power, sexual knowledge and desire and self-centered sexuality. And she appears to challenge gender norms by her unruliness and willingness to deregulate sexual scenarios by seizing male prerogatives. Bordo thinks that since, "control and "power" are words that are invoked over and over in discussions of Madonna they become "equivalent to self-creation"[34] and that Madonna is then seen as "in control of her image, not trapped by it." The question remains how "in charge" of this material can she be? Kaplan and Stoller have taught me to be suspicious. Disruption of traditional gender categories through the powerful imagery of parodic dominance must somehow conceal the search for submission. Somewhere obscenity must reveal the hatred that Stoller says is at the core—the look of revolution hides a worse conservatism.

Madonna's video productions, like "Open Your Heart" and *Sex,* "facilitate rather than deconstruct the presentation of Madonna's body as an object on display . . . (it is ) entirely about Madonna's body. . . . a way of claiming trendy status for what is really just cheesecake—or, perhaps, pornography.[35] And Madonna's body, Bordo points out, has recently been subjected to the same disciplines of diet and exercise (and surgeries? though she denies them) that other megastars, such as Elizabeth Taylor, Cher, Dolly Parton, and that ultimate postmodern hero(ine) Michael Jackson, have made careers of. Her former voluptuousness (round belly) which she had once celebrated has been whittled down to a flat perfection "making Madonna's body-as-object, now perfectly, plastically taut and tightly managed, for display."[36] But why call Madonna to account for what she, like other performers, does with her body? Because, I think, she is not only using her body for her work, she is intent on using her body to make a cultural statement about women, women's bodies, and women's sexuality. And therefore her message and the medium of it must be scrutinized before she can be fully accepted as our heroine.

Bordo's final assessment, one that nearly redeems the "material girl," is that Madonna represents a new inscription of mind/body dualism. "What the body does is immaterial, so long as the imagination is free. This abstract, unsituated, disembodied freedom... celebrates itself only through the effacement of the material praxis of people's lives, the normalizing power of cultural images, and the sadly continuing social realities of dominance and subordination.[37] And, as Kahn noted, a disembodied imagination is what is necessary for pornographic fantasy to work. It is in Kahn's "conjuring void" of the disembodied imagination that Kaplan locates the source of our perversions. Society, she says, takes advantage of our *infantile* misinterpretations, our fantasies, and mythologies about the primal scene, (the castrated/castrating vagina, the biological superiority of the penis, the innate inferiority of the female sexual organs), to enforce traditional roles for men and women and to keep its structure of gender normality intact. Madonna, by putting it in our face in *Sex,* hopes to cure us of our one-sided views. She's not out to shock us she says, but rather to open our minds. Madonna as sex-educator?

Although she claims to want a sexuality that will take us out of the tyranny of the domination submission model, Kaplan offers no ideas on what that might look like. Citing an example of women's attempts at writing their own "democratic" erotica (i.e. erotica without the victim/oppressor dynamic) she can barely contain her contempt: she calls a volume, *Ladies Own Erotica,* a "schoolmarmish manual for nice men"[38] written by the "generous ladies of Kensington in their gender-orderly households"[39] She confesses it sent her back for the real stuff in de Sade.

Although feminist analysis gives Kaplan's understanding of female perversions a convincing ring, and her material is thought-provoking she does not, unfortunately, take her argument into the realm of "good news" for the future of women's full sexual expression. So, too, I would say for Madonna. Hers is truly a "risky business." To "do" obscenity is to risk becoming obscene. To caricature gender behavior is to risk actually upholding and supporting the standards one is trying to defy. Rebelliousness is often conservative at its core. But maybe that's the point. In the last book written before his death, *Porn: Myths for the Twentieth Century,*[40] Robert Stoller put forth his belief that "the people who create pornography embody the communications systems that make up a culture's avowed erotic desires." Thus we learn about "a culture's sexual fantasies by means of the private fantasies of those hired to represent the fantasies."[41] Somehow we are all implicated.

Bordo's examination, shows how (and why) we, as women, and Madonna, as our culture heroine, are, even now, contributing through our "self-normalizing" activities to the perpetuation of the very cultural objectification and sexualization of our bodies that we say we are fighting against. Bordo demonstrates how we participate in "the production and reproduction of sexist culture,"[42] Perhaps nothing exemplifies this trend better than what Kaplan calls "the little cosmetic surgeries of everyday life"[43]

There is, Kaplan warns, a danger for the investigator of the perverse of succumbing to the perversion investigated. Insofar as perversions are identified by monotonous, repetitive sexual fantasies, I would say that Kaplan herself, not unlike Madonna in her latest book, *Sex,* slipped over the edge. After 500 pages of Kaplan I felt pounded away by the reductive Freudian formula. After 128 pages of *Sex,* I felt fatigued by the trashy aesthetics. In Kaplan I kept looking for something that would move my embodied imagination beyond the by now worn out phrase "unwelcome news" which proceeded every new revelation of the difficulty accepting gender differences. I kept searching Madonna's work for the extreme breath-taking edge of eroticism present in Robert Mapplethorpe's work. Neither Kaplan's book nor Madonna's productions give predictions or descriptions of what is truly possible in the realm of sexual diversity, sexual identity, and intimate relationships, nothing towards how to establish what our sexuality could be or what levels of loving our relationships could attain. *Sex*, Madonna claims, shows us her "private sexual fantasies" and, following Stoller, we see that she is showing us the favorite fantasies of our culture. But I find Madonna's appropriation of the male prerogative of producing pornography, the paraphernalia of "S and M," and the emotional charge of child sexual abuse does nothing to truly undermine our sex/gender system. Masud Kahn once remarked that pornography is "the stealer of dreams." Both Kaplan and Madonna participate in the theft, by presenting us with only one sexual scenario wherein gender norms, whether perversely pursued or rebelliously resisted, can continue to ratify the domination/submission plot. It is up to us individually to dream ourselves beyond these stereotyped images. Without our dreams we cannot begin to imagine the multitude of meanings underlying our sexual lives, the complexity of our fantasies, longings, fears and hopes, and the possibilities for expression of human intimacy, power, and love.

NOTES

1. Louise J. Kaplan, *Female Perversions: The Temptations of Emma Bovary* (New York: Doubleday, 1991).

2. Robert J. Stoller, *Observing the Erotic Imagination* (New Haven: Yale University Press, 1985) 34

3. Stoller, "Hostility and Mystery in Perversion," *International Journal of Psycho-analysis*, 1974, 425.

4. Stoller, *Erotic Imagination,* 34.

5. Kaplan, *Female Perversions,* 14.

6. Ibid., 10.

7. Ibid., 12.

8. Ibid

9. Ibid., 1.

10. Ibid., 14.

11. *Rolling Stone,* "Madonna: Big Time Girl Talk" Rolling Stone Interview with Carrie Fisher, June 13, 1991.

12. Madonna *Truth or Dare* (1991).

13. Madonna *Sex* , (New York: Warner Books, 1992).

14. Regine DeForges, *Confessions of O: Conversations with Pauline Reage* (New York: Viking Press, 1979).

15. *Rolling Stone*, "Madonna: Girl Talk, Part Two" June 27, 1991.

16. Stoller, *Erotic Imagination,* 7.

17. Ibid.

18. Stoller *Erotic Imagination* 1985,90 italics mine)

19. Ibid., 90.

20. Ibid.,91.

21. Kaplan, 174.

22. Ibid., 182.

23. Stoller, *Erotic Imagination* , 78.

24. Ibid, 90.

25. Ibid., 81

26. Ibid. 76.

27. Masud Kahn, *Alienation in Perversions* (London: The Hogarth Press, 1979).

28. Brassai, *The Secret Paris of the 30s,* trans. Richard Miller (New York: Pantheon Books, 1976).

29. Susan Bordo, " 'Material Girl': The Effacements of Postmodern Culture" in *Michigan Quarterly Review* (Fall 1990) 664

30. ibid.

31. Bordo, 657 .

32. Ibid.,, 669 (emphasis mine).

33. Kaplan, p.173.

34. Bordo, 673..

35. Ibid., 675.

36. Ibid., 674

37. Ibid., 676.

38. Kaplan, 354.

39. Ibid., 359.

40. Stoller, *Porn: Myths for the Twentieth Century* (New Haven: Yale University Press, 1991).

41. Ibid., viii.

42. Bordo, 666.

43. Kaplan, 360.

*PATRICIA REIS* is the author of *Through the Goddess: A Woman's Way of Healing* (Continuum, 1991) and *Daughters of Saturn: From Father's Daughter to Creative Woman* (Continuum, 1995). She has a private practice for women in Yarmouth, Maine.

This article was published under the title "Female Gender Trouble: Pursuing the Perverse with Madonna," in *The San Francisco Jung Institue Library Journal*, Volume 12, Number 3, 1993. San Francisco C. G. Jung Institute, 2040 Gough St., San Francisco, CA 94109. Phone: (415) 771-8055. Subscription: $36/year.

# HERMES & THE
# CREATION OF SPACE

## *by* MURRAY STEIN

## THE GREEK GOD

WHO WAS HERMES? THE GREAT 19TH CENTURY GERMAN
mythographer, W. H. Roscher, identified Hermes as the wind, sub-
suming under this basic identity all of his other roles and
attributes—Hermes as servant and messenger of the sky god Zeus,
Hermes as swift and winged, Hermes as thief and bandit, Hermes as
inventor of the pipes and lyre, Hermes as guide of souls and as god of
dreams and sleep, Hermes as promoter of fertility among plants and
animals and as patron of health, Hermes as god of good fortune,
Hermes as patron of traffic and business activities on water and land.
Ingeniously, Roscher tied all of these functions to the primitive perception of a wind god. Hermes is like the wind. We can hear Shelley's
"Ode to the West Wind" as a hymn to this god:

O wild West Wind, thou breath of Autumn's being,
Thou, from whose unseen presence the leaves dead
Are driven, like ghosts from an enchanter fleeing . . .

Norman O. Brown took up the scholarly quest for the essence of this enchanter in his classic work, first published in 1947, *Hermes the Thief.* Brown does not mention wind, or any other natural elements either for that matter, but instead focuses on the human features of this complex Greek diety. Brown locates the core of Hermes in his stealth and his magic. Hermes was generally known in the ancient world as amoral and the patron god of thieves, highwaymen, travelers and traders, and businessmen. In the famous portrait of him given in the Homeric Hymn, Hermes is a merry and light-hearted trickster figure. More than a simple robber or trickster, however, Brown sees in Hermes the figure of a magician. From his magical powers flow his other functions and attributes. In Brown's brilliant account, Hermes is not meteorological but psychological, a human type, a shamanic presence.

Hermes role as psychopomp is well-known too, and emphasized by Kerenyi in his essay on this god. This deepens the image. Jung adverts to this identity of Hermes in his references to Hermes Kyllenios: "Hermes is the psychon aitios, 'originator of souls,'" he writes (1969, par. 538). Perhaps one can trace a symbolic link between Brown's shamanic-magical Hermes and Roscher's wind god Hermes in the linguistic fact that wind and spirit have the same name in Greek: pneuma.

In the cluster of stories involving Hermes passed down in Greek tradition and literature, a distinct type of human character shines through: a young man of ideal physical build, extroverted, swift in physical movement and rhetorically gifted, enchanting and seductive, ready to serve but not to be taken advantage of, friendly but independent, inventive, intelligent, generally benign and having a ready sense of humor, athletic, stealthy. In art and story he is usually depicted as a puer aeternus, along the lines written by M. L. von Franz in her book on this theme. In mythic tales he is not at the center of politics, decision-making or narrative action, but on the periphery: "Mercury stirring up the broth of air at the edge/ Of Botticelli's Spring," to use John Hollander's fine words ("Looking Ahead"). Hermes stands at the edge, an edge-person, located essentially in liminality. "Hermes' original home was not at the center but on the edge of things, on the boundary," notes Brown (p. 113). The father principle is relatively weak and absent in Hermes (he is a bastard son of Zeus who fell in love momentarily with the nymph Maia), while the mother is positive and doting. This puer aeternus has the airy swift spirit of the wind and the intelligence and a skill of a magician.

## HERMES AS ARCHETYPAL IMAGE

What is Hermes? Wind, magic, a puer spirit. But beyond that, he is a god, and to fathom what this means we need to plunge deeper into the connections between this mythic image and the arche- typal and instinctual base of the psyche from which he comes and which he represents. Why is he an immortal god? Where is his numinosity?

Brown points out what many other scholars say as well, that the "name Hermes is probably derived from the Greek word for 'stone-heap,' *herma*, and signifies 'he of the stone-heap'" (p. 33). Martin Nilsson, in his delightful little book, *Greek Folk Religion*, imagines a peasant walking through the Greek countryside. He writes:

> If our peasant passed a heap of stones, as he was likely to do, he might lay another stone upon it. If a tall stone was erected on top of the heap, he might place before it a bit of his provision as an offering. He performed this act as a result of custom, without know-ing the real reason for it, but he knew that a god was embodied in the stone heap and in the tall stone standing on top of it. He named the god Hermes after the stone heap (*herma*) in which he dwelt, and he called the tall stone a herm. Such heaps were welcome landmarks to the wanderer who sought his way from one place to another through desert tracts, and their god became the protector of wayfar-ers. And if, by chance, the wayfarer found on the stone heap something, probably an offering, which would be welcome to the poor and hungry, he ascribed this lucky find to the grace of the god and called it a *hermaion*. (p. 8)

The name Hermes is connected with the name for the stone heap that was a boundary-marker, a *herma*. This is the physical fact from which the experience of Hermes springs, in which it is grounded. Around this concrete phenomenon of the boundary-marker there grew up the many associated features and qualities that go into making this god what he is. Something about the experience of herma and boundaries and cross-roads stimulated the Greek imagination into elaborating the figure of Hermes.

Nilsson continues his imaginative presentation by saying that this stone heap at the crossroads might have marked a grave, and perhaps there was a body buried under it. This would mark a space that was a crossroad in a double sense, with one axis horizontal, another vertical: A three-dimensional cross-roads. Hermes is a god of travelers living and dead, his monument of stones a boundary marker for the world on this plane and between it and the underworld. Kerenyi, in his masterful study, *Hermes: Guide of Souls*, emphasizes the god's role in traversing the boundary between life and death, between this world and the underworld of shades, Hades. Because of his association with boundaries and with the realm of shades, Hermes takes on the features of a liminal god, or of what I have called a god of liminality in my book *In MidLife*, that is, one who inhabits interstices, a denizen of betwixt-and-between (cf. Turner). He stands at the edge not only geographically and interpersonally but also metaphysically. He is essentially in and of the world of liminality.

The element of uncanniness, which Walter Otto so forcefully stresses in his chapter on Hermes in *The Homeric Gods*, would attach to Hermes because of this close association with the spirits of the dead and the underworld. The Oxford Classical Dictionary states flatly that while Hermes appears as a youth, he ". . . is probably one of the oldest [of the gods] and most nearly primitive in origin . . . . and signifies the daemon who haunts or occupies a heap of stones, or perhaps a stone, set up by the roadside for some magical purpose" (pp. 502-3). Again, we come upon the notion of magic in connection with Hermes.

The classic statue of Hermes, called a Herm, was a later development. It was a quadratic pillar usually about 6 feet high resting on a square base, topped with a bearded head and fronted with an erect phallus. Herms first appeared under rule of the tyrant Hipparchus around 520-524 B.C., who had these figures set up as boundary markers throughout Greece. Oddly, the Herm has none of the qualities of movement and lightness usually associated with the spirit of Hermes, and the head atop it is that of an older, bearded man. It is anything but

Hermes represented in classical Greek statue.

youthful, dynamic and air-like, although it is quite charming in its own way. A marker of boundaries, it is geometric and hard-edged, exact and defining. Hipparchus set these in place, according to Brown, in order to "integrate the cult of Hermes into urban and political life of the city-state" (p. 113). This brought Hermes more centrally into Greek consciousness. A Herm was also placed at the Propyleia (entrance) to sacred precincts and temples, where he marked the boundary of the temenos. With this development, liminality moved in closer to centrality; everywhere Hermes now stood at boundaries and defined spaces, referring the citizen to horizontal and vertical dimensions of existence.

Archetypally, we can see in the image of Hermes a mythical state-ment of the psyche's innate tendency to give definition to perceptual and mental horizons, to mark edges, to define spaces. Originally Her-mes stood at the edge of known space, a pile of stones at the boundary. His sign marked the limit of consciousness. Beyond the boundary lies the unknown, the uncanny, the dangerous, the unconscious. When markers are created and limits set, however, curiosity and explorative-ness are also excited and new spaces for exploration and discovery invite the bold and courageous traveler. If Hermes marks the boundary be-tween conscious and unconscious, we have to realize that this boundary is always shifting and in flux; it is mercurial. Background and fore-ground may instantaneously reverse too, and generate new perceptions, novel insights.

Within the area of the known, containers take shape which are reserved for specific types of human activity, while beyond them lies the "other," the foreign (even if only temporarily), the taboo, the forbid-den, the unclean. Hermes standing at the boundary marks a psychological and sometimes a moral limit and calls special attention to the space being entered or left. When he first appears, he may create a new space by dividing a vast horizon into the "here" and the "beyond," and thus he creates both consciousness and a new unconscious. His intervention in the perceptual and psychological field creates new possibilities for consciousness, also new edges and boundaries beyond which lie the mysterious "others." When he disappears, there is a loss of identity and definition.

Boundaries, it must be noted, are basic to human perception, and their creation and maintenance therefore are archetypal. Boundaries create categories for thought and behavior. Fences not only make good neighbors; fences make neighbors, period. Without boundaries there are no object relations—in a sense there are no objects; without defini-tions there can be no thought; the world is ouboboric, undifferentiated, pleromatic. The appearance of herma—an epiphany of Hermes—repre-sents the introduction of the differentiating principle into the pleromatic void.

In *Seven Sermons to the Dead* (1989, pp. 378-90), Jung calls this *principle creatura*, the principle of distinctiveness:

Distinctiveness is *creatura*. It is distinct. Distinctiveness is its essence, and therefore it distinguisheth. Therefore man discriminateth because his nature is distinctiveness. . . . Our very nature is distinctiveness. . . . the natural striving of the creature goeth towards distinctiveness, fighteth against primeval, perilous sameness. This is called the *principium individuationis*. This principle is the essence of the creature. (Jung 1989, p. 380)

Hermes is the psyche etching lines into the panes of perception.

What does it add to say that this function of making distinctions is archetypal and not simply an artifact of ego-functioning? It says that the ego actually depends upon the psyche in order to function properly. By keeping Hermes out of the ego and refusing to make him ego-syntonic, we acknowledge our dependency upon archetypal powers even for our most mundane daily activities. In the agora and not only at a crossroads in the wilderness, at home and not only at the gate of the sacred temenos, Hermes is present. The archetypes undergird the ego in all of its activities and functions. This is a key to perceiving sacredness in everyday life.

## HERMES AND THE INSTINCT OF CREATIVITY

The erect phallus on Hermes monuments has perplexed scholars and amused tourists. Burkert says that a "form of territorial demarcation, older than man himself, is phallic display, which is then symbolically replaced by erected stones or stakes. To this extent, stone cairn and apotropaic phallos have always gone together" (1985 p. 156). Burkert, who seems to be a keen student of animal behavior and ethological studies, connects the phallicism of Herms to the phallic display of a certain species of monkeys: ". . . they sit up at the outposts, facing outside and presenting their erect genital organ. . . . every individual approaching from the outside will notice that this group does not consist of helpless wives and children, but enjoys the full protection of masculinity" (1982, p. 40).

To me this emphasis on Hermes' protective role and on the use of Herms to brandish claims of territoriality seems interesting but far-fetched. It is one thing to say that Hermes stands at boundaries and defines space; it is quite another to make of him a guardian of the gate.

This is not usually seen to be his role. Cerberus guards the gates of Hades, not Hermes. And Apollo would be insulted to realize that one supposed Hermes was needed to guard the gates of his sacred precincts on Delos. Hermes is a thief, not a guard. Burkert has to admit: "That a monument of this kind could be transformed into an Olympian god is astounding" (1985, p. 156).

The answer is of course that Hermes was a god long before the Herm was constructed. He is archaic and primordial. But so is territory and the sense of territoriality. Yet it was not Hermes' management of the territorial imperative—which is after all nothing more than a defense—that placed him on Olympus. It was his connection to the source of life, to archetype and instinct, to the self. Hermes states creativity. It seems to me that a better explanation for the presence of the erect phallos on Hermes' monuments has to do with his deep and indeed essential association with the instinct of creativity.

Creativity is highlighted in a number of tales and emphasized by some scholars as a major attribute of this god. Along with Hephaistos and Prometheus, Hermes was loved and honored by craftsmen. In the *Hymn to Hermes* we hear of the new-born baby creating the lyre from a tortoise shell on the first day of his life. Later he is credited with the discovery of starting fire by rubbing sticks together and with the invention of the pipes. The sheer joy and delight he experiences at his own quick and sure inventiveness are infectious as one reads or listens to the Hymn. This has reminded some readers of the gleam in the craftsman's eye as he forges a new device or solves a practical problem (cf. Brown, p. 79). You can hear this joyous craftsman's energy in Wagner's rendition of Siegried hammering his sword into shape in the third opera of the Ring cycle.

The sheer rampant energy of creativity sounds through the image of Hermes as he is classically presented in the Homeric Hymn. And his successful struggle with Apollo to attain equal rank has been interpreted to represent also the rise of craftsmen in ancient Greece and their seizure of equality with the aristocracy of Athens (cf. Brown, pp. 79ff.). Hermes is given equality in the arts with Apollo, the great god of poetry, music, dance and other artistic activities in ancient Greece. Hermes claims in the Hymn that he is a follower of Mnemosyne, the goddess of memory, and her daughters the Muses (hence his appearance in Botticelli's famous painting, Spring). His essential association with the instinct of creativity must be granted.

Brown draws an important distinction, too, when he points out that Hermes is not primarily a fertility god. The phallos on his statue is not a signifier of male procreativity and sexual prowess. Brown associates the phallos with his perception that Hermes is fundamentally a magician: "The phallus is so closely identified with magic in Roman religion that the word fascinum, meaning 'enchantment,' 'witchcraft' (cf. 'fascinate'), is one of the standard Latin terms for the phallus; no better evidence could be found for the appropriateness of the emblem for Hermes as magician. When Greek craftsmen hung images of ithyphallic demons over their workshops, it is clear that to them the phallus symbolized not fertility but magic skill at craftsmanship" (p. 37). I would agree with Brown but place the accent on creativity—the Creative itself as *fascinosum*, following Aniela Jaffe's interpretation of Jung's famous childhood dream of the underground phallus—rather than on magic, although the two can easily be associated. Creative people have often seem especially potent and magical, and their talents can be awesome and numinous. Creativity is magical, of the self and not of the ego.

The phallos on the Hermes monument, then, grounds this image in instinct, not in the sexual instinct as such however but in the instinct of creativity.

## HERMES AS A "FACTOR" IN THE PSYCHE

In my understanding of Jung's mature thought, a major mythic figure like a god represents a psychological factor that embraces an archetype and an instinct. The archetype, rooted ultimately in spirit, is represented in the psyche by an image and is a mental, and often a cognitive, object or process; the instinct, rooted in the material body, is experienced in the psyche as an urge, a drive, a force compelling one to do something. In the psychological factor that a god symbolizes, instinct supplies the drive and the dynamic force, while image orients and directs it. Instinct and archetype are wedded in the psyche, and a god is a representation of this conjunction.

To summarize what I have said so far about the Greek god Hermes: in Hermes we have a figure who signifies a union between an innate tendency on the part of the psyche to create boundaries and define spaces, to etch lines in the panes of perception (an archetypal process), and the instinct of creativity. It is this particular combination of archetype and instinct that makes Hermes so interesting psychologically. He signifies the creative instinct at work in the psyche in a particular way. A specific type of creator god, he is the creator of new spaces. It is in the creation of new spaces, novel spaces, inventive spaces, especially psychologically subtle spaces that Hermes shows his special nature and genius. Trickster and magician are suitable epithets, for often these are secret spaces of subtle interiority.

## New Spaces

When you draw a line on a blank page, you create new space. And you also destroy or transform an already existing space. In this simple act, destruction and creation take place and a new space is opened up. A new inside/outside possibility has been created, as when some people are elected to form a small group within a larger group. Yahweh, another creator god, resembles Hermes in this respect; he too creates space, divides and sets boundaries, and selects a people from among all the peoples of the earth to be his chosen.

Some spaces have magical properties, which unite inside and outside in a surprising way, like the Moebius strip. Boundaries are not what they seem. Even carefully guarded and maintained, they are both real and irreal. It is as though the boundary line is a space itself, which can open into a new space and which is permeable to the other spaces. This is Hermes space, a liminal space. Boundaries, we find again and again, both separate and unite spaces.

What Jung called "the reality of the psyche" or "the objective psyche" is such a category. The psyche has boundaries, but they are both real and irreal. They are boundary lines that expand into liminal spaces themselves. At the boundary of psyche there is a psychoid area, psyche-like but not limited to subjectivity; it is both inside and outside of the psyche. Jung's notion of the objective psyche embraces a space that is beyond the usual subject-object, inner-outer dichotomy and includes parapsychological phenomena and synchronicity (for an incisive discussion of this, cf. von Franz, 1990, chapter 9). Can we think of Hermes as being the archetypal image embedded in Jung's notion of the reality of the psyche? Was Jung really a child of Hermes? I think a good case can be made for this.

## The Space of Psychotherapy

Perhaps we can leap now over two or three thousand years of history and look at the creation of novel psychological spaces in the twentieth century. I want to refer, initially at least, to the creation of the space of psychotherapy in our present and fast-closing century, and to see this as an artifact of the Hermes archetype.

Psychotherapy exists in and depends upon the creation of a space that is a new space and yet one that does not violate the boundaries of other already established spaces. It is a space that opens in the boundary line between public and private, professional and personal. It is a space that often has magical properties reflective of the reality of the psyche, in that synchronicity and parapsychological phenomena are often constellated in this space. Winnicott wrote of the kind of space I will describe as transitional space, but I do not much care for the term. Transitional to what? has been my question. I prefer to call it "a third space."

What kind of a space is this? Is there a therapist alive who has not been struck by the frequency of the feeling and the fantasy of therapy as a love affair? Not an illicit love affair, because often the spouse knows and apparently approves of it, and it takes place in the full light of day—taxes, insurance, office hours, answering machines, and all the paraphernalia of official business life. And yet, a married (or unmarried) woman leaves her home (or office) and comes to my place at a certain hour of the afternoon once a week, full of excitement and expectation, having prepared herself emotionally and physically for this intimate encounter. She may hesitate as she pays and say that she somehow doesn't feel it's right to give money for this, nor does she want to acknowledge that this is not a purely personal relationship on both sides. What a strange relationship this is, she may remark; so personal and intimate, and yet so removed from reality. The analyst knows so much about the patient, the patient so little about the analyst.

Taking the fee, the analyst may feel a bit uncomfortable too, wondering if he is somehow illicitly involved in a subtle form of prostitution: selling his time and attention for a set fee, on a time schedule, at his place.

But this is only the beginning, the surface. For constellated within the container of the analytic sessions is a third space, a psychic world unto itself yet existing within the given world of convention, law and other relationships, and a world that recognizes its own limitations, its boundaries whose violation is absolutely taboo. This world opens up, or is created, by the mutual interplay of the psyches within it, which represent two other worlds, two persons with full lives outside of this new space. There is therefore a duality within this new space, each side of which has connections strongly fixed to the worlds outside of this one.

This third space of therapy dare not become One World, the Prime World, the only real space, or it will lose its standing in the world of solid boundaries, and this would create psychic confusion and harm, even collapse. For this is a new and fragile space. And yet this space must also insist on its own legitimacy, its own right to exist, its own birthright and equality with other already established worlds. Here in the twentieth century experience of deep psychotherapy we find a replay of the ancient story of the birth of Hermes and his rivalry with a brother, Apollo, who was already established and claimed a lot of space for himself. The third space, a new space, is a Hermes space.

Depth psychotherapy is a Hermes space in another respect as well: it connects the upper world with the underworld, the world of shades and dreams, the unconscious. In the famous diagram that Jung drew of the analytic relationship, he showed a further complication within this third space. There are four dimensions (see diagram on next page) within it: 1. conscious to conscious (horizontal); 2. conscious to unconscious (vertical); 3. unconscious to conscious (diagonal); 4. unconscious to unconscious (horizontal). It is a quadratic relationship. Of the four vectors, the fourth is the most fascinating, for it is this one that represents the underground connection and implies the field of mutuality that defies the laws of time and space, inner and outer, mine and yours. Out of this ground comes a force and a form that will define the quality of the interactive field in each unique analytic relationship. It is here that we look for the epiphany of new archetypes, mediated by the messenger god, Hermes, the creator of this new space. Here, within the third space of analysis, is yet another third space that bridges and includes the duality of the personalities involved in this complex field

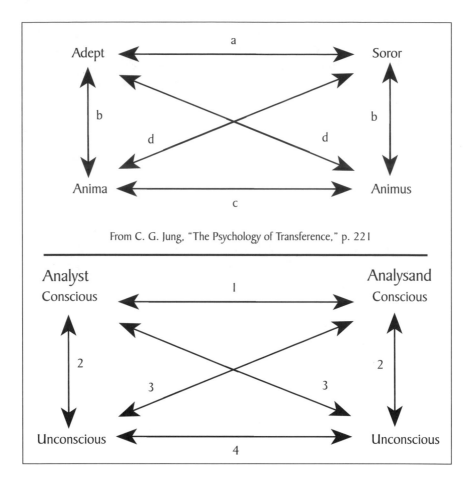

From C. G. Jung, "The Psychology of Transference," p. 221

of vectors. Like Hermes' crossroad-markers, psychotherapy marks a double crossroad, horizontally in relation to the civic world and vertically in relation to the psychic world.

Let me give a somewhat whimsical example of how this constellation of a third space manifests itself in clinical practice. A young man came to me recently for therapy because he was stuck in his life and quite seriously depressed. After several sessions in which we became acquainted, more or less (vectors 1,2,3), he had a dream in which he was in bed with a well-known but now somewhat dated movie star. The dream went on to portray some of his personal conflicts and problems in a humorous and graphic way, but the extraordinary detail that I noted in the dream was the identity of the movie star. I asked the young man whose dream this was for his associations to her, but he had none to speak of, other than some movies he had seen many years ago. He had not thought of her consciously in a long time and could hardly even remember her name after he woke up and was recording the dream.

The strange and remarkable fact was that I had seen this very movie star in a restaurant only several months previously. She may be the only movie star I have ever seen up close (to my knowledge). What this dream told me was that vector 4 was activated, that Hermes was active. He would create a unique interactive field between us. A new space was being created.

I could go on for a long time with similar examples from my own clinical experience and from the practices of colleagues and supervisees who have shared their experiences with me over the past twenty years, each of which would illustrate the activation of this fourth dimension. This is the uncanny element in analysis, that such things can and do happen in this highly protected, private, and confidential space. It is a space that is maximally sealed off from the world and yet so profoundly open to it at another level.

## Active Imagination

Jungian analysis classically uses two major methods: dream analysis and active imagination. Both of these activities encourage the constellation of Hermes and the creation, or manifestation, of a "third space" in analysis. Active imagination, however, is an activity that is undertaken in solitude, by oneself, rather than in the presence of another. It works on the vertical axis (no. 2) rather than the horizontal, and its function is to constellate a third psychic space within the individual.

Again we can see Jung as a child of Hermes as he embraces this method and refines it during his midlife years. As he tells the story of his discovery of active imagination as a method to promote individuation and to engage the unconscious, Jung entered this psychic geography for the first time with considerable fear and trepidation:

> It was like a voyage to the moon, or a descent into empty space. First came the image of a crater, and I had the feeling that I was in the land of the dead. The atmosphere was that of the other world. Near

the steep slope of a rock I caught sight of two figures, an old man with a white beard and a beautiful young girl. I summoned up my courage and approached them as though they were real people, and listened attentively to what they told me.

(Jung, 1989, p. 181)

So begins active imagination as a psychological technique in the twentieth century. This led to the creation of a space that Jung was to occupy time and again for the rest of his life, a Hermetic space in which he conversed with a teacher named Philemon and with a host of other figures.

Active imagination opens a "third space" within the interpsychic matrix, which contains, again, a polarity—the I (ego) and an other (an archetypal image, typically)—and opens out in a Moebius-strip-like twist to the object world. This is the reality of the psyche, inside and outside related in synchronistic unison.

Jung tells of a happening not long after this discovery of the third space of active imagination in which the objective psyche was constellated and parapsychological and psychoid phenomena became active.

It began with a restlessness, but I did not know what it meant or what "they" wanted of me. . . . Around five o'clock in the afternoon on Sunday the front door-bell began ringing frantically. It was a bright summer day; the two maids were in the kitchen, from which the open square outside the front door could be seen. Everyone immediately looked to see who was there, but there was no one in sight. I was sitting near the doorbell, and not only heard it but saw it moving. We all simply stared at one another. The atmosphere was thick. . . "For God's sake, what in the world is this?" Then they cried out in chorus, "We have come back from Jerusalem where we found not what we sought." That is the beginning of the Septem Sermones.

(ibid., pp. 190-91)

In this example we can see the confluence of inner and outer phenomena in a highly charged liminal space, a typical Hermes space lying between the daylight world of a calm Sunday afternoon on Lake Zurich and the spirits of the dead who hunger for new meaning and arise from the depths of history and the unconscious in search of it. It would take

Jung the rest of his long and productive life to try to satisfy them. As he portrays himself in the autobiography, he was a man who lived a good deal of his life in this "third space" of verticality.

## More New Spaces

Psychotherapy itself and active imagination are two instances of the creation of new space in the modern world. But we can certainly find Hermes at work in many other locations as well. Wherever he is constellated, a new space opens up. He both creates and marks the space, sets it apart, and gives it an aura of numinosity and fascination. Where creativity and distinction-making come together, there Hermes appears.

In the University, a new cross-disciplinary committee is born; in communications, a new space called virtual reality suddenly pops up on the screen and draws awe and fascination, even addiction to itself; in business, advertisers create a space between producers and consumers and ply their trade, while multi-national corporations define new spaces for commerce, traversing national and ideological boundaries and sending financially charged electrons back and forth into banks around the world. This is, in fact, the space age and new spaces are being created at a rate of speed that surpasses our capacity to follow them all. Hermes is everywhere, alive and active. One might even call this the Age of Hermes!

REFERENCES

Brown, N.O. 1969. *Hermes the Thief.* New York: Vintage Books.

Burkert, W. 1982. *Structure and History in Greek Mythology and Ritual.* Berkeley: California University Press.

_____. 1985. *Greek Religion.* Cambridge: Harvard University Press.

Hollander, J. 1985? "Looking Ahead." *The New Yorker.*

Jaffe, A. 1972. *The Creative Phases in Jung's Life.* In Spring. Dallas: Spring Publications.

Jung, C.G. 1969. *The Archetypes of the Collective Unconscious.* Coll.Wks. 9/2. Princeton: Princeton University Press.

_____. 1989. *Memories, Dreams, Reflections.* New York: Vintage.

Kerenyi, K. 1987 *Hermes Guide of Souls.* Dallas: Spring Publications.

Nilsson, M.P. 1978 *Greek Folk Religion.* Philadelphia: University of Pennsylvania Press.

Otto, W. 1979. *The Homeric Gods.* London: Thames and Hudson.

Roscher, W.H. 1886-1890. *Ausfuehrliches Lexikon des griechischen und roemischen Mythologie.* Leipzig: B.G.Teubner.

Shelley, P.B. 1901. *The Complete Works of Shelley.* Boston: Houghton Mifflin.

Stein, M. 1983. *In MidLife.* Dallas: Spring Publications.

Turner, V. 1987. *Betwixt and Between. In Betwixt and Between* (ed. L. Mahdi). LaSalle, IL.: Open Court.

von Franz, M.L. 1970 *Puer Aeternus.* Zurich: Spring Publications.

_____. 1990. *Projection and Re-Collection in Jungian Psychology.* LaSalle, IL.: Open Court.

*MURRAY STEIN* is a Jungian Analyst in Chicago and a leading writer in archetypal theory. He is author of many groundbreaking books, including: *In Midlife: A Jungian Perspective, Solar Conscience, Lunar Conscience,* and *Jung's Treatment of Christianity.* The books he has edited or co-edited include: *Jungian Analysis, Psyche and Sports, Jung's Challenge to Contemporary Religion,* and *Psyche's Stories.*

This is an original essay published for the first time in *SAGA.* It is used by permission of the author.

# PITFALLS IN FAËRIE

## by VERLYN FLIEGER

### from Mythos Journal

"Faërie is a perilous land, and in it are pitfalls for the unwary and dungeons for the overbold. . . . In that realm a man may, perhaps, count himself fortunate to have wandered, but its very richness and strangeness tie the tongue of a traveller who would report them. And while he is there it is dangerous for him to ask too many questions, lest the gates should be shut and the keys be lost." (*MC*, p. 109)

So WROTE J. R. R. TOLKIEN IN HIS ESSAY "On Fairy-stories" in 1936. Nearly 30 years later he wrote a short story, *Smith of Wootton Major*, about a man who went to Faërie and had exactly that experience. He could not report his wanderings, the gates ultimately shut on him, and the key, although not lost, had to be handed on.

As a work of art, *Smith of Wootton Major* is itself not unlike Tolkien's characterization of Faërie. Too often those who try to analyze it take on the roles of the unwary and overbold. Attempt to explain it and you risk stumbling into a pit, assume that you know what it "means," and you may have imprisoned yourself in a dungeon. Try to unlock its magic and the gates may shut and the key be lost.

The action of the story is fairly simple. A magical star is baked into a cake by an apprentice Cook who is in reality the King of Faery.[†] Without knowing it, a boy named Smith swallows the star with his piece of cake and thereby gets a passport into Faery. Under the star's protection he wanders through the perilous realm until at last the King tells him it is time to give it up and pass it on to someone else. He does give it up, and in time it passes to another child. This is a slender story line, and like most plots, gives by itself little hint of any special magic.

Roger Lancelyn Greene was on the right track when he said of *Smith* that "To seek for the meaning is to cut open the ball in search of its bounce" (*Letters*, p. 388). More than one critic has cut open the ball, but the bounce continues to elude detection. What Greene termed bounce—the ephemeral, magical air and effect of *Smith*—is elusive largely because it is less a thing in itself than the space between things, not one specific meaning but tension between meanings. This tension is in its turn the product of tensions in its author, tensions between opposing ideas which lead to concomitant tensions in the story itself. Keeping a wary eye on the pitfalls and the dungeons, I would like to look at three such tensions—one structural, one technical, one emotional.

The first tension, the structural one, arises out of the genesis of *Smith*, which occurred in the context of a preface that Tolkien had been asked to write for George MacDonald's *The Golden Key*. Although he always said he disapproved of allegory, he began his preface with one, to explain to children the meaning of the term "fairy":

---

[†]The spelling of this important word in Tolkien's lexicon is as elusive as the bounce. It appears in his writing variously as Faery (as above), Fairy (see quote below), Faërie, and Fayery. However changable the spelling, the meaning remained constant, it was "the Perilous Realm itself and the air that blows in that country."

*Fairy* is very powerful. Even the bad author cannot escape it. He probably makes up his tale out of bits of older tales, or things he half remembers and they may be too strong for him to spoil or disenchant. Someone may meet them for the first time in his silly tale, and catch a glimpse of Fairy, and go on to better things. This could be put into a short story like this. There was once a cook, and he thought of making a cake for a children's party. His chief notion was that it must be very sweet. (Carpenter, p. 242)

The preface never got finished, but the idea took on a life of its own. The boy replaced the cake as the focus, and the Smith—the craftsman, the creator—became a more important figure than the Cook. Nevertheless, Tolkien's original allegorical impulse left its ghost in the narrative, a ghost which has haunted the tale ever since, for nearly every critic has succumbed to the temptation to allegorize it.

Allegory is a strict mode, relying on a basic structure of one-to-one correlation between the surface level—the plot—and the more important deeper level—the meaning. However primary in importance, the deeper level must underpin and support the surface level. Herein resides the first tension, for Tolkien's story invites allegory and at the same time refuses to support it. This is largely his own fault, for he also invited allegory, yet refused to support it. Rather, he both disclaimed allegory and yet toyed with the concept. In an ancillary essay now part of the Tolkien collection in the Bodleian Library he wrote to clarify in his own mind the story's theme, action, characters, and surrounding history he started off declaring unequivocally:

This short tale is not 'allegory', though it is capable of course of allegorical interpretation at certain points. It is a 'Fairy Story', of the kind in which beings that may be called 'fairies' or 'elves' play a part and are associated in action with human people, and are regarded as having a 'real' existence, that is one in their own right and independent of human imagination and invention.

He continued in this vein, assuring his reader (and reassuring himself) that:

There is no need to hunt for allegory. Such teaching as this slender story contains is implicit, and would be no less present if it were a plain narrative of historical events.

Yet almost immediately he conceded that:

> The Great Hall is evidently in a way an allegory of the village church: the Master Cook with his house adjacent, and his office that is not hereditary, provides for its own instruction and succession but is not one of the 'secular' or profitable crafts, and yet is supported by the village, is plainly the Parson and the priesthood. 'Cooking' is a domestic affair practiced by men and women: personal religion and prayer. The Master Cook presides over and provides for all the religious festivals of the year, and also for all the religions occasions that are not universal: births, marriages, and deaths.

The critics were no less allegory-tempted than the author, some seeing the story as outright allegory, and almost all reaching for a level of meaning outside the plot. Jane Chance Nitzsche found *Smith* to be Christian allegory showing, "the reward of grace for humility and suffering" (Nietzsche, p. 67). Clyde Kilby saw it as an allegory of "the creative process and the special problems of a fantasy writer" (Kilby, p. 37). Humphrey Carpenter saw in the story "Tolkien's anxiety over the future and his growing grief at the approach of old age" (Carpenter, p. 242). T. A. Shippey saw Tolkien wrestling with his own contradiction, the scholar-fantasist torn between philology and fiction. Of all the allegorical readings Shippey's is the most outright, for he assigns specific roles to Tolkien's characters, calling the Master Cook a "philologist-figure," Nokes the baker a "critic-figure" and Smith himself a "Tolkien-figure" (Shippey, p. 204).

All of these interpretations are plausible. Each focuses on an identifiable element in the narrative (though the focus may say more about the critic than the story). But none accounts for the whole picture, for the enduring appeal of the piece, or its haunting effect on its readers. Tolkien himself said "Faërie cannot be caught in a net of words," and yet he kept on trying to catch it, and in so doing gave his critics license to do likewise. The story began as allegory but almost immediately became larger than an allegorical structure could accomodate. The result is that the more you try to define it the less you see.

This brings up the second, the technical tension, which has to do not with catching Faërie either in a net or in an allegory, but defining its relationship to the ordinary world. Tolkien wanted to show both the "otherness" of Faërie and its closeness to humanity. Further than that, he wanted to show how the two separate worlds and times remain separate yet interpenetrate one another. This is a tall order. It is greatly to his credit that he came as close as he did to succeeding. Of all his works, it is in *Smith of Wootton Major* that the two worlds and times most explicitly touch and interact. The point of intersection is Smith—that figure who passes between the worlds—the figure through whom Faery time and space and human time and space are made to touch. That they do touch is unquestionable. *How* they do it is less clear.

In the same essay in which he vacillated so indecisively between allegory and no allegory, he tried once again, as he had tried in *The Lord of the Rings*, and in the (at that time) unpublished *The Lost Road*, and *The Notion Club Papers*, to characterize and codify, not for his readers but for his own satisfaction, what he conceived to be the actual relationship between the real world and Faërie. That he was unable, finally, to do so is more a comment on the length of his reach than the inadequacy of his grasp. He was trying for a synthesis which has eluded theologians, mystics, and physicists—the union of the actual with the transcendent. He began with a consideration of space and time relationships.

> The geographical relations of Wootton and Faery are inevitably, but also intentionally left vague. In such stories there must be some way or ways of access from and to Faery, available at least to elves as to favoured mortals. But it is also necessary that Faery and the world (of Men), though in contact, should occupy a different time and space, or occupy them in different modes. Thus though it appears that Smith can enter Faery more or less at will (being specially favoured), it is evident that it is a land or, world of unknown limits, containing seas and mountains; also it is plain that even during a brief visit (such as one on an evening walk) he can spend a great deal longer in Faery than his absnce [sic] counts in the World; on his long journeys an absence from home of, say, a week is sufficient for exploration and experiences in Faery equivalent to months or even years.

For all his concern with the relationship of space and time, Tolkien was not attempting a coherent theory of space-time, but simply trying to find a sound enough theoretical base on which his Faërie and the ordinary world could believably stand together and co-exist. Time, he asserts, is different in Faërie. But here he finds himself almost at once in deep water and struggling to keep his head up:

> In many Fairy Tales use is made of the idea that time passes quickly in Faery, so that a man who finds his way there may come out after what seems a brief episode to find that years, even centuries have passed. Except as a mere device to bring a man out of the past into contact with a (to him) future time—that is in a tale of which this is the real point, and Faery as such is not seriously considered—I have always felt this to be a mistake: a mistake in credibility, if Faery of any kind is taken seriously.

It is plain that this discussion has a direct bearing on Tolkien's treatment of time in other, similar instances, most specifically in the Lórien chapters in *The Lord of the Rings*, and that such instances are based on the same, still unresolved, theoretical premise. He could not make it work on a practical level, but he could not forego the beauty and the (for him) utility of the concept. This forced him, finally, to adopt an untenable rhetorical position, for while on the one hand he rejected the faërien time-warp as a "mere device," and a "mistake in credibility," yet on the other hand he went on to declare that:

> The Faery of the tale is a particular one. If one accepts it while 'within' the tale, then clearly the Rulers of Faery . . . must be able to arrange that the experience in Faery of favoured human persons may be enjoyed without dislocation of their normal human life. The time of their Faery must be different, even though it may be at points contiguous. For them human time is or may be also longer than that of Faery.

This will not do. He cannot have it both ways. To declare so positively that the time-warp is a mistake in credibility and at the same time to maintain the principle that a sojourn in the Faery world should bring about "no dislocation of normal human life" is to try to have your cake and eat it. It creates a tension between logic and imagination similar to that between allegory and no-allegory, a tension that even the Rulers of Faery would find hard to sustain.

As it always does, space proved easier for Tolkien to deal with than time. Space lends itself more naturally to travel than does time, and such travel, being more traditional, is easier to account for.

> As for place. Entry into the 'geographical' bounds of Faery also involves entry into Faery time. How does a mortal 'enter' the geographical realm of Faery? Evidently not in dream or illusion. It is common in Fairy tales for the entrance to the fairy world to be presented as a journey underground, into a hill or mountain or the like. . . . My symbol is not the underground, but the Forest: the regions still immune from human activities, not yet dominated by them (dominated! not conquered!). If Faery time is at points contiguous with ours, the contiguity will occur in related points in space—or that is the theory for purposes of the story. At certain points at or just within the Forest borders, a human person may come across these contiguous points and there enter F. time and space—if fitted to do so or permitted to do so.

For the continuation of his story there had to be a point or points at which Faërie time and space are contiguous with that of mortals. It was not merely romance of setting that led Tolkien to a Wood. His preference for a wood over the more usual fairy-story topos of the underground (usually in the form of a fairy mound or hill) as the place of entry is surely connected to the meanings of Anglo-Saxon *wode* and Middle English *wood* as both "wood" and "mad," that is, outside ordinary experience. The convention of the wood as the predictable setting for unhuman, extraordinary experience is a standard of medieval and Renaissance narrative. Tolkien knew this, as Shakespeare knew it, as Dante knew it.

Moreover, the acceptablilty of this poetic convention offered a way around the unsolvable temporal mechanics of the situation. It allowed him to move out of time and into space, and to conceive a geography both magical and mappable. In the case of *Smith* Tolkien used both terrain and direction to seat his otherworld comfortably in a tradition of myth and legend. This Faery, he stated, "is situated (or its entrances are) westward." The forest lies on the western edge of Wootton Major, whose one inn bears over its door a stone with a worn and faded carving of three trees and the inscription "*Welcō to be Wode.*"

The nearby but smaller village of Wootton Minor is deeper in the forest, being described as "a village in a clearing," and the even smaller village of Walton (cited in the pre-history but not in the story proper) is "a distant village beyond Wootton Minor." The key to the significance of these names is in their etymology. All three place-names mean "town in or near a wood." Wootton (both Major and Minor) comes from Old Elglish *wudu-tun*, "TUN in or by a wood," and Walton has its source in Old English *W(e)ald-tun*, "TUN in a wood or on a wold." Thus all three villages are by name and by design in close proximity to the wood of Faery. Walton, even deeper in the forest than Wootton Minor, is apparently the specific point of entry into Faery for those humans who venture there.

So much is background leading up to the part of the history that comes into the story proper. But behind this background is a deeper background, more specific to Faery and to its relationship with the human realm. As Tolkien imagined it, this relationship was one of love:

> The Elven Folk, the chief and ruling inhabitants of Faery,have an ultimate kinship with Men and have a permanent love for them in general. Though they are not bound by any moral obligation to assist Men, and do not need their help (except in human affairs), they do, from time to time try to assist them, avert evil from them and have relations with them, especially through certain men and women whom they find suitable.

Within the story proper, the chief person found suitable to to gain entry to Faery is, of course, Smith. His home after his father's death was the "Old Smithy House," described in the essay as being "on the West Road, the last house in the village on that side," that is to say, on the westward edge of Wootton Major, and therefore on the edge of the forest. The practical reason for the smithy's proximity to the forest was presumably for easy access to fuel, but the more profound reason was surely for easy access to Faery, which as we have seen, is situated (or its entrances are) westward. Geographically, at least, Smith is halfway to Faery even when he is in the ordinary world. Tolkien is on firmer ground with space than with time, for the earth's topography can be both different and contiguous, with wood and meadow, ocean and shore abutting one another. This is less easy with time, and for Tolkien to assert that Faery time must be both different and contiguous, to state airily that this can be "arranged by the Rulers of Faery" and at the same time to call such an arrangement "a mistake in credibility" creates unsolvable contradiction and unresolvable technical tension.

The third, the emotional tension, concerns Tolkien's own feelings about Faërie, and about the very nature of the world and its relationship to our own. The two extremes are contained in the "Fairy-Story" essay, which expresses the position quoted at the beginning of this paper, and the *Smith* essay and story, which take a somewhat different position. For while in *Smith* Tolkien concedes that Faery is perilous to the traveller, he also wants to show it as necessary to humankind. Where the Fairy-story essay spoke of the dangers, the *Smith* essay concentrates almost entirely on its beauty, on its spiritual value, and its beneficent and necessary influence on the human world. It is in this essay that Tolkien makes what may have been his clearest, latest attempt at a personal definition. He wrote that:

> Faery represents at its weakest a breaking out (at least in mind) from the iron ring of the familiar, still more from the adamantine ring of belief that it is known, possessed, controlled, and so (ultimately) all that is worth being considered—a constant awareness of the world beyond the rings. More strongly it represents love: that is, a love and respect for all things, 'Inanimate' and 'animate', an unpossessive love of them as 'other'. This 'love' will produce both ruth and delight. Things seen in its light will be respected, and they will also appear delightful, beautiful, wonderful even glorious. Faery might be said to represent Imagination (without definition because taking in all the definitions of this word): esthetic, exploratory and receptive; and artistic; inventive, dynamic (sub)creative. This compound—of awareness of a limitless world and a desire for wonder, marvels, both perceived and conceived—this 'Faery' is as necessary for the health and complete functioning of the Human as is sunlight for physical life . . .

This seems clear enough, direct, unequivocal, positive in its attitude. And yet the most powerful episode in *Smith of Wootton Major* functions as a direct contradiction of this statement, and calls into question Tolkien's own concept of the necessary relationship between the two worlds. This is the episode of the birch tree whose branches are stripped bare when it shelters Smith from the wind which tries to hunt him down. Smith's encounter with the wind and the birch tree is far and away the most compelling, most daunting scene in the story. It is at once the most direct and the most forbidding of his experiences in Faery, for while the star hidden in the cake invites him into Faery, the birch tree tells him bluntly and vehemently to get out and stay out. Here is no firm but gentle invitation to relinquish his right of entry and yield place to another, such as Smith later gets from the King, but a summary dismissal, a notice to quit.

The scene is one of the most vivid in the whole story, and marks a noticeable shift in tone. In his wanderings, Smith has come upon a lake whose depths contain "strange shapes of flame" and "fiery creatures" going to and fro. So far, so good. We are in the perilous realm, and must expect some danger, or the adventure would not be worth the having. The atmosphere here is not unlike some of the more ominous scenes Smith has already observed, the waves on the Sea of Windless Storm, the ships, the "tall and terrible" elven mariners. Stepping on to the lake's surface, he finds that it is not water, but "harder than stone and sleeker than glass." But just here there is a change. He falls on the hard, unyielding surface, and with the fall suddenly shifts from being an observer of the scene to being a participant, perhaps even an agent in it. With his entry into the action the tone and the mood change dramatically. With his fall a "ringing boom" runs across the lake, awaking the Wind, which harries and drives him back from the lake, "whirling and falling like a dead leaf." It is then that he finds the birch.

> He put his arms about the stem of a young birch and clung to it, and the Wind wrestled fiercely with them, trying to tear him away; but the birch was bent down to the ground by the blast and enclosed him in its branches. When at last the Wind passed on he rose and saw that the birch was naked. It was stripped of every leaf, and it wept, and tears fell from its branches like rain. He set his hand upon its white bark, saying: 'Blessed be the birch! What can I do to make

amends or give thanks?' He felt the answer of the tree pass up from his hand: 'Nothing,' it said. 'Go away! The Wind is hunting you. You do not belong here. Go away and never return!'

As he climbed back out of that dale he felt the tears of the birch trickle down his face and they were bitter on his lips. (PS, p. 321).

The reply to Smith's "Blessed be the birch," and to his offer to repay is the stark, uncompromising "You do not belong here!" The tree has paid dearly for its kindness, and its only response to Smith's thanks is to reject them and him, and tell him to get out. The hardness of the lake is replicated in the hardness of the birch tree's judgment. The fury of the Wind, the bitterness of the tree's tears all speak of a world beyond Smith's mortal experience or mortal ability to understand, and mark him clearly as an intruder in the enchanted land, unwanted, unwelcomed, and punished for his presence. The vehemence of the episode cuts sharply across the mood of the story, and leaves the reader puzzling how to fit it in. It is enigmatic at the very least, at once provocative and problematic to those probing the story for more meaning than may be readily apparent.

Though it is by far the most powerful, this was not Tolkien's first treatment of the birch tree. Two of his early poems in *Songs for the Philologists* deal with the birch. One is in Anglo-Saxon, "Éadig Béo Þu" (Good Luck to You). The other is in Gothic—the only Gothic poem in the lot. In fact, as Shippey points out, although it is by a modern writer it is the only poem extant in Gothic by any writer. It is called "Bagme Blome" (Flower of the Trees). Both poems praise the birch. "Bagme Bloma," an unusually beautiful lyric, far lovelier in the Gothic than in in English translation, hails the birch as "bagme bloma, blauandei / fagrafhasa, liÞuinÞi," (the flower of the trees in bloom, fair-haired and supple-limbed,) and includes a line strongly reminiscent of the scene in *Smith*: "*Andanahti milhmam neipiÞ, / liuteib liuhmam lauhmuni; / laubos liubai fliugand lausai, / tulgus, triggwa, standandei / Bairka baza beidiÞ blaika / fraujinondei fairguni,*" [Evening grows dark with clouds, the lightening flashes, the fine leaves fly free, but firm and faithful the white birch stands bare and waits, ruling the mountain.]

Here, however, the tree is free of any human contact. "Éadig Béo Þu" takes a different approach, "herian Beorc and byrcen cynn,/ láre' and láreow, leornungmann," praising "the Birch and the birch's race, the teacher, the student, and the subject."

Shippey connects these "birch poems" with Scottish folklore. In the Scottish ballad of "The Wife of Usher's Well," the Wife's drowned sons, called back from the dead, wear hats of birch, the tree that grows "at the gates o Paradise." He also cites a tale reported by Sir Walter Scott of an apparition who wore the birch so that "the wind of the world" might not have power over him. Moving from the poems to the birch tree episode in *Smith,* and allegorizing all the way, Shippey suggests:

Smith's Wind, then could be the world; the birch is its traditional opponent, scholarly study; but that study, like the birch hats of the drowned sons, also acts as a passport, into and out of Middle-earth. It is a kind of Golden Bough; not between Earth and Hell, like Aeneas's bough, but between Earth and Paradise.

All this has a bearing on Tolkien's fable, and on his state of mind. The birch protects Smith, but is left naked and weeping. Did Tolkien feel he had exploited philology for his fiction? It also tells Smith to 'go away and never return', a command he cannot obey. Did he feel, perhaps, that in writing his fiction he was trespassing in a 'perilous country' against some unstated law?

(Shippey, pp. 206-07).

Bearing in mind that it is more prudent to frame ideas as questions (Did Tolkien feel he had exploited philology? Did he feel that in writing fiction he was trespassing?) than as statements of opinion, we may still grant Shippey the plausibility of his interpretation. But it adds little to the story. To describe the birch, as Shippey does, as a representation of "learning, severe learning, even discipline," to make the Wind into "the world" and the birch into "its traditional opponent, scholarly study," to turn the tree into "a kind of Golden Bough between Earth and Paradise," these translations do little to account for the effect of the episode *within the story itself.*

Moreover, such speculations cannot approach the emotional power of the episode, which connects more with the lightening flashes of "Bagme Bloma" than with scholarly emphasis of Éadig Béo Þu, or the hat-wearing apparition of the Scottish ballad. Nor do they add materially to an understanding of the story. Smith has already got his passport into the Otherworld. It is the star. He doesn't need another one. There is no need, moreover, to see the episode as representing Tolkien's sense of transgression for venturing into Faery—that is, into fiction—"against some unstated law," since Smith does, as Shippey himself points out, return again to Faery.

The episode with the birch does not appear at all in Tolkien's early (and much shorter) drafts of the story. And it is worth noting that when it did appear it exhibited some notable differences from the published text. The lake, the birch, the leaves, the tears, all are there, but with a slightly different flavor. To begin with, the lake is not hard, nor does Smith venture on (or in) to it. There is no fall, no "ringing boom," which in the published story seems to be what wakes the Wind. Instead, Smith tastes the water from which it gets its name, Lake of Tears, and finds it bitter. He walks on the hillside among many trees, "young and fair and in full leaf," and when the Wind comes "roaring like a wild beast," it tears up "all that had no roots," and drives before it "all that could not withstand it." Only one of these is Smith, who then is not the sole victim, but part of a general storm. All the trees are stripped of their leaves, leaving them naked, and the leaves' whirl like clouds in the sky." All the trees weep, not just the birch, and their tears "flowed from their branches and twigs like a grey rain, and some gathered into rivulets that ran down into the lake," thus giving the lake its name and (presumably) its flavor.

The birch tree is still Smith's shelter from the Wind, but its reply to his offer of thanks is not a verbal one. Smith feels it "pass up his arm." The answer is similar, but not so emphatic as in the final version. "Go away from here!" the birch tells Smith. "The Wild Wind is hunting you." This is considerably less sweeping than "You do not belong here!" as in the final version. Here nothing at all is said about Smith not belonging in Faery. Moreover, the birch gives Smith a message for the King. "If you see the King tell him. Only he can still the Wind once it is aroused." In this draft the anger of the Wind seems to be more general than in the published text. Though it is hunting Smith, it is also attacking all the trees, not just the birch which shelters him. The Wind has clearly done this sort of thing before, as the Lake of Tears bears witness.

There is no doubt that Tolkien's final version is more intense, more sharply focused, and considerably more ominous. It is certainly closer in quality to the Faërie described in his Fairy-story essay than to the one in his *Smith* essay. Like the story of which it is a part, it both invites and defeats attempts to interpret it, for no explanation can match the power of the scene itself. It demands attention, but it defies exigesis. Or rather, exigesis, explanation, allegorization, can add little or nothing to the value of the scene, whose impact is all the more powerful for being inexplicable. The passage is unique, however. Nowhere else does Tolkien draw so stern a picture of Faery's attitude toward humanity. The moment stands on its own as Tolkien's clearest picture of the "otherness," the utter strangeness to the human experience of this unhuman world.

Sometimes the human figure cannot bridge the gap between the two worlds. Sometimes the human author cannot bridge the gap. Tolkien didn't altogether succeed in bridging any of the gaps this paper has pointed out, but his failures are more memorable than the successes of many a lesser author. If he vacillated between allegory and no-allegory, if he could not rationally connect Faery time and human time, if he wavered between the beauties and the dangers of the perilous realm for the unwary traveller, if he sought ways to reconcile all of these while sensing deeply that they were unreconcileable, nevertheless, nevertheless, his attempt led him to create a work of great beauty whose ability to expand the mind and imagination still leads its readers ever on and on.

REFERENCES

Bodleian Ms. Tolkien 9.

Carpenter, Humphrey. *Tolkien: A Biography.* Boston: Houghton Mifflin Co., 1977.

Ekwall, Eilert. *The Concise Oxford Dictionary of English Place-Names.* Oxford: The Clarendon Press, 1964.

Kilby, Clyde. *Tolkien & the Silmarillion.* Wheaton: Harold Shaw, 1976.

Nitzsche, Jane Chance. *Tolkien's Art.* London: the MacMillan Press, 1979.

Shippey, T. A. *The Road to Middle-Earth.* London: George Allen & Unwin, 1982.

Tolkien, J. R. R. *The Letters of J. R. R. Tolkien*, ed. Humphrey Carpenter with Christopher Tolkien. Boston: Houghton Mifflin Co., 1981.

————. "On Fairy-stories," in *The Monsters and the Critics*, ed. Christopher Tolkien. London: George Allen & Unwin, 1983.

————. *Smith of Wootton Major* in *Poems and Stories*. London: George Allen & Unwin, 1980.

Author's note: I wish to acknowledge and thank both the Bodleian Library for allowing me access to the unpublished material quoted in this essay, and the Trustees of the Tolkien Trust as copyright owners for giving me permission to use it.

VERLYN FLIEGER is one of the foremost Tolkien scholars in the U.S. and the author of **Splintered Light**, a widely-praised etymological study of Tolkien's mythology in the **Silmarillion**. Professor Flieger teaches literature and mythology at the University of Maryland.

Reprinted from *Mythos Journal*, Winter 1995, P.O. Box 13296, Minneapolis, MN 55414. (612) 379-0872. Subscription: $30/3 issues.

# ALLEN GINSBERG
# IN INDIA

*An Interview with* ALLEN GINSBERG

*from ARIEL: A Review of International English Literature*

ALLEN GINSBERG'S ASSOCIATION WITH
India began in 1962, when he spent over a year there with Peter
Orlovsky, traveling and looking for a spiritual teacher. There were visits
to the Himalayas with Gary Snyder and Joanne Kyger, to the caves of
Ajanta and Ellora, to Buddhist shrines in Sanchi and Sarnath, protract-
ed stays in Calcutta and Benares, and meetings with mystics, yogis,
poets, writers, musicians, and religious leaders like the Dalai Lama. He
also met, without knowing, Chogyam Trungpa Rinpoche, the Tibetan
lama who would come to the U.S. in the 1970s, set up the Naropa
Institute at Boulder, Colorado, and become Ginsberg's teacher. In
1970, Ginsberg published the journals he had kept during his stay, and
the following year he was back in India in the aftermath of the Bang-
ladesh war. While planning his third trip, Ginsberg gave this interview
in the apartment he rents each summer in Boulder while teaching at the
Jack Kerouac School of Disembodied Poetics at the Naropa Institute.

*So in February 1962 Peter Orlovsky and you arrived in Bombay with only a dollar. . .*

Very little money. Did we only have a dollar? We went looking for mail, and there was probably some money waiting for us. We'd been out of touch for a long time, going on a boat to the red Sea to Dar es Salaam and Mombasa and then to Bombay.

*Was there already the 60s craze to go East, to "spiritual India" and all that?*

I had already been to Europe and spent several years there and that was a traditional thing as in the nineteenth century and early twentieth century—the American in Paris. By 1961, I was more interested in going beyond the traditional expatriate role or voyage, of wandering out in the east, particularly India, the most rich and exquisite and aesthetically attractive culture. And also least expensive . . . . But at that time India was pretty well unknown. There weren't that many people who went there. There were rare people, famous rare people who did that, but it wasn't a whole generation that took it on. It became a stereotype almost instantly when *Esquire* sent some photographer to take pictures of us and put out a fake cover with a guy who looked like me, and a piece on beatniks in India. And that apparently was a model for a lot of people going there. And then I published my Indian journals and that encouraged a lot of poor people to go looking for drugs . . . . But, then, I think it was a very valuable experience for many Americans. You will find any number of advanced Canadian and American practitioners who were there in the 60s and learnt Tibetan and who translated major works and were interpreters for visiting lamas. So there was a whole network of understanding, of experience, of education that led ultimately to things like the Naropa Institute, to an institutionalization of the meeting of Eastern and Western minds.

*What did you associate India chiefly with?*

You know, it was thirty years ago and I don't remember very clearly except snake charmers and . . . I really didn't know what to ask for, but I had the idea of going there to look for a teacher. That was definitely the purpose. I had read the Bhagavad Gita and Ramakrishna's *Table Talk*, the Tibetan Book of the Dead and a lot of Buddhist writing. I had some idea of yoga but not much. Actually, when I was twelve years old I heard an American give a lecture on yoga in Patterson, New Jersey. That always intrigued me and it's still vivid in my mind. . . . I had read some Krishnamurti, some saint poetry, some Yogananda, a little of the Mahabharata, some of the Vedas, and translations by Isherwood and Prabhavananda of the Upanhishads. I had also read Lin Yu Tang's *Wisdom of the East*. Then on the ship I read *A Passage to India* and *Kim*, and Jataka tales and some Ramayana.

*What about the cultural scene—for example, did you see Satyajit Ray's films in New York in the 50s?*

Oh yeah, but not that many. I remember *Pather Panchali* and being very impressed by that. But on our way to India, at Mombasa, I saw a film which outdid Disney and would make millions of dollars if shown in America. It was called *Sampoorna Ramayana*, and it was my real introduction to Indian mythology, to specific Indian attitudes. Boy! It was amazing! Ganesh was so pretty and amusing and sophisticated compared to the very heavy-handed, very serious Western regard for god—only one of them, watch out![1] An interesting, sweet and innocent film, probably more culturally wise than anything by Disney.

*Were you familiar with the Indian classical traditions in music and dance?*

I had seen Uday Shankar, an old man, dancing at City Center, New York, and there was some Shiva dance that he did that was absolutely astounding. I had never seen anything like that—such absolute and subtle control of the whole body so that a wave of energy could pass, beginning at the top of the skull and move down, go up the arm, and down to the belly, and from left to right. It was like a current of electricity. It was one of the most extraordinary and ecstatic artistries I had ever seen.

*Did the books you read provide a framework for such experiences?*

In the Bhagavad Gita, there is a visionary moment when Krishna shows himself with armies flowing from his mouth. That's a little bit like the high point of vision that you get in Dante's *Inferno* or some of Blake's "Last Judgment" or other poems, and to me it seemed immediately universal. . . . the Gita is really a universal poem, really archetypal. I had had some similar visionary experiences on my own—in the late 40s they were related to Blake, and then in the early 50s and late 50s I had some minor experience of psychedelic drugs—peyote, mescaline, the cactus, and then in '59 lysergic acid.[2] So I'd seen a lot of internal mandalas in my mind that reminded me of the pictures I'd seen in Tibetan Buddhism and of the universal form of Krishna in the Gita. So I was tuned into that kind of mythologic archetype as a real experience of consciousness, and I was looking for some way of making it more permanent, or mastering it or getting clearer about it in my own mind . . . . I was interested in what that older culture still had as a living transmission of spiritual and visionary energy because in the West there didn't seem to be one.

*Since you mention drugs, did you know about soma, a god and a hallucinogenic plant in ancient India, with roots in heaven?*

I was very interested in soma. I had met Robert Gordon who had a lot of experience of mushrooms and who had a theory that soma was a certain mushroom. So I was prepared to take that mythology a little more literally than most Westerners, as signifying something more literal on a spiritual level. There were realms of modalities of consciousness that were available and real, that were not within the Western psychological category except maybe in William James's *The Varieties of Religious Experience* or in the hermetic tradition of Blake.

*Was there a sense that the West had failed you in certain respects?*

Well, as I had written six-seven years before in "Howl": "Moloch whose fate is a cloud of sexless hydrogen." I had read Spengler's *The Decline of the West* in 1945-46 and was already anticipating the decline of empire which took a long time to happen, but in half a century it was almost gone, almost over. . . . So there was a realization that the West was impermanent, that the entire Western rationalistic, Aristotelian mind was causing chaos, and I was interested in Eastern thought, all summed up in that gesture—the very Indian gesture—when you ask, "Are you enjoying yourself?" and an Indian will shake his head . . . shakes his head. It could be either yes or no depending on the context, and I was interested in that context with its subtlety of expression rather than in a Western context. . . . Then there was something else I was interested in: the notion of the Kali Yuga.[3] I had read Vico's theories of Golden Ages, Stone Ages, Iron Ages, and Bronze Ages, of the cyclical nature of things, so I was curious about the idea of eternal return and the cyclical evolution of *kalpas* and also, about the staggering number of *kalpas*.[4] That fitted in with my idea of the decline of empire, of an aeon being over. The scope of the cycles of consciousness an incarnation in Hindu and Buddhist mythology was very attractive given the smaller historical cycles of the American century.

*So after almost a year and a half in India, what did you find there that you had not found in the West?*

A more intimate awareness of the relation between people and God. Just the very notion of Ganesh with a noose in one hand and a *rasgoolla* in the other, and his trunk in the *rasgoolla*, riding a mouse . . . .[5] Such an idea of a god, such a sophisticated, quixotic, paradoxical combination of the human and the divine, the metaphysical and the psychological! You don't often get that in Christianity, except maybe in some esoteric Christianity. The idea of an entire culture suffused with respect for that mythology, that religion and its practices, that poor people could understand its sophistication and grant things that hard-headed Westerners are still trying to kill each other over. That was a revelation: how deeply the sense of a spiritual existence could penetrate everyday relations, the streets and street signs . . . Naga sadhus walking around naked—people who would have been arrested in America[6] . . . or for that matter—I remember writing to Kerouac—everybody walking around in their underwear, in striped boxer shorts. What would seem outrageous or strange to Americans was just normal—it was hot and people wore very light cotton—it seemed so obvious. That showed me the absurd artificiality of some American customs . . . . and then just the notion of somebody being a businessman and then renouncing the world and being a *sannyasi* and going around with an intelligent expression looking for *moksha*, that was such a switch from the American notion of business, such a good model, but it doesn't work for even Indians now.[7] . . . And then the availability of ganja and its use in religious festivals and ceremonies was a great source of release for an American used to government dictatorship of all psychedelic drugs (even marijuana), to prohibitions, murders, beatings, corruption.[8] At least in India there was some familiarity with what it was.

*But did you find the same kind of tolerance for sex, given India's notorious homophobia?*

In Bombay someone took us to a district where there were many transvestites, but whatever the situation, it was familiar, domesticated . . . . They don't have transvestite districts in America, of course! Although I was in India for a year and a half, I never had a love affair with an Indian. It was just that I was so absorbed in whatever I was seeing that I wasn't able to connect emotionally with any particular Indian. During our last days in Calcutta, somebody took me to a gigantic beer hall of a basement. . . . All homosexuals. I didn't realize it even existed. Maybe I didn't ask about it. I wish I had known.

*Since you mention Calcutta, were you, like most foreigners, over-whelmed by the city at first?*

I had no idea about Calcutta except I had heard of the Black Hole of Calcutta, but I didn't know what it was. I met a soke fakir there, who just appeared at my hotel one day and became my guide. He was both a fool and at the same time a devotional man, in some respects the most intelligent person I met in Calcutta, who knew what we wanted to see—low life, religious life, tantric life. I wanted to go to some place where people smoked a little ganja and were serious, so he took me on a walk along the banks of the Hooghly to Howrah Bridge and to Nimt-allah burning ghat.[9]

*What was your experience of the burning ghats?*

I went there several times a week and stayed there very late at night. For one thing I was amazed by the openness of death, the visibility of death which is hidden and powdered and roughed and buried in a coffin in the West. To suggest the opposite, the openness of it is like an education which is totally different from the cultivation of the notion of the corpse as still relevant and alive and "don't kick it over." There they just lay it out and burn it and the family watches the dissolution; they see the emptiness in front of them, the emptiness of the body in front of them. So I had the opportunity to see the inside of the human body, to see the face cracked and torn, fallen off, the brains bubbling and burning. And reading Ramakrishna at the time: the dead body is nothing but an old pillow, an empty pillow, like burning an old pillow. Nothing to be afraid of. So it removed a lot of the fear of the corpse that we have in the West. And then I saw people singing outside on Thursday nights and other nights too. That was amazing, and the noise was rousing, very loud, and I would sit around, pay attention and listen, and try and get the words. I saw lady yogis meditating in the ash pit. I remember one lady who I thought was defenseless and poverty-stricken, so I offered her some coins and she spit on them and threw them back at me. And there was one very strange evening when I drank some *bhang*—it must have been mixed with *datura*—and went there with a completely screwed-up head, hallucinating.[10] And I thought I was in the used Vomit Market, everybody was so poor that they were selling vomit! Slept on a stone bench inside the temple all night and woke up and found my slippers gone. Pretty funny.

*In the journals, there are so many graphic details of bodies burning—as if you were getting high on death.*

I don't think I was. After all death is half of life. I was just describing life as I saw it.

*What did you think of the literary scene in Calcutta?*

We poets—Sunil Ganguly, Shakti Chatterjee, and others—met a lot in the coffee houses.[11] Peter and I were excited by the idea of there being a whole gang of poets like there were in New York and San Francisco, who were friends, and that we could communicate across the Pacific Ocean, and that East could meet West, and that they knew our work, and that we could interpret it more and show them poets like Gregory Corso and others they might not have heard of.

*If you were to go back to India, which cities would you revisit?*

I've a tremendous nostalgia mostly for Calcutta and Benares, and Benares particularly because I was very happy there learning a lot, and I had good friends. We had a beautiful house right above the market place and Dasaswamedh Ghat. There was a balcony looking down on the river and an alleyway that went down to the steps. That's where the beggars would gather. . . . And I remember getting really hung up on puris and potatoes.

*Now wasn't it in Benares that the Criminal Investigation Department of India got onto your backs?*

Yes. I don't know why. I think Blitz newspaper said that we were CIA spies. India was then at war with China over a border dispute, so . . . . Peter had a girlfriend, a mysterious Bengali lady, who was staying with us, and it was considered shocking by of all people secular Marxists, whereas her family was much more sophisticated, less questioning.

*Since you were living in a poor section of the city, how did you react to the squalor and human misery around you?*

The poverty was striking, but I don't know why we weren't repelled or angry. We were more interested in what we could do, how to relate to it, how to report it back to the Western world in a way that would rouse sympathy and action rather than horror. Peter was once an ambulance driver so he was not afraid of the homeless and the sick. Also, his own relatives had been in mental hospitals, so he was used to dealing with the mentally-disturbed. He was the heroic type, interested in attempting something. So I just followed Peter and he took utmost care.

*All this was thirty years ago. What did India give you that has mattered most, that has stayed with you and will always be there?*

The Indian influence was first of all on the voice itself and on the notion of poetry and music coming together. Pound had revived that notion and shown how for the ancient Greek poets song and poetry were one, even one with dance. The Greek choruses sang and danced and chanted, and Homer and Sappho sang with a five-stringed lyre. So India helped me to rediscover that relationship between poetry and song. I heard people singing in the streets, chanting mantras, so I began singing mantra too—"Hare Krishna Hare Rama" or "Hare Om Namah Sivaye."

*And you had never heard such chanting in America?*

I first heard it in India, not in America. I had never been to any Hindu temple here where people sat and chanted. I owned books that dealt with Buddhist mantras, but there was no place in America where there was mantra chanting or singing except maybe in the Vedanta temples. So it was not until I got to Bombay that I saw people singing together on the street; and in Calcutta, at Nimtallah burning ghat, people would gather, as I said, particularly on Thursday night, which was kali night to sing amazing, beautiful choral stuff, and they would pass around a chilam and sing continuously, "Siya Rama Jai Jai Rama" or "raghu Pati Raghav." But it was at the Magh Mela at Allahabad that I heard a Nepalese lady singing "Hare Krishna Hare Rama" and the melody was so beautiful that it stuck in my head, and I took it home to America in 1963 and began singing it at poetry parties, after poetry readings with finger cymbals first and later the harmonium.[12] And that began to develop into singing and chanting as part of my poetry readings and led to a deepening of my voice, which slowly began to fill up my body and resonate in the breast area (you might say by hyperbole, "heart chakra"), so that I could talk from there, and that reminded me of the voice of Blake that I had heard, as if my youthful apprehension of that voice was a latent resonance of my mature voice. So at public poetry readings I sang a great variety of mantras both Buddhist and Hindu, "Shri Rama Jai Rama Jai Jai Rama," "Hare Krishna" or "Om Shri Maitreya" or "Om Mani Padme Hum" or "Om" or "Gate Gate Paragate" which I sang quite a bit, the Prajnaparamita sutra. Then singing led to transferring my obsession with mantra to sacred song, to Blake, and I began making melodies from Blake's *Songs of Innocence and Experience* in 1968, and by 1969 I was writing my own folk songs and also recording the Blake songs I had set to music. In 1963, I met Bob Dylan and got interested in the new poetry that was in the form of song, influenced by the earlier Beat generation, by Kerouac and myself, and by 1970 I was recording songs with him. So things came together with the seed mantra planted. In that respect, India helped me to recover the relationship between poetry and music, offered me a model as well as gave me saint poetry in song.

*I notice when you sing you play the harmonium which is very popular in India. Any particular reason?*

Because I'm not a musician. I can't play anything. And this is like a child's instrument; it's so simple I can make out American chords and sing blues. It's actually a Western instrument, and oddly enough the larger harmonium, the foot pedal harmonium, the church organ, is probably the instrument that Blake used for his songs; so my first project in English was to set Blake to music.

*Why is it that at public readings you don't chant mantra that much anymore?*

In 1970, in America, I ran into Trungpa Rinpoche, the Tibetan lama who founded Naropa. I was showing him on the harmonium how I sang, and he put a paw on my hand, drunk, and said, "Remember the silence is just as important as the sound." He then suggested that I not sing all the mantras for they would raise some kind of expectation or neurological buzz in the audience; but he didn't have any teaching to give to stabilize that or to develop it, and he suggested that if I were to sing in public, to sing "Ah," the mantra appreciation of the voice, or "Om Muni Muni Maha Muni Sakyamuni e Swaha" about the human Buddha of the Sakya family, a wise man, or "Gate Gate Paragate"— gone, gone to the other shore gone, completely gone, vacant mind, salutations—something which didn't require a structured sadhana or practice to have some effect and would not confuse people.

*I'd like to go back to something you said at the start of this inter-view—that you were looking for a teacher in India. Did you find one?*

No. Well, yes and no. I found teaching there and I found teachers there who really became my teachers in America. There is a photograph of Peter and I visiting a monk and it turns out that the young monk who showed us the altar was Trungpa Rinpoche. Then I met the Dalai Lama later at Dharamsala and had some teachings from him. And on a visit to Kalimpong, I met Dudjom Rinpoche, who was the head of the N'yingma sect of Tibetan Buddhism. I was having a lot of difficulty with LSD—bum trips, hell trips, hungry ghost realms—so I asked him about it, and he gave me some very good advice, which was: If you see something horrible don't cling to it, and if you see something beautiful, don't cling to it. Basically that's the essence of Buddhist teaching, and it has stuck with me all these years. It is still the seed. And I met others like Swami Sivananda, who said: "Your heart is your guru"; and Bankey Behari, who said: "Take Blake for your guru"; and Citaram Onkar Das Thakur, an old Vaishnav, who said: "If you want to find a guru, eat certain kinds of food and diet and repeat the mantra, 'Guru Guru Guru Guru Guru Guru' for three weeks."[13]

*Did you try it?*

Yes, sure, of course I did. I also met a lot of interesting yogis. Someone taught us *pranayam*, which was helpful for a while since it creates some kind of mental stabilization.[14] But it wasn't until 1970 through Ram Dass—Richard Alpert—who was an old friend from the 60s that I met Muktananda, and he asked me if I had a meditation practice, and, since, as a matter of fact, I still didn't have one, he invited me to Dallas for a weekend and taught me a practice which I did for a year and a half until I met Trungpa, who suggested a more rounded form. So from 1972 I worked with the Trungpa in the Tibetan Vajray-ana style.[15]

*Shortly after you left India, you wrote "The Change: Tokyo-Kyoto Express" in Japan and it's widely regarded as a poem that describes what India did to you.*

Well, that's a little corny. It's a change from a sort of a preoccupa-tion with the absolute to a preoccupation with the relative, accepting the body. . . . I renounce all forms of attachment—"in my train seat. I renounce my power"—I will no longer be eternal or immortal or anything. I'll just be me. In a sense, it's a transition, but I don't think it's that well-expressed. People make a lot of it, but I don't think it's that good a poem because the references are too obscure, some of them like quasi-kundalini neurological buzzings or zappings. It's really a head trip with some emotion.

*What do you think of the rise of Hindu fundamentalism in India today?*

The greatness of India I saw was the absorption into Hinduism of all the gods—the Western ones and the Buddhist ones—and the open space, the accommodation to all varieties of human nature, and I would imagine the curse of India would be this exclusiveness.


NOTES

1. Ganesh is a Hindu god with the head of an elephant.

2. In 1948, Ginsberg had a visionary experience in which he heard a voice—which he assumed to be Blake's—reciting "Ah Sunflower."

3. In Hinduism time is structured in terms of cycles, each cycle subdivided into four ages or yugas, the last of which is Kali Yuga, the age of discord.

4. In Jainism, time is also treated as cyclical, divided into recurring periods called *kalpas* or aeons. A *kalpa* has two phases, each of which consists of six eras.

5. A rasgoolla is an Indian sweetmeat made of ricotta cheese dipped in syrup.

6. The Naga ("naked") sadhus are holy men who do not wear clothes and belong to a sect that was originally militant.

7. A *sannyasi* is an ascetic who has renounced society and seeks *moksha*, which in Hinduism represents liberation from karma (one's deeds and consequences) and *samsara* (rebirth).

8. Ganja is marijuana smoked usually from a chilam, a clay pipe, passed around by smokers.

9. Hindus cremate their dead at Nimtallah Ghat on the banks of the Hooghly (as the Ganges is called in Calcutta).

10. *Rhang* is hemp mixed with almond milk, drunk usually during religious festivals. The seeds of the *datura* plant serve as an intoxicant.

11. Two distinguished contemporary Bengali poets. Sunil Ganguly is also a well-known novelist.

12. The Magh Mela is a fair held every year in January.

13. A Vaishnav is a worshiper of Vishnu, the Hindu god who pervades the universe, holding it together.

14. *Pranayam* is a yogic breathing exercise.

15. Vajrayana is the school of Tibetan tantric Buddhism.


*ALLEN GINSBERG* is among the most noted living poets. His trailblazing epic poem ***Howl*** was a vanguard work of Beat literature of the fifties. Since then, his books have included: ***Old Love Story***, and the recent Cosmopolitan Greetings. A boxed set of recordings of his readings and performances has been released, entitled: ***Allen Ginsberg—Holy Soul and Jelly Roll: Poems and Songs 1949-1993***.

Reprinted from *ARIEL*, October 1993, University of Calgary Press, Calgary, Alberta, Canada T2N 1N4. (403) 220-4657. Subscription: $17/year.

# COMING BACK
# FROM THE SILENCE

*An interview with* URSULA LE GUIN

*from* Whole Earth Review

**Jonathan White:** What attracted you to science fiction?

**Ursula Le Guin:** *I* didn't exactly choose science fiction. I went where I got published, which took a long time because my work is so odd. For the last fifty or sixty years, literature has been categorized as "realism," and if you weren't writing realism, you weren't respectable. I had to ignore that and say to myself that I could do things in science fiction that I could never do in realism. I tend to be prickly about this subject because I get tired of being put down as a science fiction writer. The fact is, in the postmodern era, all the barriers are breaking down pretty fast.

Science fiction is a child of realism, not of fantasy. A realistic story deals with something that might have happened but didn't, right? Many science fiction stories are about worlds that don't exist, but could exist in the future. Both realism and science fiction deal with stories that might be true. Fantasy, on the other hand, tells a story that couldn't possibly be true.

With fantasy, we simply agree to lift the ban on the imagination and follow the story, no matter how implausible it may be.

*JW:* Didn't you say once that fantasy may not be actual, but it's true?

*UL:* Wouldn't you say any attempt to tell a story is an attempt to tell the truth? It's the technique you use in the telling that is either more or less plausible. Sometimes the most direct way to tell the truth is to tell a totally implausible story, like a myth. That way you avoid the muddle of pretending the story ever happened, or ever will happen.

Who knows how stories really work? We're so used to stories with all the trappings of being real that we've lost our ability to read anything else. When you read a native American story, you have to relearn how to read. There's nothing in them to draw you in. There's no sweetening of the pill. Maybe there's a coyote, but there's no description. We're used to a lot of fleshing out, and we're used to being courted and drawn into the story.

*JW:* Nora Dauenhaeur, a Tlingit woman and coauthor of *Haa Shuka, Our Ancestors* reminded me last summer that native American stories are usually told to an audience that already knows them. In fact, they've heard the stories over and over again, through many winters. As a result, the storyteller often uses shorthand—a single word or phrase—to remind the audience of a larger event with many details. She pointed out that we are telling stories like this all the time, particularly among friends and family with whom we share a history. We may say, "Remember that time we were caught in a dust storm outside of Phoenix?" And that's the story, all of it.

*UL:* Yes, exactly. You don't describe the sky or the clouds or what you were wearing. There isn't any of the scene-setting in native American stories. It bothers me when I read gussied-up native American stories. They're no longer sacred. When we embellish a native American story, it turns into just another story. Our culture doesn't think storytelling is sacred; we don't set aside a time of year for it. We don't hold anything sacred except for what organized religion declares to be so. Artists pursue a sacred call, although some would buck and rear at having their work labeled like this. Artists are lucky to have a form in which to express themselves; there is a sacredness about that, and a terrific sense of responsibility. We've got to do it right. Why do we have to do it right? Because that's the whole point: either it's all right or it's all wrong.

*JW:* We tend to have a linear, cause-and-effect way of looking at the world. I wonder if one of the things that attracts us to stories is their ability to change our way of seeing?

*UL:* The daily routine of most adults is so heavy and artificial that we are closed off to much of the world. We have to do this in order to get our work done. I think one purpose of art is to get us out of those routines. When we hear music or poetry or stories, the world opens up again. We're drawn in—or out—and the windows of our perception are cleansed, as William Blake said. The same thing can happen when we're around young children or adults who have unlearned those habits of shutting the world out.

The tribal storyteller is not just providing spiritual access but also moral guidance. I think much of American writing today is an exploration of ethical problems. I'm thinking particularly of novels by black women such as Paula Marshall, Alice Walker, Gloria Naylor, and Toni Morrison. The stories these women write are gaining literary praise, but they're also doing something terribly important for their people, who are not just black Americans but all Americans. In a sense, these women are fulfilling the ancient role of tribal storytellers, because they're trying to lead us into different spiritual and moral realms. They're intensely serious about this, and that's why they're so beloved as novelists.

*JW:* Stories can also help us remember who we are. In *The Book of Laughter and Forgetting,* Milan Kundera says, "What is the self but the sum of everything we remember?"

*UL:* Yes. To *remember,* if my Latin is correct, actually means to put the parts together. So that implies there are ways of losing parts. Kundera talks about this aspect of storytelling, too. In fact, he says that history, which is another kind of story, is often deliberately falsified in order to make a people forget who they are or who they were. He calls that "the method of organizing forgetting."

History is one way of telling stories, just like myth, fiction, or oral storytelling. But over the last hundred years, history has preempted the other forms of storytelling because of its claims to absolute, objective truth. Trying to be scientists, historians stood outside of history and told the story of how it was. All that has changed radically over the last twenty years. Historians now laugh at the pretense of objective truth. They agree that every age has its own history, and if there is any objective truth, we can't reach it with words. History is not a science, it's an art.

There are still people who insist on teaching history as a science, but that's not how most historians work anymore. My husband, Charles, who is a historian, says, "I don't know the difference between story and history. I think it may not be a difference in kind, but a difference in their attempts to be truthful."

The history of the last hundred years still has a tremendous intellectual bias toward the white European point of view. Defined by historians as the written record, it conveniently illegitimizes all oral traditions and most indigenous people right from the start. In fact, in its view, everybody but white Europeans is "primitive." If you don't have a written language, you aren't part of history.

*JW:* Are the current changes in how we look at history also changing the way we look at indigenous cultures?

*UL:* Absolutely. It's a de-centering process. We've been pretending that Europe was the center of the world for too long. With the help of anthropologists, and now historians, we are finding that there is no center, or that there are many centers. Nobody has "the answer." It's amazing how much resistance there is to this. Everybody wants to be "the people," everybody wants to be "the center." And everybody *is* the center, if only they'd realize it and not sneer at all the other centers.

*JW:* Because history, as it has been practiced, concerns itself only with the written record, language acquires a loaded role in terms of our perception of reality. Like history, language can become a tool of forgetting, a tool of estrangement. As a writer, how do you work against that?

*UL:* This is a tricky area. As a writer, you want the language to be genuinely significant and mean exactly what it says. That's why the language of politicians, which is empty of everything but rather brutal signals, is something a writer has to get as far away from as possible. If you believe that words are acts, as I do, then one must hold writers responsible for what their words do.

One of the strangest things about our culture is our ability to describe the destruction of the world in exquisite, even beautiful, detail.

The whole science of ecology, for instance, describes exactly what we're doing wrong and what the global effects are. The odd twist is that we become so enamored of our language and its ability to describe the world that we create a false and irresponsible separation. We use language as a device for distancing. Somebody who is genuinely living in their ecosystem wouldn't have a word for it. They'd just call it the world.

We can't restructure our society without restructuring the English language. One reflects the other. A lot of people are getting tired of the huge pool of metaphors that have to do with war and conflict. The "war against drugs" is an obvious example of this. So is the proliferation of battle metaphors, such as being a warrior, fighting, defeating, and so on. In response, I could say that once you become conscious of these battle metaphors, you can start "fighting" against them. That's one option. Another is to realize that conflict is not the only human response to a situation and to begin to find other metaphors, such as resisting, outwitting, skipping, or subverting. This kind of consciousness can open the door to all sorts of new behavior.

I am struck by how much we talk about rebirthing but never about rebearing. The word itself is unfamiliar to most people. Yet both women and men are capable of rebearing, women literally and men metaphorically. A door opens just by changing the name. We don't have to be reborn; we can *rebear*. This is part of the writer's job, either to rebear the metaphors or refuse to use them. Gary Snyder's lifelong metaphor is *watershed*. How fruitful that is! Another of his is *composting*, which is a lovely word that describes the practice of creating.

*JW:* The use of language to name the world seems to have two sides. On one hand, things are given names as an expression of intimacy and respect; and on the other hand they are given names to create distance and separation. In your story, "She Unnames Them," for example, barriers are broken down as the names for animals are taken away.

*UL:* "She Unnames Them" is really an Adam and Eve story that I subverted. Eve takes all the names back because they were either wrong from the start or they went wrong. As she does this, the barriers between herself and the world are dismantled. At the end of the story, she has no words left. She's so close to the animals that she feels vulnerable and afraid, yet full of new desire to touch, smell, and eat.

Why do I feel like the way we give names is wrong? I don't want to flog that little story to death, because it was meant partly as a joke, but we do use names to cut ourselves off. Talking about a dog is different from talking about Rover. In the language of war, we don't talk about killing or even casualties anymore. We use strange euphemisms instead, like "body count" and "friendly fire." The language of pretended objectivity is often used this way, too. We manipulate names as categories of reality, and the names then become screens between ourselves and the world. The names become a tool of division rather than of community.

My father worked with the Yurok Indians of California, among other tribes. If you read his Yurok myths, you learn that every rock and every tree had its name. It was a small world they lived in, not a planetary one. They were in intense community with it, and their naming was a way of respecting their independence. But anything is reversible, and naming can become the destruction of community, where we hide from the real world by using more and more words. I know people who refuse to learn the names of trees. They have a concept of "tree," but the names simply get between them and the real tree.

I grew up in the Napa Valley without learning the English names for many of the plants and animals. When I started writing *Always Coming Home*, which takes place there, I had a wonderful time learning the flora and fauna of the area. For a while, I knew the name of every wildflower. But what you learn late doesn't stick. Now when I come across a flower whose name I've forgotten, I say, "How do you do, little yellow flower, whatever your name is." I used to crave to know the names, and I enjoyed learning them. It's funny, by naming a thing, do we think we get control over it? I think we do. That's how magic works. If you know the name of a thing, then you know its essence. At some level, I think we all must believe that.

We're naming creatures, but we need to respect that some things are beyond names. Like the mysterious essence of an animal in the wild. If our names make them appear tame or petlike, as in Walt Disney's world, then it's degrading. Some of the California Indians knew that when you name an animal, such as a deer, you are addressing its metaphysical nature. They called that universal quality "Deerness" or "The Deer." It's a profoundly mysterious and important matter, and very hard to put into words, but I feel I know what they're talking about. When these Indians hunted, they asked Deerness to help them. The deer that comes to the hunter is related physically to all other beings, but it is also an embodiment of Deerness. It's the gift of Deerness. This way of looking at the world can apply to every living being. When we name something we are naming its essence, and therefore its sacredness.

*JW:* In *Buffalo Gals*, you say that all creatures talk to one another, whether we are able to hear or not. But this conversation—this community— is not a simple harmony. "The peaceable kingdom, where lion and lamb lie down, is an endearing vision not of this world": What do you mean by that?

*UL:* The vision of the "peaceable kingdom" denies wilderness. In the Christian tradition, the denial of violence, of the fact that we eat each other in order to live, removes you from this world. Heaven is supernal bliss where there is no violence, no eating, no sex. When lions and lambs lie down in the wilderness, the lamb ends up inside the lion. That's how it is. You can deny that in order to gain another world. But if the only world you want is this one—and this one seems quite satisfactory to me—then the myth of the "peaceable kingdom" is only a charming painting.

*JW:* You continue in *Buffalo Gals*: "Some rash poets get caught in the traps set for animals and, unable to endure the cruelty, maim themselves to escape." You give the example of Robinson Jeffers. Was Jeffers maimed because he took too personally his disappointment in the dark side of nature?

*UL:* Jeffers was a very strange man and poet, with an enormous component of cruelty and violence in his work. He had incredible sympathy with animals. He could give you an animal in a word or two like very few poets can. I think he honestly felt them, even though he often perceives them through violence. I can't explain Jeffers, he has always awed and annoyed me. I'm grateful to him as one of my predecessors writing about California. Even as a teenager, I knew he had California right.

The poem that most reveals Jeffers' self-hatred is the one about the cavemen who torment a mammoth to death. They trap it and roast it alive. He's full of this kind of disgust for humanity. Yet he soars out into a great vision; never a happy vision, but a great vision. He's a difficult case when you're talking about animals.

*JW:* The trap of shamefulness seems like an easy one to fall into. If we want to be alert, we have to take all this in—the violence, the killing, the cruelty. . . .

*UL:* Yes. But since we're capable of compassion, we know it hurts. This causes all sorts of difficulties. My aunt was a biologist, and I watched her drop an artichoke into a pot of boiling water and say, "I wonder if it can feel that?" She was a very hard-headed biologist. Humans have to think about these things, whether we like it or not. It's the nature of our humanity to feel uncomfortable and full of guilt and shame and confusion. But we still participate, because we have to eat. Much of what animals do naturally we have to do consciously. That's our gift and our curse. All we can do is be conscientious about it—do it rightly, not wrongly.

*JW:* In *Always Coming Home*, hunting for food and skins was primarily done by children and adolescents. Under the supervision of adults, young girls and boys were allowed to hunt rabbit, possum, squirrel and other small game, and deer. Why was hunting considered inappropriate for adults?

*UL:* You're supposed to outgrow it. The same thing is true of war. In one chapter, I describe a small war with the Pig People. It's modeled on the warfare of the Northern California Indians, which was usually just a matter of standing on a hill and shouting insults. Sometimes people got mad enough to hurt each other, and occasionally someone was killed. Mostly it was the young boys who engaged in war, not the whole tribe. What comes up in the chapter or on the Pig war is the report that there were adults involved in the war. That's a shameful thing in the Kesh society. Both hunting and war are looked upon as occupations for adolescents—adolescents who are already a little out of control and needing to prove themselves. You can continue to hunt into adulthood if you're really good at it, of course, but I was implying that it's something most people outgrow.

People should be able to figure out their place in the life-death cycle without killing animals. The trouble is that it relates to what Hemingway said: "You can't be a man until you've killed another one." I say bullshit! Why don't you try it without a gun? Maybe there's a gender difference there. Maybe a woman can do it and a man can't. I hate to say that, but you wonder. It isn't built into women to be hunters in our culture. Even a fisherwoman is unusual.

Having a close relationship with an animal, particularly one that lives a short life, can be an intense, constant reminder of mortality. Cats only live ten years, so most of us see a lot of cats die in our lifetime. Going through the death of a pet, particularly for children, can put us through the same emotional process that hunting does. We don't have to kill an animal to get there. It's a very interesting subject, and I hope the difference is cultural and not inherent to gender.

*JW:* Another aspect of hunting is that it teaches us where our food comes from.

*UL:* That's a different subject. That's not a spiritual process but a matter of facing the facts. What are you willing to do for your food? Most of us would kill an animal to eat it, if we had to. I could, and would, if I were hungry or defending myself. I'm not saying I would enjoy it, but for those two reasons I would kill an animal. I have Buddhist friends who don't even swat flies. I can't go that far. If something is biting me, I squash it. A pest is a pest.

*JW:* It's clear from your work that language and writing have become sharp tools for reestablishing human society's (and humanity's) place in the larger household. Much of that effort to envision anew, at least in the last thirty years, has been inspired by feminist principles. You say your goal is always to subvert, to create metaphors for the future "where any assumption can be tested and any rule rewritten. Including the rules of who's on top, and what gender means, and who gets to be free." How were you introduced to the feminist movement? What role has it played in your writing?

*UL:* My introduction was slow and late. All my early fiction tends to be rather male-centered. A couple of the Earthsea books have no women in them at all or only marginal woman figures. That's how hero stories worked; they were about men. With the exception of just a few feminists like Joanna Russ, science fiction was pretty much male-dominated up to the 1960s. Women who wrote in that field often used pen names.

None of this bothered me. It was my tradition, and I worked in it happily. But I began coming up against certain discomforts. My first feminist text was *The Left Hand of Darkness*, which I started writing in 1967. It was an early experiment in deconstructing gender. Everybody was asking, "What is it to be a man? What is it to be a woman?" It's a hard question, so in *The Left Hand of Darkness*, I eliminated gender to find out what would be left. Science fiction is a wonderful opportunity to play this kind of game.

As a thought experiment, *The Left Hand of Darkness* was messy. I recently wrote the screenplay version, where I was able to make some of the changes I wish I could make to the novel. They're details, but important ones, such as seeing the main character, Genly, with children or doing things we think of as womanly. All you ever see him doing are manly things, like being a politician or hauling a sledge. The two societies in the book are somewhat like a feudal monarchy and Russian communism, which tend to be slightly paranoid. I don't know why I thought androgynous people would be paranoid. With twenty years of feminism under my belt, I can now imagine an androgynous society as being much different—and far more interesting—than our gendered society. For instance, I wouldn't lock the people from the planet Gethen, where the story takes place, into heterosexuality. The insistence that sexual partners must be of the opposite sex is naive. It never occurred to me to explore their homosexual practices, and I regret the implication that sexuality has to be heterosexuality.

I gradually realized that my own fiction was telling me that I could no longer ignore the feminine. While I was writing *The Eye of the Heron* in 1977, the hero insisted on destroying himself before the middle of the book. "Hey," I said, "you can't do that, you're the hero. Where's my book?" I stopped writing. The book had a woman in it, but I didn't know how to write about a woman. I blundered around a while and then found some guidance in feminist theory. I got excited when I discovered feminist literary criticism was something I could read and actually enjoy. I read *The Norton Book of Literature by Women* from cover to cover. It was a bible for me. It taught me that I didn't have to write like an honorary man anymore, that I could write like a woman and feel liberated in doing so.

Part of the women's experience is shared with men and part of it isn't. Experiences that are only women's, like childbirth, have been described a thousand times, mostly in novels by men. These descriptions have nothing to do with the actual experience. Generally, I don't think men in our culture want to hear from women about childbirth because men want to have their way. So, women's stories have been cast in the form of men's stories. A women's story has a different shape, different words, different rhythm. Theirs is the silent crescent of experience that we are just beginning to find words for.

The incredible upsurge of woman writers and poets in the 1980s is a sign that women are finding their voices. They're beginning to talk about their experiences without using a male vocabulary or meeting male expectations. It's sticky, because the language is so male-centered that it excludes much of the feminine experience. Sex, for instance, is always described from a male point of view, as penetration, insemination, and so on. A lot of women still deny that their experience is different than a man's. They do this because it's scary to realize you don't have the words to describe your own experience. The few words we do have we get from our mothers and the women who taught us when we were young. Virginia Woolf says, "We think back through our mothers."

One of the functions of art is to give people the words to know their own experience. There are always areas of vast silence in any culture, and part of an artist's job is to go into those areas and come back from the silence with something to say. It's one reason why when we read poetry, we often say, "Yeah, that's it. That's how I feel." Storytelling is a tool for knowing who we are and what we want, too. If we never find our experience described in poetry or stories, we assume that our experience is insignificant.

*JW:* The natural landscape is another of those vast silent areas you speak of. As a writer, have certain landscapes had a particularly strong influence on you?

*UL:* Mostly I don't know where my writing comes from. Experiences are composted, and then something different and unexpected grows out of them. In 1969, my husband and I spent a couple nights in French Glen, the mountainous area of southeastern Oregon. It was my first sight of that sagebrush high-desert terrain, and it got into me so instantly and authoritatively that a book grew out of it—*The Tombs of Atuan.* The book isn't about the desert but about a community surrounded by a terrain similar to what you find in southeastern Oregon.

The desert is a buried metaphor in the book. I have no idea of the reason for the emotional economy of it, but I know the book came to me as I was driving back from French Glen.

The central landscape of my life is the Napa Valley in Northern California. I grew up there and I consider it my home. I've often thought, "How can I get this beautiful valley into a book?" That was the main impulse of *Always Coming Home*. I wanted to write about people living in the Napa Valley who used it a little more wisely than we do now. When I was a child, it was the most beautiful and diversified agriculture you ever saw. There were vines and orchards and truck gardens. It was the way a cultivated valley ought to be. But there was too much money in vines, so they pulled up the orchards and truck gardens. The only thing growing there now is money.

*JW:* What role has your interest in indigenous people played in your work?

*UL:* I wasn't aware that it played any role at first. Although my father was an anthropologist and an archaeologist, my entire formal training in this area amounts to one physical anthropology class. Obviously I have some temperamental affinity with my father, but I often say that he studied real cultures and I make them up. He had an eye for exact concrete detail, and an interest in it. He also had a respect for tools and the way things work. I got a lot of that from him.

When I started thinking about *Always Coming Home* I took a lot of time to discover what the book was going to be. Once I realized I wanted it to grow out of the Napa Valley I looked around for a literary precedent. I couldn't find anything except a couple of swashbuckling romantic novels about Italian wine-growing families. The only literature of that earth was native American oral literature. The people of the valley itself, the Wappo, are gone. Even the name they used for themselves is gone. There are people with a little Wappo blood, but there is no language, no tradition, and there are no stories left. So I read other Northern California myths and legends and songs. There's a good deal of information available there. My father collected much of it himself. I read widely from traditions all over the United States. My problem was to find a way to use the literature without stealing or exploiting it, because we've done enough of that to native American writing. I certainly didn't want to put a bunch of made-up Indians into a Napa

Valley of the future. That was not what I was trying to do. What I got from reading California oral literature was a sense of a distant and different quality of life. You can't hear the voices but you can pick up the feeling.

*JW:* In *Always Coming Home*, the historical period, which followed the Neolithic era for some thousands of years, is referred to by the Kesh as the time when people lived "outside the world." What do you mean by that?

*UL:* I was playing with the idea of our present growth technology from the Industrial Revolution on through the present—the last two hundred years. We don't know when this period will end, but it will. We tend to think of our present historic era as representing the highest evolution of human society. We're convinced that our exploitive, fast-growing technology is the only possible reality. In *Always Coming Home*, I put people who believe this into one little capsule where the Kesh could look at them as weird aberrations. It was the most disrespectful thing I could do, like wrapping a turd in cellophane. That's sort of a Coyote metaphor.

*JW:* Speaking of Coyote, she wanders in and out of much of your recent work. How did you meet up with her?

*UL:* She trotted through a project of mine in 1982. It was an essay on utopia called "A Non-Euclidean View of California as a Cold Place to Be" and when the tracks of utopia and Coyote crossed, I thought, "Yes, now I'm getting somewhere!" The idea of utopia has been stuck in a blueprint phase for too long now. Most of the writing you see is similar to Callenbach's *Ecotopia*, which is another "wouldn't the future be great if we did this or that?" Or, in science fiction, it's been dystopia: utopia gone sour. These blueprints aren't working anymore.

Coyote is an anarchist. She can confuse all civilized ideas simply by trotting through. And she always fools the pompous. Just when your ideas begin to get all nicely arranged and squared off, she messes them up. Things are never going to be neat, that's one thing you can count on.

Coyote walks through all our minds. Obviously, we need a trickster, a creator who made the world all wrong. We need the idea of a God who makes mistakes, who gets into trouble, and who is identified with a scruffy little animal.

*URSULA LE GUIN* is one of the most widely read and most prolific writers in North America. She won the National Book Award (*The Farthest Shore*, 1973) and was an NBA finalist for *The Left Hand of Darkness* (1970), *The Tombs of Atuan* (1972), and *Always Coming Home* (1985). She has also received the Hugo, Kafka, and Nebula Awards. In addition to her many novels, she has written several collections of short stories, poetry, and literary theory.

Reprinted from *Whole Earth Review*, Spring 1995. Subscription: $20/year from FULCO, 30 Broad St., Denville, NJ 07834, (800) 783-4903. Excerpted from *Talking on Water*, © 1994 by Jonathan White (San Fransisco: Sierra Club Books).

# Language Alone Protects Us

### The Nobel Lecture by Toni Morrison

### from World Literature Today

"**O**nce upon a time there was an old woman. Blind but wise." Or was it an old man? A guru, perhaps. Or a griot soothing restless children. I have heard this story, or one exactly like it, in the lore of several cultures.

"Once upon a time there was an old woman. Blind. Wise."

In the version I know the woman is the daughter of slaves, black, American, and lives alone in a small house outside of town. Her reputation for wisdom is without peer and without question. Among her people she is both the law and its transgression. The honor she is paid and the awe in which she is held reach beyond her neighborhood to places far away, to the city where the intelligence of rural prophets is the source of much amusement.

One day the woman is visited by some young people who seem to be bent on disproving her clairvoyance and showing her up for the fraud they believe she is. Their plan is simple: they enter her house and ask the one question the answer to which rides solely on her difference from them, a difference they regard as a profound disability: her blindness. They stand before her, and one of them says, "Old woman, I hold in my hand a bird. Tell me whether it is living or dead."

She does not answer, and the question is repeated. "Is the bird I am holding living or dead?"

Still she doesn't answer. She is blind and cannot see her visitors, let alone what is in their hands. She does not know their color, gender, or homeland. She only knows their motive.

The old woman's silence is so long, the young people have trouble holding their laughter.

Finally she speaks and her voice is soft but stern. "I don't know," she says. "I don't know whether the bird you are holding is dead or alive, but what I do know is that it is in your hands. It is in your hands."

Her answer can be taken to mean: if it is dead, you have either found it that way or you have killed it. If it is alive, you can still kill it. Whether it is to stay alive, it is your decision. Whatever the case, it is your responsibility.

For parading their power and her helplessness, the young visitors are reprimanded, told they are responsible not only for the act of mockery but also for the small bundle of life sacrificed to achieve its aims. The blind woman shifts attention away from assertions of power to the instrument through which that power is exerted.

SPECULATION ON WHAT (other than its own frail body) that bird-in-the-hand might signify has always been attractive to me, but especially so now, thinking, as I have been, about the work I do that has brought me to this company. So I choose to read the bird as language and the woman as a practiced writer. She is worried about how the language she dreams in, given to her at birth, is handled, put into service, even withheld from her for certain nefarious purposes. Being a writer, she thinks of language partly as a system, partly as a living thing over which one has control, but mostly as agency—as an act with consequences. So the question the children put to her—"Is it living or dead?"—is not unreal because she thinks of language as susceptible to death, erasure, certainly imperiled and salvageable only by an effort of the will. She believes that if the bird in the hands of her visitors is dead, the custodians are responsible for the corpse. For her a dead language is not only one no longer spoken or written; it is unyielding language content to admire its own paralysis. Like statist language, censored and censoring. Ruthless in its policing duties, it has no desire or purpose other than maintaining the free range of its own narcotic narcissism, its own exclusivity and dominance. However moribund, it is not without effect, for it actively thwarts the intellect, stalls conscience, suppresses human potential. Unreceptive to interrogation, it cannot form or tolerate new ideas, shape other thoughts, tell another story, fill baffling silences. Official language smitheryed to sanction ignorance and preserve privilege is a suit of armor, polished to shocking glitter, a husk from which the knight departed long ago. Yet there it is: dumb, predatory, sentimental. Exciting reverence in schoolchildren, providing shelter for despots, summoning false memories of stability, harmony among the public.

She is convinced that when language dies, out of carelessness, disuse, and absence of esteem, indifference or killed by fiat, not only she herself but all users and makers are accountable for its demise. In her country children have bitten their tongues off and use bullets instead to iterate the voice of speechlessness, of disabled and disabling language, of language adults have abandoned altogether as a device for grappling with meaning, providing guidance, or expressing love. But she knows tongue-suicide is not only the choice of children. It is common among the infantile heads of state and power merchants whose evacuated language leaves them with no access to what is left of their human instincts, for they speak only to those who obey, or in order to force obedience.

THE SYSTEMATIC LOOTING OF LANGUAGE can be recognized by the tendency of its users to forgo its nuanced, complex, midwifery properties for menace and subjugation. Oppressive language does more than represent violence; it is violence; does more than represent the limits of knowledge; it limits knowledge. Whether it is obscuring state language or the faux-language of mindless media; whether it is the proud but calcified language of the academy or the commodity-driven language of science; whether it is the malign language of law-without-ethics, or language designed for the estrangement of minorities, hiding its racist plunder in its literary cheek—it must be rejected, altered, and exposed.

It is the language that drinks blood, laps vulnerabilities, tucks its fascist boots under crinolines of respectability and patriotism as it moves relentlessly toward the bottom line and the bottomed-out mind. Sexist language, racist language, theistic language—all are typical of the policing languages of mastery, and cannot, do not permit new knowledge or encourage the mutual exchange of ideas.

The old woman is keenly aware that no intellectual mercenary, no insatiable dictator, no paid-for politician or demagogue, no counterfeit journalist would be persuaded by her thoughts. There is and will be rousing language to keep citizens armed and arming, slaughtered and slaughtering in the malls, courthouses, post offices, playgrounds, bedrooms, and boulevards; stirring, memorializing language to mask the pity and waste of needless death. There will be more diplomatic language to countenance rape, torture, assassination. There is and will be more seductive, mutant language designed to throttle women, to pack their throats like paté-producing geese with their own unsayable, transgressive words; there will be more of the language of surveillance disguised as research; of politics and history calculated to render the suffering of millions mute; of language glamorized to thrill the dissatisfied and bereft into assaulting their neighbors; arrogant, pseudoempirical language crafted to lock creative people into cages of inferiority and hopelessness.

Underneath the eloquence, the glamour, the scholarly associations, however stirring or seductive, the heart of such language is languishing, or perhaps not beating at all—if the bird is already dead.

She has thought about what could have been the intellectual history of any discipline if it had not insisted upon, or been forced into, the waste of time and life that rationalizations for and representations of dominance required—lethal discourses of exclusion blocking access to cognition for both the excluder and the excluded.

The conventional wisdom of the Tower of Babel story is that the collapse was a misfortune. That it was the distraction, or the weight of many languages that precipitated the tower's failed architecture. That one monolithic language would have expedited the building and heaven would have been reached. Whose heaven, she wonders? And what kind? Perhaps the achievement of Paradise was premature, a little hasty, if no one could take the time to understand other languages, other views, other narratives. Had they, the heaven they imagined might have been found at their feet. Complicated, demanding, yes, but a view of heaven as life, not heaven as postlife.

She would not want to leave her young visitors with the impression that language should be forced to stay alive merely to be. The vitality of language lies in its ability to limn the actual, imagined, and possible lives of its speakers, readers, writers. Although its poise is sometimes in displacing experience, it is not a substitute for it. It arcs toward the place where meaning may lie. When a President of the United States thought about the graveyard his country had become and said "The world will little note nor long remember what we say here. But is will never forget what they did here," his simple words were exhilarating in their life-sustaining properties because they refused to encapsulate the reality of 600,000 dead men in a cataclysmic race war. Refusing to monumentalize, disdaining the "final word," the precise "summing up," acknowledging their "poor power to add or detract," his words signal deference to the uncapturability of the life it mourns. It is the deference that moves her, that recognition that language can never live up to life once and for all. Nor should it. Language can never "pin down" slavery, genocide, war. Nor should it yearn for the arrogance to be able to do so. Its force, its felicity is in its reach toward the ineffable.

Be it grand or slender, burrowing, blasting, or refusing to sanctify, whether it laughs out loud or is a cry without an alphabet, the choice word, the chosen silence, unmolested language surges toward knowledge, not its destruction. But who does not know of literature banned because it is interrogative, discredited because it is critical, erased because alternate? And how many are outraged by the thought of a self-ravaged tongue?

Word-work is sublime, she thinks, because it is generative; it makes meaning that secures our difference, our human difference—the way in which we are like no other life.

We die. That may be the meaning of life. But we do language. That may be the measure of our lives.

"ONCE UPON A TIME. . . . ," visitors ask an old woman a question. Who are they, these children? What did they make of that encounter? What did they hear in those final words: "The bird is in your hands"? A sentence that gestures toward possibility or one that drops a latch? Perhaps what the children heard was "It's not my problem. I am old, female, black, blind. What wisdom I have now is in knowing I cannot help you. The future of language is yours."

They stand there. Suppose nothing was in their hands? Suppose the visit was only a ruse, a trick to get to be spoken to, taken seriously as they have not been before? A chance to interrupt, to violate the adult world, its miasma of discourse about them, for them, but never to them? Urgent questions are at stake, including the one they have asked: "Is the bird we hold living or dead?" Perhaps the question meant: "Could someone tell us what is life? What is death?" No trick at all; no silliness. A straightforward question worthy of the attention of a wise one. An old one. And if the old and wise who have lived life and faced death cannot describe either, who can?

But she does not; she keeps her secret, her good opinion of herself, her gnomic pronouncements, her art without commitment. She keeps her distance, enforces it, and retreats into the singularity of isolation, in sophisticated, privileged space.

Nothing, no word follows her declarations of transfer. That silence is deep, deeper than the meaning available in the words she has spoken. It shivers, this silence, and the children, annoyed, fill it with language invented on the spot.

"Is there no speech," they ask her, "no words you can give us that help us break through your dossier of failures? Through the education you have just given us that is no education at all because we are paying close attention to what you have done as well as to what you have said? To the barrier you have erected between generosity and wisdom?

"We have no bird in our hands, living or dead. We have only you and our important question. Is the nothing in our hands something you could not bear to contemplate, to even guess? Don't you remember being young when language was magic without meaning? When what you could say, could not mean? When the invisible was what imagination strove to see? When questions and demands for answers burned so brightly you trembled with fury at not knowing?

"Do we have to begin consciousness with a battle heroines and heroes like you have already fought and lost, leaving us with nothing in our hands except what you have imagined is there? Your answer is artful, but its artiness embarrasses us and ought to embarrass you. Your answer is indecent in its self-congratulation. A made-for-television script that makes no sense if there is nothing in our hands.

"Why didn't you reach out, touch us with your soft fingers, delay the sound bite, the lesson, until you knew who we were? Did you so despise our trick, our modus operandi, you could not see that we were baffled about how to get your attention? We are young. Unripe. We have heard all our short lives that we have to be responsible. What could that possibly mean in the catastrophe this world has become, where, as a poet said, 'nothing needs to be exposed since it is already barefaced.'? Our inheritance is an affront. You want us to have your old, blank eyes and see only cruelty and mediocrity. Do you think we are stupid enough to perjure ourselves again and again with the fiction of nationhood? How dare you talk to us of duty when we stand waist deep in the toxin of your past?

"You trivialize us and trivialize the bird that is not in our hands. Is there no context for our lives? No song, no literature, no poem full of vitamins, no history connected to experience that you can pass along to help us start strong? You are an adult. The old one, the wise one. Stop thinking about saving your face. Think of our lives and tell us your particularized world. Make up a story. Narrative is radical, creating us at the very moment it is being created. We will not blame you if your reach exceeds your grasp, if love so ignites your words they go down in flames and nothing is left but their scald. Or if, with the reticence of a surgeon's hands, your words suture only the places where blood might flow. We know you can never do it properly—once and for all. Passion is never enough; neither is skill. But try. For our sake and yours, forget your name in the street; tell us what the world has been to you in the dark places and in the light. Don't tell us what to believe, what to fear. Show us belief's wide skirt and the stitch that unravels fear's caul. You, old woman, blessed with blindness, can speak the language that tells us what only language can: how to see without pictures. Language alone protects us from the scariness of things with no names. Language alone is meditation.

"Tell us what it is to be a woman so that we may know what it is to be a man. What moves at the margin. What it is to have no home on this place. To be set adrift from the one you knew. What it is to live at the edge of towns that cannot bear your company.

"Tell us about ships turned away from shorelines at Easter, placenta in a field. Tell us about a wagonload of slaves, how they sang so softly their breath was indistinguishable from the falling snow. How they knew from the hunch of the nearest shoulder that the next stop would be their last. How, with hands prayered in their sex they thought of heat, then suns. Lifting their faces as though it was there for the taking. Turning as though there for the taking. They stop at an inn. The driver and his mate go in with the lamp, leaving them humming in the dark. The horse's void steams into the snow beneath its hooves, and its hiss and melt is the envy of the freezing slaves.

"The inn door opens: a girl and a boy step away from its light. They climb into the wagon bed. The boy will have a gun in three years, but now he carries a lamp and a jug of warm cider. They pass it from mouth to mouth. The girl offers bread, pieces of meat, and something more: a glance into the eyes of the one she serves. One helping for each man, two for each woman. And a look. They look back. The next stop will be their last. But not this one. This one is warmed."

IT'S QUIET AGAIN when the children finish speaking, until the woman breaks into the silence.

"Finally," she says, "I trust you now. I trust you with the bird that is not in your hands because you have truly caught it. Look. How lovely it is, this thing we have done—together."

Stockholm, 8 December 1993

*TONI MORRISON* received the Nobel Prize for Literature in 1993. Her novels include *The Bluest Eye, Song of Solomon, Sula, Tar Baby, Beloved,* and *Jazz.* She has also won the National Book Critics Award and the Pulitzer Prize. Ms. Morrison is a professor at Princeton University. Her newest novel is *Paradise.*

Used by permission of the Nobel Foundation. Copyright © The Nobel Foundation 1993. Reprinted from *World Literature Today,* Winter, 1994; 110 Monnet Hall, University of Oklahoma, Norman, OK 73069. Subscription: $30/year.